Life Story Research in Sport

What is life *really* like for the elite athlete? How does the experience of being a professional sports person differ from the popular perceptions of fans, journalists or academics? Why might elite sports people experience mental health difficulties away from the public gaze?

In the first book-length study of its kind, Kitrina Douglas and David Carless present the life stories of real elite athletes alongside careful analysis and interpretation of those stories in order to better understand the experience of living in sport. Drawing on psychology, sociology, counselling, psychotherapy and narrative theory, and on narrative research in sports as diverse as golf, track and field athletics, judo and hockey, they explore the ways in which the culture of sport interacts with the mental health, development, identity and life trajectories of elite and professional sports people in highly pressurised and sometimes unhealthy environments.

By casting light on a previously under-researched aspect of sport, the book makes a call for strategies to be put in place to minimise difficulties or distress for athletes, for support to be tailored across the different life phases, and highlights the potential benefits in terms of athlete well-being and improved performance. The book also considers how these important issues relate to broader cultural and social factors, and therefore represents important reading for any student or professional with an interest in sport psychology, coaching, sport sociology, youth sport, counselling, or exercise and mental health.

Kitrina Douglas is Director of the boomerang-project.org.uk, an ambassador for the National Co-ordinating Centre for Public Engagement (NCCPE), a member of the National Anti-Doping Panel for Sport, has a visiting fellowship at the University of Bristol, UK and a .2 contract at Leeds Beckett University. She played elite and professional golf for twenty years, was British amateur, English Open and twice European Masters Champion. For a decade she was a member of the BBC's 'Radio Five Live' award winning outside broadcasting team.

David Carless is a professor at the Research Institute of Sport, Physical Activity and Leisure at Leeds Beckett University, UK. His research uses narrative, performative and arts-based methods to understand how identity and mental health can be developed or threatened through sport and physical activity.

Routledge Research in Sport and Exercise Science

The *Routledge Research in Sport and Exercise Science* series is a showcase for cutting-edge research from across the sport and exercise sciences, including physiology, psychology, biomechanics, motor control, physical activity and health, and every core subdiscipline. Featuring the work of established and emerging scientists and practitioners from around the world, and covering the theoretical, investigative and applied dimensions of sport and exercise, this series is an important channel for new and ground-breaking research in the human movement sciences.

Available in this series:

Mixed Methods Research in the Movement Sciences
Case studies in sport, physical education and dance
Edited by Oleguer Camerino, Marta Castaner and Teresa M. Anguera

Eccentric Exercise
Physiology and application in sport and rehabilitation
Hans Hoppeler

Computer Science in Sport
Research and practice
Edited by Arnold Baca

Life Story Research in Sport
Understanding the experiences of elite and professional athletes through narrative
Kitrina Douglas and David Carless

Life Story Research in Sport

Understanding the experiences of elite and professional athletes through narrative

Kitrina Douglas and David Carless

 Routledge
Taylor & Francis Group

LONDON AND NEW YORK

First published 2015
by Routledge
2 Park Square, Milton Park, Abingdon, Oxon OX14 4RN

and by Routledge
711 Third Avenue, New York, NY 10017

Routledge is an imprint of the Taylor & Francis Group, an informa business

British Library Cataloguing-in-Publication Data
A catalogue record for this book is available from the British Library

Library of Congress Cataloging-in-Publication Data
Douglas, Kitrina.
Life story research in sport : understanding the experiences of elite
and professional athletes through narrative / Kitrina Douglas and
David Carless.
  pages cm. – (Routledge Research in Sport and Exercise Science)
  Includes bibliographical references and index.
  1. Professional athletes–Biography. 2. Professional athletes–Public
  opinion. 3. Narrative inquiry (Research method) I. Carless, David,
  1970– II. Title.
  GV733.D68 2015
  796.023–dc23   2014018131

ISBN: 978-0-415-70900-2 (hbk)
ISBN: 978-1-315-88581-0 (ebk)

Typeset in Times New Roman
by Wearset Ltd, Boldon, Tyne and Wear

Printed and bound in Great Britain by
TJ International Ltd, Padstow, Cornwall

Dedication from Kitrina:
In memory of Jack Thomas (1924 to 2009): A remarkable
cyclist and storyteller.

Dedication from David:
To Mum and Dad, with love and thanks.

Contents

Acknowledgements

Without a great number of people sacrificing their time on our behalf it would have been impossible to carry out this research, not least to write this book. First, our gratitude and respect go to participants from the Ladies European Tour (LET), who were known to Kitrina before this research began. It has been your encouragement, interest and frank openness which made it possible to explore in more depth the experiences of professional sportspeople. You have each demonstrated 'sisterhood' throughout this process. Thank you. We are also indebted to the athletes and professional sportspeople who have become known to us in the course of carrying out this research. Some, like women from the LET, have contributed over several years and have given feedback on multiple occasions, others less frequently. We are indebted to you all for the time, expertise and candid reflections.

The opportunity to present our work, gain feedback and engage in in-depth conversations with academic colleagues, students, other professional sportsmen, sportswomen and coaches over more than a decade has made it possible to expand, test and deepen our understanding about life in professional sport from the perspectives of those who have a different lens or who perform different roles. We want to acknowledge here your contribution to our work: thank you. We have also highly valued the opportunities afforded us by Dr Kyle Phillpots, Director of Training and Education (PGA) at the Professional Golfers Association of Great Britain, The Ladies Golf Union of Great Britain, Professional Golfers Association of Europe, the Dutch Golf Federation, Dutch Golf PGA, *Women & Golf* magazine, and English Golf Union South-West. Added to the above, we are mindful of the benefits we have gained since we first began researching elite sport in 2000 from in-depth discussions with sport science, sport psychology, and qualitative research students and peers. In this regard we would like to extend special thanks to Brett Smith, now at Loughborough University, and Pedro Ferreira, University of Coimbra, for the multiple invitations to present at their institutions. We would also like to thank Helen Owton, Shaunna Burke, Hilary McDermott, colleagues from the National Anti-Doping Panel for Sport (UK), Anne Flintoff, Martyn Joseph, Joanne Foreman, Simon Jenkins, Guy Thomas, James Hutchinson, Karen Hutchinson, Peter Hutchinson, Kandis Ip, Pauline Douglas, Lucy Foster, Peggy Conley, Alison Smith, Edd

Vahid, David Gilbourne, Alec Grant, Andrew Sparkes and Ken Fox who have invested time reading, reflecting or discussing issues with us. Jerry Bingham at UK Sport made it possible to widen and extend our initial research by providing funding for two projects in 2006, and what researcher isn't grateful for funding? We also thank Kelsey Erickson, Lorena Lozano and Suzanne Peacock for offering feedback on draft chapters, and Ashley Cooper for extending Kitrina's visiting fellowship at the University of Bristol across the course of this research. We reserve a very special thanks to Emeritus Professor Kim Etherington for her gentle admonitions and calls to reflexivity and ethical research relationships.

Introduction

Why would an athlete who has a newborn baby, a loving husband and a seemingly thriving sport career try to take her own life at 28 years of age? Why might another successful athlete risk jeopardising his sport performance by going on a recreational skiing trip immediately before a major event? How does an athlete who never wins an event remain positive, upbeat and even joyful, while another, who regularly wins international championships, experiences life as a roller-coaster, where mood swings cause them to become depressed and sometimes violent?

As you can see, I have had a lot of questions mulling around in my mind since walking off the golf course and out of the 1996 English Open Championship following a minor injury. At the time, I was a multiple tournament-winning professional on the women's European golf tour, had been a member of the first-ever winning European Solhiem Cup Team, and – courtesy of my wins – had a position in the top-ten all-time order of merit which guaranteed me a place in major professional events for years to come. Perhaps it was these questions that prompted me to enrol in a sport and exercise science degree a few weeks after playing my last professional event. Perhaps it has been my desire to address these same questions that has led me to continue researching the lives of elite and professional athletes for the past 15 years. I am not alone in wanting answers to my questions – others too, it seems, want answers to *their* questions about the lives of elite sportspeople: 'Why did you stop playing golf?' is a question I'm often asked by colleagues in academia, curious to make sense of my actions. 'Why don't you play golf now?' is a question I am asked by nearly everyone I meet. 'What a waste of all that talent!' is a common response when I say that I no longer play.

By walking away from professional golf without announcing any particular intention to do so, I would be categorised in academic literature as a 'drop-out'. I find this both ironic and strange, given the positive experiences I had in sport and the negative connotations generally associated with 'dropping out' of anything, let alone sport. Before I 'dropped out', however, I was aware of what I can only describe as a massive gulf between how life in sport is generally talked about in the academic literature, in public discourse and in the media, and how I experienced life in professional sport. In short, the reality of my life in sport did not fit well with how sport psychologists, sport sociologists, coaches, journalists, media commentators and fans typically portrayed the reality of athletes' lives.

Observing, interacting, and building relationships on a day-to-day basis with other golfers over 20 years strengthened this sense of tension or disparity. It wasn't just me who was different – others' lives too were at odds with 'received knowledge'. Over time, I became increasingly aware of many contradictions and ambiguities between the behind-the-scenes behaviour of other athletes compared to how they were when performing on show in the public gaze. Like those colleagues and acquaintances who were curious about my sport career and life choices, I hoped that studying sport and exercise science would answer these questions, and that the answers would help me understand and make sense of other sportspeople's lives as well as my own.

The undergraduate course I began in 1996 was interesting and diverse – I enjoyed nearly every aspect of it. I learned about ageing and physical activity, about how to design exercise referrals, how to take blood samples, collect anthropometric data, how to use an ECG machine, an isokineticdynomometer and force plates, analyse running gait and golf swings, how to design sport programmes for children with learning disabilities, and a whole lot more. Yet when it came to the lectures on sport psychology – and in particular on elite athletes – my 'insider' experiences and knowledge about performing at the highest level in sport were notably at odds with what I was being taught, what the academic literature told us. While there was a truth to this research, it seemed simplistic and failed to adequately represent what I had experienced myself and observed in other professional athletes. Added to this, the research didn't seem to answer the questions that, to me at least, seemed most important – and there were a whole host of issues left untouched. As an undergraduate, studying the sport psychology and sociology literature only widened my sense of a gulf between how athletes' lives were represented by people *outside sport*, and what I knew in an embodied sense from *living in sport*. The more I picked at the surface, the more deeply I became interested and committed to both answering the questions that were important to me as an athlete *and* making sense of why these answers were missing from the existing sport literature.

So, in 2000, I started my doctoral studies – which explored the kinds of questions that had been plaguing me – by researching the lives of other professional golfers. At the time, I shared an office with another doctoral student – David Carless – who was studying the ways in which a small group of men with severe and enduring mental health difficulties, such as schizophrenia and bipolar disorders, used sport and physical activity in their recovery. Together we formed a small research team and throughout our Ph.D. studies read and discussed each other's interview transcripts, provided feedback on content as well as techniques of interviewing, and acted as critical 'outsiders' to each other's projects.

This way of doing research had many benefits. One benefit was that we were each exposed to alternative methodologies and populations, which allowed us to compare and contrast the developing insights we were each gaining through our own research. It also challenged many of our assumptions regarding mental health, elite sport and social science research methods. Most significantly perhaps, during the hours we spent reading and discussing each other's interviews, one strange finding across our two cohorts of participants began to emerge: at times, the life stories shared by the people with serious mental health problems in David's study suggested greater well-being compared to the stories shared (anonymously and in confidence) by some of the professional athletes in my research. Yet, culturally speaking, people with the most severe forms of mental health problems are often stigmatised, seen as deficient or even dangerous, while elite athletes are typically held up as role models for how to live well and succeed in life.

This paradox struck us both powerfully: *what was going on here?* Why might elite and professional sportspeople come to experience mental health difficulties? Why do accounts of these experiences so seldom surface in public discourse, in the media or in sport psychology literature? Of course, sport has many positive aspects and effects that are clearly apparent across societies. While we in no way wish to deny these strengths, we are aware that less is said about the darker side of sport. Recent years have seen the beginnings of an awareness that problems exist in terms of athlete well-being – through, in football, for example, the highly publicised suicides of Robert Enke and Gary Speed – and the beginnings of a concerted professional and policy response which takes seriously the mental health of elite and professional sportspeople. This response is, in our view, both necessary and timely, and this book contributes directly to informed debate around these issues.

In our first book together – *Sport and Physical Activity for Mental Health* (Carless and Douglas, 2010) – we presented one strand of our continuing research focusing on the therapeutic and life course benefits of regular leisure-time participation in sport and physical activity for people with diagnosed mental health difficulties. In contrast, in this book we turn our attention to the other side of the coin: the ways in which sport can compromise or threaten the mental health, well-being and development of athletes. By drawing on our ongoing narrative life story research with elite, professional and Olympic athletes from sports as diverse as rugby union, track and field athletics, swimming, judo, netball, canoeing, hockey, rowing, cricket, and golf, we aim to unpack the ways in which the culture of sport interacts with not only mental health but also the development, identity and life trajectories of elite and professional sportspeople.

Our first aim in taking this approach focuses on the *individual person* and relates to our belief that if the lives of athletes and professional sportspeople are better understood, strategies may be put in place to minimise difficulties or distress and support may be tailored across different life phases. Recent research suggests that this in itself is likely to have positive effects on the individual in a holistic sense: both well-being and sporting success stand to improve. Our secondary aim is to move beyond a focus on the individual to consider how these issues relate to broader cultural and social factors. Insights from this focus have important implications for family life, school and youth sport participation, and the aspirations we set for the future generation of sportspeople – be they interested in medals, friendship, personal development, health or pushing the boundaries of human performance.

Our approach to the book

The material we present throughout the book draws on life story research we have conducted to understand the experiences of high-level sportspeople over time. This approach allows us to explore the ups and downs of life, the ebbs and flows, the highs and lows through the stories each person tells across their life span. Projections, hopes, fears and dreams for the future can also be explored in ways that connect these possible futures to the concrete events and lived experiences of the individual's life to date. Throughout the book, we present stories of sportspeople's experiences alongside analysis and interpretation of these stories. Doing so allows us to move – tentatively – from the visceral and emotional impact of individual stories to also offer more general interpretations and conclusions on the basis of psychological, sociological and, in particular, narrative theory. By doing so, we shed light on what life in sport is like for diverse athletes to raise awareness of not only the problems and possibilities but also the ways in which things might be different.

The 'dual' perspective of *insider–outsider* has, we think, been a strength of our research but it has brought a degree of complexity to our writing. In particular we have become aware that there are limits to when we can write as 'we' and when, as the insider with experience of living in sport, it is necessary for Kitrina to write in the first person. We have been able to negotiate this difficulty by Kitrina writing certain sections of the text in the first-person 'I' while in the remainder of the book we write about *our* research findings, interpretations and understanding in the third-person 'we'.

The book falls into three parts. The first part – comprising Chapters 1, 2 and 3 – provides a backdrop for the research that we present and discuss in later chapters. In Chapter 1, 'Public portrayals of elite athletes', we explore how high-level sportspeople are portrayed in the media, sport literature and public discourse. We suggest that a particular master narrative underlies most public portrayals. This narrative not only represents, but also *shapes* the lives of athletes. In Chapter 2, 'Life story research and the contribution of the insider', we reflect on how the unique possibilities of 'insider' status, when combined with a narrative life story approach, can contribute a more complete understanding of the lives of elite and professional sportspeople. In Chapter 3, 'Our research journey', we share a series of stories about selected moments that occurred while we conducted our research. This story contributes a critical reflexivity to our project, revealing important issues around power, ethics, research relationships and methodology.

In the second part of the book – Chapters 4, 5 and 6 – we present our theoretical conception of three narrative types that we see as underlying the personal stories we witnessed through our research. We draw on Arthur Frank's (1995: 75) conception of a *narrative type* as 'the most general storyline that can be recognized underlying the plot and tensions of particular stories'. We use this concept throughout the book as we try to make sense of the sometimes challenging, troubling or surprising stories we have witnessed. In Chapter 4 we explore what we consider to be the dominant narrative type within elite sport culture: the *performance* narrative. In Chapters 5 and 6 we present two alternative narrative types – *discovery* and *relational* – that serve as counter-stories which explicitly challenge and destabilise the dominant narrative.

In the third part – Chapters 7 through 11 – we use this theoretical concept as a lens to better understand different phases across sportspeople's lives, from childhood through retirement. In each chapter we focus on two or more individuals whose different stories, when placed alongside each other, give rise to a dialogue that extends understanding of high-level sport. In these chapters we offer accounts of individuals who both conform to and resist the dominant performance narrative. In Chapter 7, 'Learning the story: enculturation of young athletes', we focus on the processes through which aspiring youngsters become socialised into the culture of elite sport. In Chapter 8, 'Living, playing or resisting the part of "Athlete"', we explore three ways in which established high-level athletes negotiate sport culture. In Chapter 9, 'The consequences of stories at retirement', we focus on how the stories an individual tells across a lifetime in sport shape their withdrawal experiences, particularly in terms of their future horizons and mental well-being. In Chapter 10, 'Asylum and the conditions for story change', we explore the conditions that are necessary for a performance storyteller to change their life story in the direction of an alternative narrative type. We conclude, in Chapter 11, with some reflections and responses to questions we are regularly asked concerning the research that underpins the book. By doing so, we hope to stimulate further dialogue around the ways in which high-level athletes might, in future years, live, develop and experience sport.

1 Public portrayals of elite athletes

> Joe Public just doesn't have a clue what tournament golf is like. They haven't got
> any idea.
>
> (Golfer on the Ladies European Tour)

If a spaceship hovered over The Earth and its inhabitants watched through a high-powered telescope to see exactly what it is that human beings get up to, we wonder what they would make of sport. What sense would they make of people facing each other with foils and fists, or hitting things at each other, or chasing round after one another on foot, in boats, on bikes, on horses, and sometimes sitting in chairs? Would they be curious why large numbers of earthlings gather together in vast arenas to stare, shout, scream and applaud a small number of other humans? What would they make of the *Haka* or the singing of national anthems? What sense would they make of all the data collected about sports and sportspeople – on laptops, with stopwatches, through blood and urine samples, in newspaper articles, documentaries and films? Would they wonder why some of these individuals are placed aboard open-topped buses, paraded through streets lined with more humans doing more shouting and applauding while throwing tickertape into the air? Would the visitors' sophisticated lenses deduce that some members of this small minority of earthlings influence the behaviour and consumer choices of many others? Would they be able to discern the magnitude and meaning of the inspiration and entertainment enjoyed by millions around the world as spectators and fans? Would they conclude that the men and women who play sport at this level are special – superhuman, perhaps?

We are inclined to see high-level sport as a *strange* phenomenon that has, for many of us all over the world, come to be seen as *normal*. While we humans typically look on, join in or try to avoid the circus of professional sport, mostly with a degree of acceptance of its ways, our imagined intergalactic visitors are more likely to be puzzled, surprised, concerned, shocked, amazed, appalled or confused. Unlike us, they have not had a lifetime of socialisation and enculturation into sport. They have not, over a period of years, reached an acceptance of the sometimes strange ways of elite and professional sport as 'just the way it is'. Instead, they come to it fresh; devoid of assumptions and the received wisdom that, whether we recognise it or not, influences our experience, responses and understanding of more or less everything.

Most of us have, for a time at least, been personally immersed in sport in some capacity. In much of Europe, North America and Australasia, young people are exposed to sport at school through physical education, typically from the age of five or six through to 16 or 18. For some, leaving school signifies the end of their personal involvement in sport. Others continue to be involved in sport, perhaps recreationally, for health reasons or as a spectator. A smaller number continue to work in sport, perhaps as a coach or teacher, or as part of a support team (e.g. physiotherapist, psychologist, sport scientist). A smaller number still go on to play sport at the elite or professional level. All of these forms of personal involvement serve to socialise individuals into sport. They provide lessons on what sport *is*, what it is *for*, what *matters* in sport and what involvement in sport *means*. They teach what it is to *be* a sportsperson: what is required and what is expected. They define what is 'normal' when it comes to sport. Through these experiences we also learn about our own (potential) place within sport, our worth, our ability, our possible futures. All of us – to some extent – have learnt lessons through our personal experiences in sport. And all of us, should we wish, have the potential to reflect on these moments as a way of exploring our own assumptions regarding the 'reality' of high-level sport.

Aside from these personal experiences, there exist a multitude of public portrayals of sport. Perhaps more so than almost any other area of life, sport is represented to the public on a daily basis through thousands of public portrayals. These include television coverage, interviews, documentaries and features; newspaper, magazine and online articles; autobiographies and biographies; films and plays; policy documents; research papers and academic texts; 'how-to' manuals ... the list is endless. The splashes these public portrayals create go on to stimulate or provoke further ripples in the form of conversations in pubs, debates in universities, arguments in changing rooms, twitter conversations, online posts and so on. Through these channels, public portrayals have a wide reach and exert a powerful influence, serving as a potent means of socialisation and enculturation into sport. They reach above and beyond personal experience, to shape the assumptions of not only those who live or work in sport but also of those who are not involved. It is hard to imagine anyone who has not, in some way, had their understanding of sport moulded by portrayals in the public domain.

These shaping processes are, we suggest, important and worthy of serious consideration, not least because they provide a key route through which *assumptions* regarding sport are seeded, germinated, fed and developed. It is precisely because they have *not* been exposed to public portrayals of sport that our imagined intergalactic visitors can come to sport afresh and with an open mind. They would be likely to see what is strange in the 'normal' – and, potentially, what is normal in the 'strange'. In this book, we strive – as best we can – to place ourselves in a similar position of openness. We want to hear stories of sport anew, as our alien visitors might. Of course, this is not entirely possible, as we cannot completely divest ourselves of our assumptions. And at times the cultural legacy that underpins our assumptions can be useful in making sense of the stories we hear. There is, however, much to be gained from trying to become aware of our assumptions, by allowing them to become visible for a moment, so that we might appreciate how they can act as 'blinkers' or a 'lens' that shapes our understandings and expectations of high-level sportspeople. We invite you to do the same.

Thus, in this chapter, we step back to take a broad view across the sporting landscape, beyond disciplinary boundaries, to consider how sport and sportspeople are publicly portrayed. We hope to show that *how* we come to learn about what it means to be an elite athlete is coloured by a number of powerful social and cultural mores, those accepted traditional customs and usages of a particular social group that are passed down and embedded before we become aware of how they influence our expectations and understanding. This wide-angle view provides a social and cultural backdrop for the material we present in the rest of the book. It also provides part of our rationale for the methodological approaches we have chosen to use in our work (which we discuss in Chapters 2 and 3).

Within a single chapter we can only really skim the surface of the multitude of public portrayals of sport and sportspeople. Space constraints imply that we must focus ourselves to provide a brief account which, we hope, cuts to the heart of the issue. To this end, we focus on four particular characteristics that are evident in many public portrayals of high-level sport and sportspeople. Of course, each portrayal is somewhat unique – the many different stories are not all the same! However, many portrayals demonstrate recurring hallmarks. While not the *only* hallmarks, we think these four hold particular significance when it comes to understanding high-level athletes. In short, these characteristics have very real implications for the development, expectations, behaviours and lives of high-level sportspeople. In what follows, we consider each of these characteristics in detail, concluding with some reflections on how these forms of portrayal can come to shape 'reality' and influence people's lives.

The sportsperson as hero

Irish golfer Christie O'Connor was one of the all-time greats of European golf. In the eyes of the Irish public at least, his status and reputation made it unnecessary to refer to him by his name. He was just known as *Himself.* You didn't ask, 'What did O'Connor score?' You just asked, 'What did Himself score?' When the Spanish golfing sensation Severiano Ballesteros first arrived on Irish shores, he was recognised as the new star of the European tour – he was the upstart. Ballesteros was referred to as *Yer Man.* So, the story goes, when a fan arriving after the event had finished enquired, 'Who won?' he was told, '*Yer Man beat Himself.*'

This is merely an illustration of the ways in which the 'big names' in sport typically acquire a status that seems to elevate them above – often, *way* above – the average person in society. Among Irish golf fans at least, O'Connor and Ballesteros were simply *too great* to be referred to by name. Closely allied to this perceived 'greatness' is a strong sense of high-level sportspeople being lauded and held up as heroes (see Anderson, 2009; Sparkes, 2004). For some, heroism remains within the limits of their locale (e.g. particular sport, geographical location, period in time). For others, heroism seems to transcend beyond not only time and place but sport itself.

In Greek mythology, where we first encounter 'the hero', we learn that the role is associated with an individual who has developed highly refined skills, ability and who has courage. For Campbell (2008), who studied heroes across a variety of cultures, the 'hero myth' could be reduced to a singular story plot where 'The protagonist undertakes a hazardous journey (for example, into Hades) in pursuit of truth and meaning' (cited in McLeod, 1997: 60). The concept of valuing highly an individual who overcomes obstacles and challenges hasn't been lost in our contemporary value system and is particularly garnered in sport. Autobiographies and biographies abound with stories that follow this narrative arc and these types of journeys provide models for others, especially young people, to follow and to which to aspire.

To give a flavour of the typical hero script we briefly draw on the story of round-the-world yachtswoman Emma Richards, as told in her autobiography *Around Alone*. The hero myth is predicated on overcoming obstacles, but Richards writes: 'I don't like to dwell on obstacles.... I take on challenges one step at a time, one mile at a time' (2004: ix). Yet at the beginning of her voyage she reminds us of the obstacles that await her: broken bones, bandits, blows to the head and so on. She asks: is it feasible to expect to be rescued in the middle of an ocean should something go wrong? She chooses to set the scene for her epic voyage by speaking to her readers from atop the 80-foot mast, in the middle of the South Atlantic, in high winds and terrified by an image in her head of someone breaking the news to her parents that she had been killed. Nearly 300 pages are devoted to describing hardships, dedication to her goal and her disciplined focus. Then she writes: 'For eight months and tens of thousands of miles I have been inching towards an imaginary peak. Now I was there. I'd done it' (2004: 302). She was the youngest person to finish the Around Alone event and the first-ever woman. 'It wasn't a mountain that I'd scaled, but a roller-coaster', she writes. She is immediately catapulted into the limelight, invited to parties and award ceremonies, where more glory is bestowed. She sips champagne on a luxury power boat off the Monaco coast with *her* sporting hero, Sebastian Coe, and reflects on a life that has become surreal, surrounded by the biggest names in sport, movie celebrities and royalty.

Richards' journey – like the hero stories of many other athletes told through autobiographies and biographies, documentaries, interviews, movies and mass media – progresses from a challenge, through hardship and setbacks, to eventual triumph against the odds. It culminates with the individual being invited to join a select group of heroes through whom many in society expect to have their aspirations raised and their values affirmed, perpetuated and solidified (Klapp,

1962). As a special object of adulation, Smith (1973: 70) suggests, 'the sports hero is both the instrument of and the mirror for a variety of social processes'. While the preferred type of hero may change – at times we want moral heroes, at other times, prowess heroes – these changes roughly parallel changes in societal values (Smith, 1973).

With hero status comes the potentially intoxicating effects of adulation and glory. Patricia and Peter Adler experienced its power to seduce during their research among college athletes. They describe, in the opening chapter of *Backboards and Blackboards* (Adler and Adler, 1991), how a student of Peter's gave them complementary tickets to a basketball match. At this stage of their research they knew little about the player or the team but went along primarily because Peter was a basketball fan. They then describe the moment when the young student ran on to the court to be greeted by the fans chanting his name, or at least the name the fans had bestowed upon him: *Apollo* – the Greek god of light, god of truth, the archer with a silver bow. Late in the game, after a foul, they describe how 'Apollo' stepped forward to take the penalty. The moment is full of tension and anticipation. He paused, wiped his sweaty hands. At this moment the expectation of the huge crowd – as well as Patricia and Peter Adler – was that Apollo would take the shot. But no – he turned and looked directly at the two researchers sitting up in the stands. *Then* he took the shot. The two researchers tried to describe what they experienced in that moment, amidst the thousands of fans, to have the star player, the god of light, look upon them. They write, 'the glance' was 'intoxicating' (Adler and Adler, 1991: 3). It is the experience of this type of glory and adulation, or the lure of it, they learn later through their research, that the young men found impossible to resist: becoming a hero in the sport environment is just too seductive for many.

War metaphors

Lakoff and Johnson (1980: 5) describe metaphor as 'understanding and experiencing one kind of thing in terms of another'. They influence the way in which we make sense of and interpret the world, ourselves and others (Richardson, 1994). They are bridges between what we recognise, understand and is familiar to us, and that which is unrecognisable. That is, metaphors 'act as relays for transferring meaning, myth, and ideology from one pocket of cultural understanding to another' (Bloor (1977), cited in Jansen and Sabo, 1994: 8). 'They embody, exhibit, police, and preserve the withered mythologies that create social order and make communication possible' (Jansen and Sabo, 1994: 8). Nisbet (1969: 5) suggests that:

> It is easy to dismiss metaphor as 'unscientific' or 'non-rational,' a mere substitute for the hard analysis that rigorous thought requires. Metaphor, we say, belongs to poetry, to religion, and to other more or less 'enchanted' areas of thought. So it does. But metaphor also belongs to philosophy and even to science.

The linking of sport and war through metaphor is commonplace in broadcasting, journalism and film as well as in the spoken word, both public and private. A large degree of the language of sport and war seems to be used interchangeably. Jansen and Sabo (1994) and Jenkins (2013) provide insights into this symbiotic relationship between war-speak and sport-speak, illustrating how, during war, soldiers, generals and politicians often adopt sport metaphors to make points, explain issues and illuminate their ideology. During the First World War, the following excerpt appeared in print:

> Cricketers … can help to bowl out the Germans, who started hitting hard before some of their opponents could take their places in the field. The Allies are hoping to 'have a knock' on the other side of the Rhine.
> (*Athletic News*, 7 December 1914, cited in John, 2013: 20)

More recently, during the Gulf War, United States President George Bush accused Saddam Hussein of 'stiff-arming' (a footballing term meaning to fend of an opponent) while US pilots likened their bombing raids to a football game. War journalists too use sport metaphors as they describe 'the play' for their audiences. This strategy 'coerces citizens into displays of patriotism and national unity when it may not exist and to quiet political dissent when it arises' (Jenkins, 2013: 258).

Conversely, in sport, journalists routinely adopt the language of war to create different yet no less powerful allegiances and images that help make sport appear serious and dramatic. A rugby player, for example, has 'a mission' to score, running towards a pair of upright posts he or she might be 'weaving through a minefield' of defenders. These kinds of metaphors help provide an awareness of the danger to the player and how her or his objective may be thwarted by the defence of the opposition – 'the enemy'. A golfer's shot to the pin becomes a 'guided missile' to communicate the accuracy and consistency of the professional. There is a sense of speed and propulsion in the metaphor that is not conveyed with the words, 'Davis hit her drive towards the pin'.

Some coaches, too, propagate war stories when, for example, they tell players to 'go in for the kill' or 'take no prisoners'. For England's cricket captain Alistair Cook, a direct war analogy was used to portray the relationship between the Australian and English cricketers. 'On the pitch,' he said, 'it's pretty much a war, isn't it?' We were both shocked some years ago when we read, on a whiteboard in the 'hot-desk' area of a sport and exercise department we were then affiliated to, the slogan: 'Hurdle the dead and trample the weak.' Even the BBC cannot help but engage in war mentality to promote their sports coverage, for example, by advertising the Oxford and Cambridge boat race on their website as 'the annual rowing battle along London's River Thames' (BBC, 2013). For athletes, the use of a war metaphor or two often seems a seductive option for providing colour and emotional content during interviews or on a website.

Even athletes in non-contact sports, where there is little potential benefit from hostility, are sometimes drawn into talking about their sport as if it were war.

Snowboarder Hannah Teter, who is known for her 'peaceful demeanour' and donated all of her 2009 prize money to charity, is even lured into using war imagery. Teter 'has a secret weapon' that she calls 'the bomb'. Her bomb may only be syrup to pour over breakfast cereal, but describing it as 'the bomb' evokes far greater severity, seriousness, significance and consequence. Jenkins (2013: 265, citing Ratto, 2001) provides some insight into why war metaphors are particularly favoured, suggesting that 'the players like the mythology of athletes as warriors, the coaches, who liked the mythology of coaches as generals and military strategists, and to the fans, who just liked the imagery'.

Generally, analogies and metaphors slip by unnoticed. Most of us have come to accept them as normal, and see high-level sport as essentially a 'conflict' between two or more 'enemies'. At other times, and especially during times of real war or following events where the horrors of war have become more obvious and raw, the use of war metaphors crosses the border of social acceptability. Broadcasting networks are of course aware of this. During Kitrina's commentary work for the BBC, she was sometimes reminded that certain words should be avoided on a particular day. 'Don't use "tragedy" or "disaster" today', Rob Nothman, the producer of BBC Radio Five Live Open Championship Golf, told the correspondents one morning because other events in the news rendered their use unacceptable at that time.

The social acceptability doesn't always filter down to athletes, however, as is the case in the following three extracts:

> 20+ games left in phase 2. I'm ReFOCUSED! No prisoners, I have no friends when at WAR besides my Soldiers.
> (LeBron James Tweet, March 2011, cited in Jenkins, 2013: 255)

> It's war.... They're out there to kill you, so I'm out there to kill them. We don't care about anybody but this U. They're going after my legs. I'm going to come right back at them. I'm a ... soldier.
> (Kellen Winslow, cited in Drape, 2003)

> This is it. It's all for the marbles. I'm sitting in the house loading up the pump, I'm loading up the Uzis, I've got a couple of M-16s, couple of nines, couple of joints with some silencers on them.
> (Kevin Garnett, cited in Jenkins, 2013: 255)

These examples reflect how war-speak has become embedded in a way of thinking about and communicating sport. It speaks to the type of courage and commitment that is expected from an athlete, that the fans want to see from their heroes. When used by sportspeople, it also potentially shows teammates that the speaker is committed and passionate, and that he or she has a 'you can count on me' attitude.

The use of war metaphors and language connects the specific sporting tale being recounted to a much larger historical and cultural repertoire of war stories.

Stories of battles and wars have permeated the culture of many (if not all) nations for centuries. They are part of each of our inherited cultural legacy or, in Mark Freeman's (2010) terms, one of the many sedimentary layers that shape our lives even if we have no personal experience of war. Seemingly innocent phrases such as 'to the victor go the spoils' mask a history of domination through, for example, the 'right' to own or destroy the property of those defeated, to rape and pillage their families and homes, and to enslave or govern their descendants. While we of course are not suggesting that these practices equate to contemporary sport, we are suggesting that the use of war-speak at times makes a subtle and implicit connection between the meaning of the outcome of a sport contest and a battle.

Stewart *et al.* (2011: 587) observe that 'in all sports winning a game is never simply winning, it is a victory, as losing is being defeated'. Critically, war metaphors and language significantly 'up the stakes' when it comes to the outcomes of a sporting contest. They bring to the event a greatly heightened sense of meaning and significance. Yet in sport whether or not a team or individual wins or loses is *not* a matter of life and death. The health and well-being of entire populations is *not* threatened by the result of a sporting contest. Countries are not bankrupted on the basis of losing a match. But in war stories, winning is *survival* while losing is *death*. Losers are humbled, shamed, and forced to submit to the will of the victor. Everything can depend on whether or not the war is won. In this sense, using the language of war to describe sport provides a way of dramatically and artificially heightening the importance and the consequences of winning and losing. War metaphors are an important and commonplace linguistic device that allow this *particular* way of doing sport to appear 'normal' – the *only* way of doing sport.

Winning is everything

> According to the sports programming that boys consume most, a real man is strong, tough, aggressive and above all, a winner in what is still a man's world. To be a winner he must be willing to compromise his own long-term health by showing guts in the face of danger, by fighting other men when necessary ... he must be the aggressor on the 'battlefields' of sport and in his consumption choices.
>
> (Messner *et al.*, 1999: 11)

> Like good and evil, you use whatever means you have, they will always be the enemy.
>
> (Oxford Blue and Olympic Gold Medallist Andrew Triggs Hodge;
> University of Oxford, 2012)

> 'You any good?' He came back after sipping his gin, and turning lightly toward her in his seat. She observed his actions wondering, *'Aren't you going to put a little more tonic in that?'* and then *'Why are they always so*

predictable.' She could answer his question truthfully by saying, 'Yes I'm brilliant,' or she could be a little more humble, perhaps not so truthful and say, 'Not bad.' But you see, whichever way she played it, however she answered, brilliant or bad, they would always ask, 'Oh, so have you won anything?' and then 'What have you won?'

(Douglas, 2013: 83)

'Have you won anything?' and 'What have you won?' are questions that every high-level athlete is likely to be asked. Winning, it seems, is of interest to people who are not elite athletes, just as it appears to be for those who are. But *how* important is it for an athlete to win? Put another way, to what lengths would an athlete go in order to reach their goal? Would an athlete be prepared to risk their health, as Messner and colleagues (1999) suggest above, or perhaps even their life in order to win? How far do Andrew Triggs Hodge's words 'use whatever means you have' extend? Just how far would an Olympic rower be prepared to go? Is there a limit? In the case of round-the-world yachtswoman Emma Richards, who we mentioned earlier, *Around Alone* does endanger life, but the risks are minimised and managed through meticulous planning, robust equipment, life support strategies, and excellent sailing and navigation skills. The result is that although there are dangers, the chances of survival are good. But what if injury, ill-health or premature death was a certainty? Would athletes still pursue the win?

In the 1970s, sports medicine practitioner Gabe Mirkin polled a group of athletes with this type of question. He asked: would you take a pill if it gave you a win but meant death in five years' time? Half of those polled said they would take the pill. Later, between 1982 and 1995 Robert Goldman tested his version of the question on athletes from a number of sports. Fifty-two per cent of athletes again said yes (Goldman *et al.*, 1984). These studies have been questioned by Connor *et al.* (Connor and Mazanov, 2009; Connor *et al.*, 2013) on a number of counts: no comparable measure exists, there is positive response bias in the wording of the question, no mention in the article about recruitment and representativeness of the sample, and no consideration of political climate. Yet the World Anti Doping Agency for sport (WADA) use what has become known as 'the Goldman dilemma' as a base from which to judge whether anti-doping measures are working. Flawed or otherwise, these studies have become a baseline. Irrespective of WADA's interest, or the justified concerns of Connor and colleagues, we are still left with a sizeable number of athletes who, even if it was just during dinner-table chat, say they would put their life on the line in order to win a big sport event. If we are in any doubt about the centrality of winning or being the best, these observations should alert us to a prevalent belief in high-level sport that winning is *everything*.

At the elite level of sport – likely influenced by the use of aggressive and dominating war metaphors in public portrayals – other valuable dimensions of sport have all but disappeared for some. As Eric Anderson (2009: 48) observes:

the existing structure is so powerful in its influence, basked in decades of 'tradition,' that many maintain that without winning, there is no purpose to sport. This ethos moves sport far from the field of leisure and recreation, and closer to the act of war.

Absent are accounts of high-level athletes being captivated by sport for its ludic and creative qualities. Absent too are accounts of professional sportspeople being motivated or engaged simply 'for the love of the game'. Sage suggests that these have been eclipsed 'by an obsession with victory above all else. Broadcast sports tends to be unbridled odes to winning' (Sage, 1990, cited in Trujillo, 1995: 409).

For some, there is nothing wrong with unbridled odes to winning – we *should* celebrate both the hard work and the success of our athletes. Some point to the desire to win being a 'natural' dimension of our humanity, a more complex and evolved dimension perhaps, but nonetheless embedded within a 'survival of the fittest', 'kill or be killed', 'it's in the genes' ideology. Further, success of athletes and unbridled 'odes to winning' are reported by some to improve the health of the nation through a 'feel-good factor', bring people together, and encourage solidarity and national pride (Forrest and Simmons, 2003; Hallmann *et al.*, 2013). Public portrayals, in our experience, tend to assume the tone that *we should all accept, embrace and promote these values.* They typically portray a hunger to win as desirable and natural. Anything else is seen as deficient.

It is not only the athlete who is expected to win – coaches and managers must get results too. The choice of to which athletes to give an opportunity therefore becomes a dangerous one, as the coach cannot afford too many mistakes. What coach would want to own up to training a failure or investing huge amounts of money (either from private or government funds) in those who win no medals? The quest to find winners means the coaches and performance team must intensify their strategies to find 'new talent', spreading their nets wider and looking at increasingly younger ages, and by employing more intense testing strategies in the search for potential. The pressure on coaches and performance directors, like the athlete, is always there. In response, athletes and those who have been identified with potential are expected to 'give everything', leave their family, home and sometimes countries to train with top coaches at leading institutes where their 'gifts' can be 'best developed', sometimes risking injury or health to pursue victory (see Malcolm and Sheard, 2002; Therberge, 2008).

We detect that, even within cultures where a hunger to win has not historically been predominant, a change in ethos has slowly been taking place over the past two decades. For example, for those of us who have been steeped in the British sporting culture, we don't have to dig too deep to remind ourselves of a British trait for supporting the underdog. It seems that, in the past at least, the UK often fostered a spirit of 'playing the game' as opposed to 'winning the game'. Journalists, especially prior to the 2012 Olympics and the huge medal tally for the UK, would often point to the USA or Australia and ask: *'What's the matter with British athletes?' 'Why don't our sportspeople have the killer instinct?' 'Why aren't we more like them?'*

Forging a U-turn in attitude seemed to be the aim of the UK's Secretary of State for Sport who voiced how the government would support these changes in attitude through a change of policy. 'When you play sport,' he suggested, 'you play to win. That is my philosophy' (Department for Culture, Media and Sport, 2008). A philosophy, he suggested, that was at 'the heart' of a plan to 'change the culture of sport in England'. What was needed, *he* believed, was records broken, medals and tournaments won. This change in attitude and culture was decreed as necessary not just at the highest levels of sport, but *throughout* sport. The subtext was that is was necessary for everyone in sport, all of the time. Government policy for sport in England, from this time forward, was about winning.

Of course we don't need to look too far to find examples of the type of 'winning attitude' we were expected to mirror. Australia has for some time been renowned for its ethos which is reflected in the words of Professor Peter Frickes, onetime Director of the Australian Institute for Sport, broadcast in a prime-time television documentary:

> The main drive of the AIS is we are here to win. Getting a personal best and trying your hardest is fantastic and you would never knock an athlete for doing that, but you are here to win. Getting on the Olympic team is fantastic and getting a green and gold tracksuit is fantastic, but you're here to win. No athlete comes in here without fully understanding and being absolutely committed to winning, winning and winning. That's what it's all about.
>
> (BBC, 2006)

If winning is everything, winners become the heroes who inspire, motivate and lead, while those who are successful in performance terms become society's role models. But what becomes of those who do not win? During my (KD) Ph.D. I was still working as part of BBC Radio Five Live's on-course commentary team. At the PGA championship I was to follow and commentate on the 10.20 a.m. group, which included Ballesteros and two other Ryder Cup players. It was the late 1990s and all three players were at the peak of their careers. I went to the first tee a little earlier than I needed to and stood among the crowd watching a number of other groups tee off, soaking up the atmosphere and waiting for my match. After one group teed off a man in front of me turned to his friend and asked: 'Who's up next?' The reply is an example of the disparity between 'the gods' and 'the rest' in the eyes of many fans. After scanning the programme his friend replied: 'Ah, nobody.' Because the three (very good golfers by the virtue of the fact that they were on tour) hadn't won, they were 'nobodies'.

To use another war analogy, the 'casualties' of sport are those who are unable to win or sustain success in performance terms. They are widely expected to feel shame and may be the butt-end of jokes. Those who fail at sport in performance terms cannot survive financially in competitive sport; they are unlikely to gain media attention or secure lucrative endorsements. They are not recognised, we don't know their names, and they are typically not deemed worth following or supporting or writing about. While movies, documentaries and books describe the lives of winners, we know very little about those who do not win. Those who 'lose' seem to become invisible. Do we see only the disgrace of the loser? Do we draw merely further impetus to strive harder ourselves? Or are we missing potentially important lessons?

Perhaps curiosity, to understand more about human behaviour, has been behind research targeted at understanding – and ultimately predicting and controlling – winning behaviour. In psychology, research has attempted to identify effective cognitive strategies (e.g. Gould *et al.*, 1981; Mahoney and Avener, 1977), and psychological variables affecting performance (e.g. Gould *et al.*, 1992, 1999; Greenleaf *et al.*, 2001). These studies have spawned further research to explore the traits of winners and the characteristics associated with peak performance and then how these characteristics might be developed (Gould *et al.*, 2002; Williams and Krane, 2001). From this reservoir of research more refined strategies have been created aimed at nurturing skills believed to be essential to win in sport – such as becoming mentally tough (e.g. Jones *et al.*, 2002).

Over the past decade or so numerous studies have been used to develop and design programmes, interventions and strategies targeted at young performers, at talent development or aspiring athletes who want to develop the psychological 'strengths' associated with enhanced performance outcomes. Performance is the name of the game and the *raison d'être* of the research and the interventions it informs. While this focus does not coincide with our interests, we don't particularly have a problem with its goals. What could be wrong with trying to help aspiring sportspeople improve their sport performance? On the face of it, nothing. However, we (and many others) are concerned when this becomes the *only* or *primary* focus; that is, when performance enhancement in the quest to win takes over from all other interests, needs, goals and aspirations. When this happens, there is the very real potential of obscuring or normalising a host of maladaptive practices and behaviours.

A subgroup of researchers in sport psychology and related disciplines have explored the darker side of sport, sometimes being vocal in warning of the dangers of extreme performance-enhancement practices (e.g. Andersen, 2009; Gilbourne and Richardson, 2006; Gilbourne and Andersen, 2011; Ingham *et al.*, 2002; Therberge, 2008). In response to their opposition and the concerns expressed by some practitioners and sportspeople, governing organisations have more recently begun to introduce policies and measures to ensure that attention is given to the bigger picture. Athlete welfare, education and lifestyle support through 'holistic' programmes and 'athlete-centred' models are key examples of this (Miller and Kerr, 2002; Cruickshank and Collins, 2013). We welcome these initiatives and see, at a minimum, their continuation and development as a moral and ethical necessity.

Winston Churchill was reported to have said: *'Without victory, there is no survival.'* This saying, it seems to us, holds true nowhere more so than in public portrayals of professional sport. Those who lose do not survive. Even for those who make it to the top and win at the highest level, every athlete knows that *you are only as good as your last win.* You cannot let up, you have to keep pushing, striving, ever higher, ever faster. *No athlete can sit back on their laurels.* The pressure to win is always on, day in, day out. Can it ever be possible to reconcile these brutal truths with a morally and ethically informed position? If so, the pressing question at this point in time is: *how?*

Body as machine

> Discipline in sport requires control of athletes' bodies through the acquisition of skill and a sophisticated body of knowledge focused on how to produce skilled athletes. Coaches realize that athletes become disciplined in the performance of skills as a consequence of a meticulous observation of detail in which coaches' knowledge about skill acquisition completely fills the time and space available with its required activity.
>
> (Shogun, 1999: 18)

> The British team has used computational fluid dynamics (CFD), a technique which harnesses computer processing power to model airflows and see how even the tiniest change to a bike will affect how the air behaves around it.
>
> (Williams, 2012)

Within a culture in which winning is everything, then doing 'whatever it takes' to maximise performance outcomes becomes a reasonable course of action. Performance enhancement is typically glossed over as 'natural' and 'normal' within most public portrayals of high-level sport. It is a widely shared assumption that it is both possible and desirable to shape performance through specific interventions. While this applies in a very literal sense to equipment an athlete may utilise in their sport, it has also more recently come to apply to the athlete's *body* as well. As Shogun's words in the excerpt above suggest, the athlete's body has come to be seen as a machine amenable to control in much the same way that the bicycle is described by Williams, above. Contemporary interventions routinely view the sportsperson's body – and often their mind as well – in mechanistic terms: as a machine to be developed, reworked and fine-tuned through targeted interventions.

One reason why athletes, coaches, journalists and fans migrate towards mechanistic metaphors is the lure of perceived control (Stewart *et al.*, 2011). Bikes, cars, computers and other machinery can be built, tinkered with, taken apart, fixed and rebuilt. This can be a comforting thought when one is putting one's body on the line, pushing it to the limit. It's also helpful if we are starting a journey to know that we can build the type of body that is needed – that there is a blueprint. Most people are used to having a mechanic work on their car, rather than fix it themselves. Thus the 'body as machine' metaphor also provides a potentially reassuring narrative map for the athlete by subtly reminding him or her that it is 'normal' and 'natural' to hand over the keys (responsibility) for the car (their body, training, rehabilitation) and let the experts do their thing. Then, like the racing car, each individual segment of the athlete's body can potentially be analysed, tested, scrutinised and perfected. Technological advances make it possible to monitor the athletic body during training and redesign its motion to fit a more biomechanically efficient movement pattern. It can also monitor what the individual has ingested or injected, take omega waves to measure central nervous system activation and cardiac functioning, and factor in the degree to which blood is oxygenated.

The mechanistic imagery and analogies, however, also provide a means through which athletes may become both desensitised to others (the experts) pushing, prodding and probing, while at the same time being provided with a language that rationalises the necessity of this 'work'. There is a danger that the metaphor of the machine functions to depersonalise and detach the body from the self. As Williams notes: 'even healthy athletes deal with their bodies as a sensitive piece of equipment over which they do not have total control' (Williams, 1996: 40). The body/self split facilitates the body being seen as an object to be worked on by others while making it more difficult for an individual to object to this scrutiny. The intrusion becomes so much a part of life in elite sport that many athletes refer to these interventions as being 'natural'.

Increasingly, however, it becomes more difficult to know what is and is not natural given the number of people working on the athlete's mind, body and performance at any time. *Which bit are we claiming is natural?* For Trujillo (1995), as the sporting body becomes a machine in the way we control, manage and talk about it, so too it becomes governed by principles of 'maximum output' (Brohm, 1978: 55) or 'maximum performance' (Sage, 1990: 111). Bodies, under these social and cultural conditions, come to be endlessly judged on times, distance, weight, number, size and ever-more sophisticated statistical analyses. *Are these practices, too, natural and normal?* To what extent, we might ask, does sustained immersion in testing, monitoring and targeted modification threaten subjective dimensions of their body–self relationship? In light of the prevalence in sport of eating disorders, sexual and physical abuse, and substance use (Brackenridge, 2001; Fasting and Brackenridge, 2005; Green *et al.*, 2001; Papathomas and Lavallee, in press), feelings of concern in this regard are justified.

It is not just the athlete for whom the body as machine metaphor underpins and guides practice. It goes without saying that in modern-day sport performance enhancement is the purview of not only each individual athlete but entire support teams. Those who support the performance of the athlete become performers too – or 'cogs in the machine'. At the top level, coaching staff will often coach only a specific skill. For example, teams want psychologists to teach athletes to become 'mentally tough', while others are responsible for speed or endurance, place kicks, the short or long game and so on. This picture of the performance team may perhaps be seen most obviously in grand prix motor sport. It takes a team of ten to 16 mechanics to change four tyres on a Formula One car during a pit-stop. The teams work continually to cut fractions of a second off these pit-stop times and, like the athletes they support, these teams are monitored and filmed in order to improve performance. During one pit-stop, which McLaren completed in record time at the German Grand Prix in

2012 with a stationary time of 2.31 seconds, the team changed four tyres, refuelled the car and wiped the driver's helmet. As in many sports, every split-second counts in the drive to win. Although other performance teams may be less visible, their input to victory – in both individual and team sports – is no less integral to what we now recognise as a team approach to supporting elite athletes to peak at the right time.

Like war-speak, the use of mechanistic metaphors saturates public portrayals of sport. However, Butryn and Masucci (2009) argue that the blurring of the boundary between human and machine is more than metaphoric. They note that a:

> growing number of researchers from across several disciplines have also argued that our 'humanness' has been so profoundly altered by more intimate, available, and often unavoidable engagements with technology that humans should be reconceptualized as posthuman cyborgs.
>
> (Butryn and Masucci 2009: 286)

While becoming a 'posthuman cyborg' is too big a step for many of us, we may be persuaded that it isn't too big a step for some athletes when we consider the use of blood doping, performance-enhancing drugs or anabolic steroids. Perhaps replacement knee joints, prosthetics and 'smart medicines' really do challenge the idea of a *natural* human. However, given the importance of winning, the question *'are we harming ourselves by becoming more machine-like?'* is of little interest in sport. Rather, the question that concerns athletes is: *'Is it legal?'*

Very public portrayals

The public sportsperson who emerges in the twenty-first century comes to light via a mass media and an electronically mediated age (Hughson, 2009). When Washington and Karen (2010: 47) write that 'the marriage between sports and the media has transformed sports', they touch on what is perhaps *the* most significant 'marriage' in professional sport. At the professional level, sport needs media attention to attract an audience. Sport organisations need to lure the public to buy tickets to watch events, or buy subscriptions to the sport channels. Sport *wants* the public woken up to events, to whet their appetites, to be motivated to buy the product and follow their heroes. The 'marriage' is reciprocal, too. Despite it being widely accepted that newspaper circulation is declining, the sizes of the sport sections have increased (Vincent and Crossman, 2012) and are reported to be the most read sections of newspapers (Boyle and Haynes, 2000; Coakley and Donnelly, 2009). It seems that the sporting public, fans and enthusiasts have a collective and insatiable appetite for reading sport news, commentaries and reports.

For those who work in the media, the 'bottom line' is a need for content – something to write about. The sport media does not just report the facts but strives to provide a 'good story'. A 'good story' for the media is generally a story that sells papers, gains viewers or accumulates web page hits. Perhaps the best way to achieve this is through drama. And sport – when the tale is 'well told' – offers drama in abundance. It offers heroes (and potential fallen heroes) like 'Apollo' alongside (usually) a clear and understandable outcome: win, loss or draw. This provides a live story plot without a foregone conclusion that may create tension and intrigue. Sport offers instances of interpersonal competition that may be storied as conflict, battle, combat or war and potential sci-fi accounts of 'human machines' driven to the limits of their capabilities. Modern-day sport provides all this day in, day out, across the world.

In publicly portraying these dramas, the media *amplify* what they see and, very often, *distort* what occurs. Perhaps it is impossible to do otherwise. It is, after all, naive to expect *any* story to merely mirror the events it recounts. However, it has been our experience that the media's portrayals typically misrepresent sportspeople in systematic ways. That is, the distortion that is introduced is not random, but instead is slanted towards the characteristics discussed above.

Kitrina's analysis of media reports covering her sport career (Douglas, 2014) provides a detailed exploration of some of the ways in which her life was *constructed* in a particular image through newspaper articles. In 1984, for example, an article was published in *The Sunday Times* which read, 'as soon as Kitrina finishes her round she leaves the course, eats and returns to the practice ground to work for a couple of hours. It is this relentless drill that has taken her to the top in her first season.' Here, the 'relentless drill' may not have been responsible for the success and the 'drill' may not have even been relentless. Yet the use of these links within a military coda help the reader form a picture that likely fits with *their* expectations of a dedicated athlete, working hard and making sacrifices in the pursuit of victory. Perhaps it also works to athletes' advantage – they know that being serious and working hard is valued. Either way, our point is that through their representations the media play a big part in cementing particular stories which pave the way for building the general public's expectations about what it is to be an elite sportsperson.

While other forms of portrayal also shape public understanding, the media are unparalleled in scale and reach. Theirs are *very* public portrayals. In addition to newspaper circulation, book sales and television viewing figures in the millions, the public have more recently been given opportunities to hear directly from athletes through online means. Blogs, Tweets, YouTube clips, Facebook pages and websites often receive tens of thousands of hits and sometimes much more. The public reach of the electronically savvy sportsperson was demonstrated when, in December 2013, Olympic diver Tom Daley announced publicly that he was in a relationship with a man, via a YouTube video on his website. By doing so, he bypassed journalists who he said had misquoted him in the past. In just two weeks, the clip had clocked up over ten million hits.

Such mammoth public interest in one athlete's sexuality says much about troubling heterosexist assumptions that still permeate sport in the twenty-first century. It will be interesting to see the extent to which Daley's very public announcement helps to shift sport's heteronormative culture. In the meantime, Daley's action, and the number of people who responded to it, suggests (on the surface at least) that famous athletes are now empowered to share their personal stories in sport. Perhaps the advent of the electronic age has increased athletes' freedom in this regard. Our feeling, however, is that assumptions about sport and sportspeople generally remain entrenched, based as they are on many years of media portrayals weighted in particular directions. Sustained questioning, resistance and critique are, we believe, still needed to overturn some of the more damaging portrayals.

A master narrative in public portrayals of sport?

Critically, public portrayals do not just *represent* athletes but *construct* them. Public portrayals shape what is expected of elite athletes and, often, what is demanded of them in terms of lifestyle and behaviour. Because sport is a *closed loop system* (Anderson, 2005), in that people in sport have typically been immersed in sport culture from a young age, few alternative perspectives are likely to penetrate. Public portrayals may be seen as helping create a *master narrative* within high-level sport: a particular shape of story that encapsulates what sport *is* and what it *means*.

Master narratives provide a useful function in that they 'give guidance and direction to the everyday actions of subjects; without this guidance and sense of direction, we would be lost' (Bamberg, 2004). That is, without some shared understanding between people of what we mean when we talk about any *thing*, it would be impossible to interact with others or make sense of the world. Thus:

> speakers constantly invoke master narratives, and that many, possibly even most, of the master narratives employed remain inaccessible to our conscious recognition and transformation. Master narratives structure how the world is intelligible, and therefore permeate the petit narratives of our everyday talk. If this is true, it follows that speakers generally and principally are compliant and only rarely engage in resisting or countering the grid of intelligibility provided by what is taken for granted.
>
> (Bamberg, 2004)

What Bamberg ties together is the need for a starting point, some kind of common understanding, and that this starting point is largely 'inaccessible to our conscious recognition'. As language users, we communicate by using what is passed down to us, what is around us or what is accessible to us. This process usually commences with others teaching us this coding system, and these people have, in turn, at an earlier phase of their lives, learned a complex system of communication in order to make sense of life, to commune and live with others. When we take on these communication processes we also take on their histories, as if the past was rushing through our veins. Narrative, Mark Freeman suggests (2010: 123), 'rather than being imposed on life from without, is woven into the very fabric of experience'. The word 'woven' is useful, as it provides a sense of the way in which, during the process of learning to communicate when we are children, we also learn and begin a process of learning what words, phrases and stories fit with what others can understand, expect and make sense of.

When something is too distant from our realm of understanding it is simply unintelligible. Explaining this point, Arthur Frank (2010) draws on a story about the early Canadian settlers whose understanding of Native people and their ideology made it impossible to do anything but cast them as 'savages' and, when in court, deem their actions unlawful. We need some type of common ground to make sense of life and the tools we are given have historical implications for their current usage. The term 'hero', for example, has been used across cultures and across time. When a football fan describes his favourite player as 'my hero' we understand some of the personal significance for this individual. When basketball fans named the team's star player 'Apollo' it made sense to Patricia and Peter Adler through the historical significance of Apollo the god. Master narratives provide these kinds of moorings for our life, and they tie us with other people, events and actions.

The point of labouring this issue is to highlight that master narratives are needed so that we can all, to some extent, share *something*. The problem, however, is that master narratives tend to become hegemonic, totalitarian and ultimately oppressive by constraining or limiting individuals to socially dominant roles, identities or behaviours. Therefore, there is a dark side to master narratives: they can constrict or damage an individual's moral agency, and restrict and stunt emotional, intellectual and/or physical growth (Lindemann, 2009: 418).

This can occur in three ways. First, dominant or master narratives *hide* how they subjugate people (i.e. bring them under control), 'so that nothing morally objectionable appears to be going on' (Nelson, 2001: 162). Second, dominant narratives *naturalise* an (oppressive) identity, 'making it seem inevitable that certain groups of people must occupy certain places in society' (Nelson, 2001:162). Third, dominant narratives *normalise* an identity, by focusing on the behaviour that is expected under certain conditions, which deflects attention away from the behaviour itself. In addition:

> oppressive narratives are notoriously evidence-resistant. They run roughshod over what actually happens in the world, papering over or distorting inconvenient facts that might call the narrative's credibility into question, and undermining the cognitive authority of people who are in a position to point out those inconvenient facts.
>
> (Nelson, 2001: 167)

One example of how a master narrative dominates our consciousness is the term we use for programmes meant to help those in sport avoid becoming role-engulfed by managing their life, emotions and health in a positive way. When describing these programmes or initiatives, we use the term *athlete centred* as opposed to *person centred*. It may be that as practitioners we consider the full potentiality of the *person* when delivering support under this model. But why then do we use the word *athlete*? What about all the other roles or identities the *person* may have (such as student, mother, writer, aunt, sister, board member, artist, actor and so on)? By using the word *athlete* rather than the word *person*, are we not implicitly placing sport and the sportsperson ahead of other dimensions of life? Have we fallen under the spell of a master narrative? The fact that we accept the term *athlete centred* suggests we have become complicit in privileging sport ahead of other dimensions of life.

If, as Nelson suggests, a master narrative in sport naturalises and normalises a particular view of sport and sportspeople, while hiding the processes through which this occurs, how would an athlete *see* these processes or become empowered to resist? What kind of lens might an individual adopt to make these processes visible? These questions become all the more challenging when we recognise that master narratives are often 'inaccessible to our conscious recognition', run roughshod over what 'actually' happens and undermine the authority of those who show 'the inconvenient facts' (Nelson, 2001: 167).

Our answer to this question is that we must find a way to move, in Erving Goffman's (1959) terms, beyond the 'front-stage' stories that dominate public portrayals of sport and sportspeople to access instead the 'back-stage' stories. This is the first step: to move out of the public realm into the private realm of personal stories. The second step requires us to 'lift the veil' on the lives and experiences of high-level athletes to get 'under the skin' of widely shared assumptions and conventions. By doing this, we can potentially get behind the master narrative of sport, to see what lies behind the kinds of stories we've explored in this chapter. We need to see this master narrative not as the sole truth or reality, but as a partial and situated social construction. How, though, might we access these kinds of stories? What sense might we make of them? And how might we represent them to make them available to a wider audience? It is to these questions – questions of methodology – that we turn in the next two chapters.

2 Life story research and the contribution of the insider

> Fieldwork consists of more than collecting data, something that catapults it beyond simply being there. And whatever constitutes that elusive 'more' makes all the difference. Regardless of outcome, I think the critical test is how deeply you've felt involved and affected personally.
>
> (Wolcott, 2002: 210)

At the end of Chapter 1 we set ourselves the task of getting behind front-stage public portrayals of sportspeople to access the back-stage stories of sportspeople's experiences. To do so, we have had to find ways to, first, *access* athletes' experiences (i.e. uncover and learn about them), second, *make sense* of those experiences (i.e. distil and understand them) and, third, *represent* them in a way that makes them accessible to others.

In this chapter, we describe what we have done to achieve these aims, providing a rationale for our approach. Two particular characteristics characterise our work. First is Kitrina's role as an *insider* to professional sport (golf) culture. We consider how Kitrina's embodied experience of *being* a professional tournament golfer, combined with longitudinal fieldwork that draws on her pre-existing relationships, helped generate new insights. We also discuss some of the ethical challenges that can arise in researching one's own community or culture. Second is our use of a *narrative life story* methodology. We reflect on how and why this has proved a fruitful methodology that has given us space to engage intensively and creatively with the experiences of people playing high-level sport.

A focus on experience

As long ago as 1934, Thomas Znaniecki wrote on the challenge of understanding human activity and experience:

> When I wish to ascertain at first hand what a certain activity is … I try to experience it. There is only one way of experiencing an object; it is to *observe* it personally. There is only one way of experiencing an activity; it is to *perform*

it personally. Practical men [*sic*] insist on this: they will tell you that you cannot fully realise what you are doing till you do it yourself.

(cited in Plummer, 2001: 33)

In our research we are interested in understanding a 'certain activity' (high-level sport) and the lives of those who experience it directly (high-level sportspeople). In relation to these aims, nothing has changed regarding the truthfulness of Znaniecki's remarks over the past eight decades. Perhaps the best way to understand high-level sport is still to perform it personally. Yet this seemingly self-evident truth often appears to be forgotten in much social and psychological research. The relatively recent rise – or, perhaps, return – of self-study and self-reflection through auto-ethnography (see Holman-Jones *et al.*, 2013) perhaps heralds a return to recognising the importance of direct personal experience of an activity or phenomenon. Through this methodology, personal experience becomes the basis through which a particular culture is explored. Auto-ethnographic approaches to research have been used by an increasing number of researchers in sport over recent years (e.g. Carless, 2012; Douglas, 2009; Duncan, 2000; Gilbourne, 2010; Sparkes, 1996; Smith, 1999; Tiihonen, 1994; Tsang, 2000).

In the research we present in this book, Kitrina's direct personal experience of high-level sport has been critical. Her position as an insider to professional sport culture offers an unusual perspective within this field because she has direct personal experience of (elements of) the topic of enquiry. Insights from Kitrina's immersion in professional sport culture have been shared in a number of auto-ethnographies (Douglas, 2009, 2012, 2013, 2014), permeating and informing much of the material in this book.

Yet Kitrina's auto-ethnographic work can provide only one person's experience of life as a high-level sportsperson. As much as we value and support the use of auto-ethnography, we do not see this as the only legitimate form of social research. While it offers much that cannot be gained through other methodologies, it is necessarily limited through its focus on a single life. We aspire to include the experiences and voices of others in our research, and see this as a necessary step in the context of our aims for this book. The question, then, is *how* might we access, explore and understand *others'* experiences of high-level sport? The first challenge we had to negotiate was gaining *access* to elite and professional athletes.

A few years ago we conducted a study for a local council interested in community physical activity provision. The number of Asian men participating in physical activity had been very low and it had led Asian men to be identified as a 'hard-to-reach' group. At one community day centre which had managed to attract a large group of Asian men who participated in a weekly physical activity programme we interviewed a practitioner about how he had accessed these 'hard-to-reach' men. His reply revealed the absurdity of our assumptions and categorisations. 'They're not hard to reach at all,' came the reply, 'we just go round to each house in a mini-bus, pick them up and bring them to the centre.'

Elite athletes, like these Asian men, and countless other so-called 'hard-to-reach' groups, are often considered difficult to access because they don't fit comfortably with traditional strategies regarding access and recruitment. Famous sportspeople, like 'elites' and 'celebrities' in many areas of life, may make themselves difficult to access by establishing barriers to protect their time, privacy, actions and activities. But, as we described in Chapter 1, Emma Richards, by completing a round-the-world race, was granted personal access to world-class athletes, celebrities and even royalty. So there are ways around this problem, one of which is membership of the culture of interest. In our work, Kitrina's membership status and involvement in professional sport opened doors to access and recruit elite and professional sportspeople in ways that 'outsiders' would likely find difficult or impossible.

When we began our research, this was the expected end of Kitrina's insider contribution. It was expected that after the 'making contact' and 'giving an invitation to participate' stages of the research, her input would be much the same as any other researcher. We now see this as a simplistic notion that omits many other valuable dimensions of what an insider might contribute. It wholly misrepresents how relationships developed across a life in sport might be extended for research purposes and it also fails to take account of the sportsperson's changing roles, relationships and their ethical dimensions. It omits the less predictable hazards that go along with conducting research by accessing pre-existing relationships, environments and hierarchies. We share some examples of these issues in Chapter 3.

Something is missing

When it came to the lives and experiences of high-level athletes, we began with a suspicion that *something was missing* from the existing reservoir of portrayals. Kitrina's embodied experience served as the trigger in realising that something was being omitted in public portrayals of sport. The master narrative was *not* the whole story. Narrative scholars have suggested that when our experience is at odds with the master narrative the outcome is some type of fracture. How acutely the fracture is experienced is down to its size. A small crack or initial awareness may not be enough for an individual to recognise that there are conflicting narratives at play in his or her life. One story with cracks in it may not even be enough for an individual to feel pressure or tension. Yet a bigger fracture can alert an individual to a mismatch between their own experience and the ways in which people like them are portrayed publicly.

The first time I (KD) remember a fracture between the public portrayals about what it means to *be* a professional tournament golfer (the 'available stories') and my own experience occurred after I'd been playing golf for about a year. I describe the scene in the following story.

Golf course, hotel, airport

The 15-minute drive to the course went by in a flash, the sun was up, the weather warm, it was spring and the grass was lush. The field that had been muddy all winter was now inviting, a carpet of green mown velvet. The aroma of dank, wet dirt had been replaced by a sweet, fresh lure. She wanted to pour her clean white golf balls into a neat pile and begin hitting, to feel the burst of the ball off the club face and watch it fly brightly through the morning sunshine. The radio had been on during the drive but she hadn't really noticed. That was until one of Europe's top tour players came on air live to talk about his last win. He was asked about how he'd won, the six-iron to the last hole and the tantalising three-foot putt to win. He talked about how he felt, what winning that tournament meant, what was next, about his hopes for The Open. The chat was relaxed, no tense moments, lots of laughs, he sounded upbeat, they sounded like friends. She pulled into the parking space but didn't switch off the radio with the engine; she was enthralled, interested, and wanted to listen to the end of the interview.

'Ah, you've got such a great life', the interviewer stated in envy, bringing their time to a close.

'Well it's not really that great,' the star came back. 'I only see the golf course, the hotel and the airport, there's no time for anything else.'

These final words seemed to take on a life of their own. *I only see the golf course, the hotel and the airport ... golf course, hotel, airport ... golf course, hotel, airport.* She began to ruminate in her mind how this well-known tour player encapsulated what life in golf meant for *him*. But she didn't like the sound of the story. She didn't want *that story* to be *her story*. Of course, she couldn't articulate what she *did* want, but his story didn't seem to fit with her ideas or plans about life, to *only* see the golf course, the hotel and the airport.

She switched off the radio and stepped out of the car, almost in autopilot mode. Like every other morning she took her practice balls and clubs from the boot of her car and walked over to the range a few yards away, never really thinking that she may have already begun this journey: *golf course, hotel, airport.*

Given that, as we suggested in Chapter 1, the lure of adulation, hero status, glory and money are intoxicating and irresistible to a young performer, it seems strange now that I didn't think: '*I'm going to have to give up a lot to be a pro.*' Rather, what filled my mind was the question: *Is this the only way?* Hearing the winning professional talk about life in sport as he lived it provoked a search for an alternative story in the *inner library* (Frank, 2010) of experiences that might offer a way to combine my expectations for life with the supposed reality of being a professional tour player. We have heard other participants tell this story almost word for word. At the time, I wasn't aware of other athletes providing a different story plot. It appeared that there were no alternatives. Over time, however, I became aware of stories that didn't fit this mould. The following story provides one example.

Campervan

There is something about the glow of a setting sun across an expanse of grass. What seems flat in the stark light of the midday sun becomes sea of undulations when lit by a deep red glow from the side. The carpet of dusk descending plays tricks on the eyes and on the colours of night as it settles down.

She knew she should stop, it was late, but the warm pockets of air, the dusty sand lingering like a mist, the intense sound of each hit was a melody that made her body feel alive. She swung back with a tension in her muscles, then uncoiled in a smooth and rhythmical release. Why stop and go to bed? She looked over at Annabel, who also seemed lost in the half-light. *Lucky you*, she thought, *staying in your campervan by the side of the range, sipping tea at the end of the day, relaxed, at ease, gentle, wandering up and down collecting your balls, slipping into bed and rising before the range gets busy.*

In all the years she had encountered Annabel on the practice ground, late at night, each lost in their own body rhythms, she had never really talked to her. They might nod, sometimes smile, sometimes even say something like '*Hi, beautiful evening*', or Annabel might say '*well done*' to show an awareness of her day's work. Annabel also showed awareness of something else by leaving space between them on the range, going to another patch of grass further away. She felt a kind of respect, allegiance, or perhaps they were kindred spirits, but they didn't talk, commune or interact.

Was it the fact that she was a 'winner' and Annabel a 'loser' that kept them apart? Was it the fact that Annabel toured in her campervan, doing it on a shoe-string, trying to make ends meet while she, in contrast, travelled in luxury on the Orient Express and stayed at five-star hotels? Was it the fact that Annabel never had to endure the pro-ams and the businessmen at dinners, whereas she had to smile on cue each week and lose a day of her life. She was annoyed that she had to play in every pro-am and players like Annabel didn't have to play. She knew, from the outbursts at the players' meeting, that Annabel was annoyed at not being allowed the opportunity to play with the sponsor or his guests. *How ironic*, she thought.

But, you see, on *this* evening they did talk. *This* evening they even sipped tea together, sat on camping chairs on the edge of the practice ground watching a great orange ball disappear from the sky. *Why are you so at ease with life*, she wondered. *Why are you here? Why doesn't it bother you that you don't win? How can you sound so joyful with your lot in life, no money, no wins, no glory?* These things didn't seem to saturate Annabel's motivations; there was something else more valuable, more sating, more exciting. It wasn't what she expected from someone on tour who never won. Annabel's life didn't fit the mould.

'Goodnight, and thank you', she said, as she left to drive back to her hotel room in a smoggy built-up area of town.

The press wrote of Kitrina as 'the hardest working professional on tour' and that it was 'relentless drill' that was responsible for her success (see Douglas, 2014). By rehearsing this kind of account time and time again, the media cemented in the public consciousness a particular narrative. That is, 'hard work' in terms of hitting thousands of practice balls is why a golfer is successful (in terms of wins, money, glory). However, Annabel's life and actions challenge this story on a number of counts. They challenge the *hard work equals success* plot, the *loser feels shame* plot as well as the *it's all about winning* plot. *Campervan* provides 'evidence' of a crack between the dominant storyline and life as lived. Embodied or experiential triggers, like in the story above, can be a cue to seek out answers, to *re-search* with the realisation that the dominant story doesn't hold true. That is: alternatives exist but we have to find the right lens and approach to uncover them.

Subjectivity

A first step in finding – or creating – a 'lens' that worked for our research was to understand that because we wished to explore the activity of high-level sport and the lives of those who experience it, the objective world (i.e. the world of physical entities or things) was *not* the focus of our study. We did not set out to examine, for example, the effect of sustained high-intensity training on bone mineral density among young athletes. Neither were we attempting to determine the numbers or quantities of things. For example, we did not attempt to answer questions such as: what is the proportion of youth academy footballers that make it into the professional game? For these lines of research, traditional scientific methods – methods derived from the natural sciences – are usually appropriate. These research methods operate within the positivist and post-positivist paradigms, typically taking a realist position to treat the 'reality' to be explored as a measurable and objective *thing* that can be known independently of the social and cultural context. Here, reality is assumed to be singular and potentially universal. These kinds of research approach, Andrew Sparkes (1992) has observed, usually have the aims of prediction and control. In the first example above, researchers might predict how increasing duration of high-intensity training affects young athletes' bone strength. In the second example, researchers might attempt to control drop-out rates by instigating a peer-mentor programme.

Instead, in our work we are primarily interested in how things (such as phenomena, events or occurrences) are *experienced* by individual human beings. It is less the phenomena, events or occurrences themselves that we focus upon, and more the effects, consequences, meanings and interpretations of those events for the person who lives them. Thus, our focus is directed towards *lived experience*. The only satisfactory way to gain understanding of an individual's lived experience is to try to learn from the individual herself. It is not, for us, desirable to enquire about one person's lived experience by asking a different person. While that other person is well placed to help us learn about *their* experience, they are not well placed to speak about another person's experience. How can one person ever know intimately and in an embodied manner the experience of another? While there may be times when this approach is the only available option, our preference is always to try to learn about lived experience through interacting directly with the individual himself. To do otherwise would be to invite or allow one person to speak about and for another. We prefer to let individuals speak for themselves. In this light, our overriding focus is always on *personal lived experience*.

A couple of examples may help clarify these general points. In the first example above, we would want to understand a young athlete's experience of sustained high-intensity training. We would be interested in the meaning of this behaviour in the context of their life more generally. We would want to learn about any consequences of training they experience in daily life. We may want to develop an understanding of how training affects the young athlete's feelings towards their body. In the second example, we would be interested in how youth academy footballers experience premature career cessation. We would perhaps ask: how does failure to achieve a professional contract impact upon an individual's identity, development, psychological well-being or mental health? We may want to learn about how one-off events or routine daily practices shaped the development of the individual and how they responded to these events over time.

There is little that is objective or measurable about personal lived experience. Instead, experience is subjective – it cannot be known in any meaningful way from the outside, from a distance or as a 'thing'. Neither can experience be given a numerical value that is able to adequately represent the complexity, subtlety, intensity, nuance, paradox or uniqueness that inhabit social life. Few aspects of lived experience, it seems to us, may be fairly described as fixed or stable. Instead, experience is likely to be fluid and shifting both within individuals over time and across different individuals. Even the most strongly embodied, overtly physical events are subject to individual interpretation and response that vary across individuals. Put simply, any given event will be experienced differently by different people. Further, experience of any event is likely to change across time and culture. In this sense, we consider that there is no 'right' or 'wrong' way to experience anything. One form of experience is as 'right' as any other. For us, therefore, the supposedly desired quality of validity (within positivist and post-positivist paradigms) is meaningless when it comes to researching human experience. How can one person's experience of sustained high-intensity training be 'valid' while another's is 'invalid'?

Like other qualitative researchers, we therefore favour a relativist rather than realist ontology (Sparkes and Smith, 2014) which sees the truth of human experience to be multiple and individual specific rather than singular and universal. We align ourselves within an interpretive paradigm that prioritises *understanding* and *illuminating* over the prediction and control favoured in positivism/post-positivism. A central aim within the interpretive paradigm is the elucidation of *meaning* as a way to question existing assumptions regarding social experience, striving 'to sustain conversation and debate, rather than attempt to act as a "mirror to nature", as a source of foundational, universal truth' (McLeod, 1997: 142). Within this paradigm, knowledge is accepted as socially constructed, and therefore dependent on the relationship between researcher and participant. Thus, the researcher is recognised as a *reflexive instrument* whose biography and positioning influence most, if not all, stages of a study (Etherington, 2004). The researcher's experience, too, is relevant to the research, and we explore aspects of this in Chapter 3.

Stories as a gateway to experience

Our preferred way of accessing another's experience is through inviting that individual to share *stories* of significant events in their life. Rather than focusing on constructs, opinions, perceptions or abstract ideas, storied forms of communication prioritise the individual's experience through sharing accounts of specific events and happenings that have occurred during their life. By recounting moments of personal experience in story form (detailing, for example, what happened, where, when, to whom, what were the consequences), the individual's emotional and subjective responses are also made accessible for study.

Stories recount the minutiae of concrete day-to-day events and are thereby grounded in lived experience. They are, in some respects at least, pre-analytic in that the storyteller need not explicitly summarise, interpret or analyse the events recounted. In contrast, when participants share their opinions, views, advice or conclusions there is a move towards a more abstract, analytic and distanced mode of communication. These forms of communication tend *not* to be overtly and explicitly grounded in lived experience. Instead, they typically 'hover over' the realities of life, keeping lived experience at arms' length. It has been our experience that encouraging and supporting participants to share stories characterised by rich description – as opposed to summaries, opinions or perspectives – provide the most powerful and grounded insights into lived experience.

For many years, Arthur Frank has advocated the importance of stories in social science research. For him, stories are essential in part because storytellers:

> offer those who do not share their form of life a glimpse of what it means to live informed by such values, meanings, relationships, and commitments. Others can witness what lives within the storyteller's community actually look, feel, and sound like. Storytellers tell stories because the texture of any form of life is so dense that no one can describe this form of life; the storyteller can only invite someone to come inside for the duration of the story.
>
> (Frank, 2000: 361)

Frank's remarks resonate with our research experience. While other forms of enquiry may provide us with facts, measurements, perceptions, opinions, correlations or differences, it is only through a participant's willingness and ability to share stories, combined with a researcher's willingness and ability to listen, that we can learn about an individual's values, meanings, relationships and commitments. It is true, too, that human experience – particularly around the time of the critical incidents that research often explores – tends to be 'dense' in that it is complex, messy, confusing and sometimes ambiguous or paradoxical. It is, oftentimes, not amenable to a neat summary. Stories allow all this to be preserved and included in part because, as John McLeod (1997: 112) suggests, 'in telling stories we are "telling more than we know"'.

Stories, however, cannot be considered to be the last word on an experience – they are always and at best a representation of that experience. Stories are, for us, the form of representation that allows us to get *closest* to another's experience. While some would question the extent to which we can ever fully know *our own* experience, most would agree that knowing *another person's* experience is fraught with difficulties. How can we fully understand how another person feels in response to a specific event? How can we possibly appreciate their hopes and fears? How can we recognise the ways in which their past experience may have influenced their behaviour in the present? There is no flawless way of accessing and understanding another's experience – any approach is both *partial* (in that we can never know the 'whole story') and *situated* (in that a 'God's-eye view' is impossible, we can only ever know from our own social and historical positioning).

Despite these limitations, we are not alone in appreciating stories as being one of the most effective ways to gain insights into personal experience. For Mark Freeman (2007, p. 132), 'It may very well be ... that the truest rendition of experience comes not from the immediate reality of the moment, flesh-and-bone solid though it may be, but from reflection, memory, *narrative*.' This applies equally to understanding *our own* lived experience through auto-ethnography (which typically relies on stories to make significant moments of experience available for study, as in the previous two stories) and to researching others' lived experience. In both, we invite and support reflection and the representation in storied form of personally important moments drawn from memory. Our focus on stories positions our work squarely within the tradition of *narrative research* or *narrative inquiry* (see Crossley, 2000; Clandinin, 2007; Lieblich *et al.*, 1998; Riessman, 2008). This is an approach used increasingly in sport psychology (see Smith and Sparkes, 2009a, 2009b; Smith, 2010). We agree with Freeman's (2007: 120) assertion that narrative research has a critical role to play in social science through its ability to 'lessen the distance between *science* and *art* and thereby open the way toward a more integrated, adequate, and humane vision for studying the human realm'.

Silenced stories

The use of stories to access and learn about others' experience depends on those stories being available – stories must be told before they can be heard. Yet many kinds of stories are not routinely told. Instead, they are, for one reason or another, *silenced*. For McLeod (1997: 100):

> The culture we live in supplies us with stories that do not fit experience, and experience that does not live up to the story. It may also fail to supply us with appropriate arenas for narrating whatever story it is we have to tell. The common theme across all of these circumstances is the experience of silence, of living with a story that has not or cannot be told.

Sport culture is no exception in this regard: certain stories are more 'tellable' than others. Some stories are not invited or are unwelcome while some experiences may be too difficult for the individual to share. Further, as Frank (2004: 62) points out, 'Not everything that everybody does is seen by others as worthy of a story.' Hitting balls on the range is not a worthy story for the media to report *unless* it makes a champion. In *Campervan*, Annabel isn't one of the winners – therefore her actions do not provide a worthy story for the press. The result is that her life and actions remain unreported, almost as if they didn't happen. For Frank (2004: 62):

> Stories do not merely narrate events. They convey on action and actor – either one or both – the socially accredited status of being worth notice. To render narratable is to claim relevance for action, and for the life of which that action is part. Storytelling continually redraws the boundary of a community's recognitions; it renders present what would otherwise be absent.

We would add that withholding or ignoring stories also renders *absent* what might otherwise be *present*. It isn't that Annabel was unvocal – she certainly spoke her mind at players' meetings and in informal groups. But because her life and what she has to say doesn't align with what mainstream sport culture wants to hear, her voice is silenced. Her experiences are rendered absent. Like the professionals teeing off the first tee while Kitrina was commentating, in the eyes of the fans she *becomes* a nobody. The culture of sport puts great emphasis on the stories of those who have 'been there' and these individuals are invited to tell researchers and biographers 'how they got to the top' and 'what made them successful'. They get invited on to sport programmes and to commentate on other athletes. When they do so, they understand what the culture expects in terms of a worthy story, and they draw on their own experiences of winning to provide evidence for the types of stories that are expected, which in turn propagate the master narrative, its values and its metaphors. As a result, alternative experiences are silenced.

There is a further reason that stories are silent. The experience or threat of shame can also result in silencing certain types of stories. Shame, according to McLeod (1997), is one reason why people maintain silence about traumatic events in their lives. It is reasonable to assume that if an athlete has stories that they feel contravene the master narrative, they may prefer to remain silent. If we consider a young athlete who has been sexually abused by an established coach (who in the eyes of the public may hold hero status) it's not too difficult to see how that young person could become mute – unable to voice their experience. For decades it was *always* the coach whose character was believed to be immutable and that grooming didn't exist. It took a series of scandals to shake that belief. Yet the uncovering of sexual abuse makes it no less traumatic for an individual to discuss how she or he was abused, raped or experienced sport-related bullying, because the culture remains primarily interested in conquest, battle, war, heroes and victory.

Returning to British diver Tom Daley's YouTube announcement of his relationship with a man, there appear to be some good reasons for him choosing this way of sharing his story rather entrusting it to the press. First, the media had apparently been hounding him for some time to reveal details of his personal relationship/s. Their interest was infused with heterosexist assumptions as they asked: who is your *girl*friend? Here, *their* expectations (of heterosexuality) potentially made his story more challenging to tell. Second, in his YouTube clip Daley refers to being misquoted by the press regarding his sexuality. Here, the press may be accused of sustaining the dominant assumption that elite male sportspeople are (and must be) heterosexual. Third, the media seemed to want a cemented, finalised and fixed story about Daley's sexual identity, even though he may be open to exploring his sexuality. It seems they wanted the label *gay* or *straight*. Yet Daley did not say, 'I'm gay'. His experience, it seems, was rather more complex than a single word could encapsulate. To communicate this complexity, he needed to share his *story*. The negotiations, tensions and ambiguities in Daley's story resonate with recent auto-ethnographies of same-sex attraction in sport contexts (Carless, 2010, 2012, 2013). Finally, Daley's example reveals another reason why some stories are silenced: at times it just isn't worth the hassle of sharing. For some time, as most of us prefer to, Daley kept his private life private. What a high-profile athlete may well learn is that by remaining silent about a potentially dangerous or traumatic story – keeping their 'self' locked behind closed doors – there is less danger that he or she will be attacked, humiliated, exposed, misquoted or misunderstood (see Douglas, 2009).

A question we may ask is: why have we been unable to break the silence surrounding certain taboo or hidden stories in sport? Gadamer (1975) reminds us that the things we recognise and think we know will inevitably influence and bias what *can be known* and *our interpretations of it*. In our view, a key reason why research hasn't revealed greater diversity among elite athletes is that researchers too are influenced by the dominant paradigm or story. We have a particular *horizon of interest* that limits, literally, how far we are able to see. We struggle to see beyond our interests, and our interests are informed by the dominant assumptions within our particular culture. Within the horizon of what we are able to see, we also have a *perspective of relevance*. This dictates what information we consider to be relevant to our studies. Again, this is shaped by our shared assumptions. For example, a sport psychologist wanting to learn about pre-shot routines is unlikely to be open to the sportsperson's need to talk about other issues. Perhaps many of us also feel unprepared for 'opening a can of worms', so we leave certain topics alone. By doing so we contribute to burying events, happenings and stories that need to be drawn into public awareness. We cannot, therefore, place our critique solely at the feet of the media and television, even though they have a huge influence. The way in which we conduct research has played a role in amplifying some stories while silencing others.

Life stories

One way to support participants in sharing stories that transgress mainstream assumptions is to sustain a trusting relationship with that individual over time. *Engaging* with their life and stories over time facilitates genuine and reciprocal trust, and makes it possible for particular experiences to be shared at a time of the participant's choosing. Kitrina's extended relationship with the participants in our original research – developed over 17 years at every level of golf – was the first stage. The second stage was continuing and developing this engagement through longitudinal research.

A characteristic of the research that underlies this book is an interest in stories that relate to moments across a person's life course, often shared over an extended period of time. The stories we have sought and witnessed are not a 'snapshot' of a particular moment in an individual's life, but rather a 'movie' that follows a significant portion of the storyteller's life span. They offer insights into the trajectory or arc of a life across time that permits consideration of how a particular life develops. Our work may therefore be considered as a form of *life story* or *life history* research (see Plummer, 2001).

A further rationale for a life story focus is that, for any person, *the now* only makes sense in relation to the experienced past and anticipated future. In other words, we cannot hope to develop a rich understanding of the emotions, responses and meaning of the moment without an appreciation of what has gone before and what is expected in the future. The act of narrating one's life experiences often results in connections being made across time and across events. This is an important way through which storytelling sheds light on the *meaning* of personal experience. For Susan Chase (2005: 656):

> Narrative is retrospective meaning making – the shaping or ordering of past experience. Narrative is a way of understanding one's own and others' actions, of organising events and objects into a meaningful whole, and of connecting and seeing the consequences of actions over time.

Michele Crossley (2003: 288) has argued that 'there is scant space in mainstream contemporary psychology to investigate questions of self and identity from a perspective that retains a sense of *both* psychological *and* sociological complexity and integrity'. Narrative approaches provide one route to bridging this schism, particularly when a *life course perspective* is utilised. The life course perspective:

> recognizes lives as more than mere products of some biological or psychological sequence. Rather, the life course paradigm recognizes development as a socially situated process. The life course itself, then, becomes an experiential product of a given historical order. The connection between the possible trajectories of development *and the construction of those possibilities by a given social structure* is acknowledged and, indeed, rendered necessary for study. Yet the life course perspective does not view social structure as inherently 'driving' development, for it preserves a notion of individual agency.... We do not privilege structure over agency, and in this way we argue that the relationship between culture and the individual is *reciprocal* and *coconstitutive.*
>
> (Hammack and Cohler, 2009: 11, emphases in original)

A life course perspective is central to our work, as we want to resist seeing, understanding and portraying sportspeople as *autonomous bounded selves*; that is, as disconnected and separate entities that think, feel and act on the basis of only conscious, internal, psychological processes. Instead, we understand sportspeople – like all people – as existing within a web of connections, both cultural and social. These cultural and social forces shape the cognitions, emotions and behaviours of athletes in profound (but often subconscious) ways. At the same time, we want to resist seeing, understanding and portraying sportspeople simply as 'products' of the social and cultural structures in which they are enmeshed. Sportspeople – like all people – retain a greater or lesser degree of agency in terms of how they respond to, negotiate and navigate social, political and cultural structures. It is these moments of navigation and negotiation, across the life course of a group of high-level sportspeople, that we explore throughout the book.

Ken Plummer (2001: 18–20) writes that life stories:

> refuse to be social scientists' own second-order constructs – accounts of accounts – that claim to be external and objective truth.... They are all first-order accounts which attempt to enter the subjective world of informants, taking them seriously on their own terms and thereby providing first hand, intimately involved accounts of life.... What matters, therefore, in life history research is the facilitation of as full a subjective view as possible, not the naïve delusion that one has trapped the bedrock of truth. Given that most social science seeks to tap the 'objective', the life history reveals, like nothing else can, the subjective realm.

We aspire to stay close to this orientation throughout the book. Doing so begins with an intensive *narrative engagement* (Hammack and Cohler, 2009) with participants' lives through their stories. If and when this engagement is successful, it can lead to, in Plummer's (2001) terms, an 'intimate familiarity' with a life. If, however, 'a study fails to get this "intimate familiarity" with a life, then such research must run the risk of simply getting it wrong: of speculating, abstracting and theorizing at too great a remove' (Plummer, 2001: 37). Avoiding this trap, we believe, requires a sustained effort to embody and enact an orientation well articulated by Robert Atkinson:

> All along, I have felt that it is important, in trying to understand another's experience in life or their relation to others, to let their voice be heard, to let them speak for and about themselves, and to look for the wholeness in their life. If we want to know the unique perspective of an individual, there is no better way to see this, and how the parts do fit together, than in their voice and their life story.
>
> (Atkinson, 2007: 231–232)

This point underlies our use throughout the book of first-person stories, each in a particular participant's own words. Doing so, we have found, offers the best chance of ensuring that their voice is heard when they speak for and about themselves, and communicating a sense of the wholeness in their life.

Insider relationships

Kitrina's insider status allowed her, quite literally, *inside the ropes* of professional golf culture. Todd Crosset's (1995) study of women on the LPGA Tour provides a contrasting example that helps clarify some of the possibilities that an insider perspective brings. Crosset conducted his research without embodied experiences of pro golf, without establishing relationships forged during the course of performing and without ever stepping on to the winner's podium. He had not experienced taking a trophy home, banking a winner's cheque, giving a winning speech, returning to his home town after winning, reading about his feats in the news or giving a press conference. His research began and stayed not only outside the ropes, but also outside the locker room and outside players' homes. He acknowledged that this was a limitation but, as an outsider to women's professional golf, he could do little else. The insider, in contrast, *has* been inside the ropes, on the podium, opened the mail with the selection result, has been coached, selected, rejected, funded and positioned in the minds of the public. These experiences, we suggest, create a different kind of connection and relationship with participants.

We often read, for example, when reviewing journal manuscripts, that 'trust and rapport was established' and that this was considered important. But seldom does the researcher comment on whether that trust moved beyond a one-way street (of the participant trusting the researcher) to become a reciprocal sharing. Too often, we feel, trust is *given* to the researcher (by the participant), but the 'outsider' researcher is unable or unwilling to display trust towards the participant (for example, by sharing information about themselves). Types of trusting knowledge which the insider and the participant might share are those unguarded moments of fragility, vulnerability or shame. In the same way as Kitrina will have seen Annabel attempt to change the tour's policy on who plays in pro-ams (and fail in this endeavour), Annabel would also have seen Kitrina fail to win, fail to perform, score poorly, be upset and so on. Each participant in our golf study had multiple daily opportunities to witness Kitrina's vulnerabilities as well as her successes. And, in a similar way, Kitrina had opportunities to witness each participant's vulnerabilities too.

Frank (1995: 72) writes that, 'even among the various selves that each of us is, a bedrock of the really real remains. Its name is often pain.' The kinds of vulnerability and pain that characterise moments of women professionals lives are – potentially at least – an area of common ground that is missing in 'outsider' research. For us, it is the deep levels of trust and empathy that can stem from shared or witnessed vulnerability and pain that lie behind several of the participants sharing (often for the first time) stories that deviate significantly from the 'safer' stories that we are used to hearing from high-level sportspeople.

In light of these points and those we made earlier in the chapter regarding access and embodied experience, we suggest that Kitrina's insider status brought some unusual qualities to our research. There are also, however, a number of risks with insider research. Table 2.1 outlines the key benefits and risks that applied to our work. Although we adopted a number of strategies to manage the risks, a key strategy was working closely as a research team where David's status as an 'outsider' to professional sport provided a counterpoint to Kitrina's insider position, allowing us to interrogate important moments in our research journey.

Stories, identity and behaviour

For narrative scholars, complex relationships exist between the personal stories people tell, the cultural narratives that inform their stories, the consequences of storytelling on sense of self, and the effects of all of this on actions and behaviours. A brief consideration of these relationships is necessary, we believe, to shed theoretical light on the stories – and our interpretations of them – that we share throughout the book.

While we often feel that the stories we tell of our lives are 'our own' stories, on reflection this is rarely, if ever, the case. Instead, each of our own unique stories, in some respects at least, may be considered a 'refashioning' of a wider story that circulates within our cultural habitus. In McLeod's (1997: 94) terms: 'Even when a teller is recounting a unique set of individual, personal events, he or she can only do so by drawing upon story structures and genres drawn from the narrative resources of a culture.' Whether we know it or not, we cannot help, it seems, but draw upon or make reference to a 'bigger' cultural narrative (e.g. a master narrative) when telling our personal stories. This is no less true when research participants story their lives: more general cultural narratives are invariably evoked, revealed or leant upon. These narrative forms may not, however, be immediately obvious or easy to see.

It is at this point that a distinction can be made between the terms *story* and *narrative*. While the two are sometimes used interchangeably, for the purposes of our work we sustain a distinction. Following Frank (1995), we use the term *story* when referring to an account told by a particular individual about events and happenings in his life and the term *narrative* when discussing a more general cultural storyline, plot or type of story. Thus, in general, individuals *tell stories*, but these stories draw on – or are derived from – more general cultural narratives.

Narrative theorists hold that both who we *are* as people (i.e. our identity or sense of self) and what we *do* as people (i.e. our behaviours or actions) are shaped by personal stories and cultural narratives (see Bruner, 1986; Crossley, 2000; Frank, 1995; McAdams, 1993, McLeod, 1997). In terms of identity or sense of self, it is increasingly recognised that identity is constructed through storytelling processes. In Brett Smith's (2007: 391) terms, 'people understand themselves as selves through the stories they tell and the stories they feel part of'. Likewise, Neimeyer and colleagues (2006: 128–129) see identity as

Table 2.1 Some benefits and risks of insider status

Phase of research	Benefits of insider status	Risks of insider status
Purpose of the research	Firsthand experience of the activity under investigation means the researcher can prioritise what is of concern to those in her culture (i.e. the athletes) as opposed to having the research community prioritise *their* interests and concerns. This doesn't mean that the research will be 'better' or more insightful, but it is likely to facilitate a different focus and generate alternative kinds of insights.	An insider may inappropriately impose her experience or interests upon others within the culture, assuming her own perspective to be universal.
Theory	An insider's experience can serve as the basis to test current theories. Her experience can also help make theory 'real', expanding dialogue between members of the culture in ways that enrich or challenge theory and received wisdom. These member-dialogues can critically explore and challenge the assumptions that underlie a master narrative or dominant ideology.	An insider may fail to see beyond the limits of her own experience and observations, thereby not appreciating other possible contexts in which a particular theory may be useful.
Accessing participants	A researcher who is or has been an insider to the community negates the need for a 'gatekeeper' to facilitate access. An insider is less likely to disturb the natural setting than a non-member, who may look or feel out of place (Fontana and Frey, 2000). The presence of an 'uncomfortable outsider' may constrain how members talk or act. Insider status provides access to sport settings that are off limits to the general public, media and even coaches. This can provide unique opportunities to observe participants behind the scenes in unguarded moments. It can also make it easier to talk with participants about sensitive issues. The insider also may have access to participants at other sites away from the study setting (e.g. hotels, restaurants, homes).	It is more difficult for athletes to avoid the insider researcher because she has authority to be in the environment. This may cause problems for an athlete who doesn't want to participate in research or who doesn't wish to give follow-up interviews. If there are unresolved tensions between the researcher and potential participants there is also potential bias in selection of participants. For example, the researcher may avoid inviting those individuals whom she dislikes to participate in the research. Normal barriers which elites erect to maintain distance from the public are not as effective at maintaining distance from the insider researcher. There is therefore a greater need to be sensitive and aware about participants' privacy.

Interactions are possible within participants' familiar territory rather than in isolation from their usual social setting (Wilkinson, 1998). To some extent, therefore, they are empowered through being on 'home turf.'

An insider may not only be familiar to the participants but also (as in Kitrina's case) to their families and friends as well. This can facilitate a fuller understanding of the individual's life.

An insider is also potentially the holder of *secret knowledge*. Things that are secret, Peter Adler believed, gave him 'both power and status' (Adler and Adler, 1991: 9) because they strengthened his research relationships.

Gathering data through interviews or observation

'Sister' status (LET, 2003) implies that rapport and trust are already given. As research begins with a pre-existing relationship, this can lead to less guarded comments, more 'history' to draw upon in interviews, and more opportunities to generate disconfirming questions, or to play devil's advocate. All this offers a deeper level of understanding.

A familiar face may be less intimidating.

Friendship is a potentially fruitful method.

The insider has greater understanding of culture-specific language and jargon.

Insider status alerts the researcher to how oppressed peoples may protect themselves by withholding and distorting data (Ladson-Billings, 2000).

Potentially, the interview will be less formal, meaning that the participant may feel 'normal', relaxed and less guarded.

The researcher has access to 'insider knowledge' with which to counter-pose an external view (Kemmis and McTaggart, 2000).

Knowing the researcher is familiar with their family and friends may make it less likely that participants will voice certain sensitive issues or experiences.

The insider has to recognise that participants may feel greater pressure to agree to participate in research due to cultural expectations (e.g. that we help sister/brother professionals).

The participants can access the researcher at times when she or he is not expecting it, not wanting to make contact or when she is unprepared or unsupported.

Fontana and Frey (2000) suggest that what we know about a person shapes our expectations and vision of them in the present. Once a vision on the self is *cast* it leaves a profound effect and is difficult to change. Participants may have a 'cast view' of the researcher as a sportsperson due to their prior relationship, making it impossible for them to realise the new relationship and roles. One problematic outcome of this is that some participants may acquiesce just to remain on good terms.

The researcher may be more likely to experience counter-transference upon hearing taboo or traumatic stories.

When trust and rapport have already been established, and participants feel they know the researcher, they may be less likely to consider ethical risks, such as loss of anonymity.

When researchers know their participants it can lead to *passive listening* which fails to allow the participant to fully define a situation, fails to seek fuller descriptions, draws early closure to explanations, or makes assumptions about meaning (Fielding, 1993).

continued

Table 2.1 Continued

Phase of research	Benefits of insider status	Risks of insider status
	Membership means that the researcher will already be part of participants' histories (e.g. playing alongside participants, playing on the same team, attending ceremonies, committee work, sponsorship events). This fulfils some of the ethical criteria of empowering participants so that they too have knowledge about the researcher. An insider holds potential firsthand knowledge about issues that are difficult or impossible to research or broach. In high-level sport these may include sexual abuse, self-harm, drug use or cheating. Sharing this knowledge with others in the context of a trusting relationship helps open up awareness of stories that are commonly silenced, delegitimised, trivialised or hidden. There is a degree of respect that goes with being a 'winner' in elite sport. This respect often transfers outside their specific discipline. This was evident in our work with athletes from other sports who appeared to relate to Kitrina differently, and perhaps more openly, because she too was a high-level sportsperson.	When a researcher is part of what she is researching she may be blind to some aspects of her environment, or embarrassed to ask and talk about a particular issue. Important things may be hidden because of their simplicity and familiarity.

Analysis	Insiders can use their own experience to test emerging themes and concepts, and have a greater wealth of contexts to situate developing findings. The researcher can access different ways of knowing about the research question that aren't restricted to textual and/or observational methods. Embodied knowledge gained through 'being there' can provide a basis for rich and nuanced insights.	An insider may overemphasise her own experience in interpreting participants' stories. Certain analysis methods may not be so appealing or may feel boring on the basis of the insider's pre-existing knowledge.
Representation	Insiders are likely to be more sensitive about how participants (as friends or sister professionals) are represented. Greater care for participants (while not restricted to insiders) brings dilemmas about how to represent participants in dignified ways. Insiders may be more wary of painting unfavourable pictures of participants as a result of appreciating more fully the tensions they face. Insiders are likely to have more opportunities to give feedback and share results to a wide audience of participants, governing bodies and sport culture.	An insider may feel more inclined to omit sensitive material in order to protect participants. Additional dilemmas may arise for insiders in finding a way to adequately represent the depth, complexity and diversity of experiences of the culture or topic.

constructed through narrative means as people make 'meaning of their life experiences by punctuating the seamless flow of events and organizing them according to recurrent themes ... which in turn scaffold the "plot" of one's life story'. From this perspective, identity is construed not as a static entity, but as an ongoing project continually constructed and developed as a person creates (and shares) stories of her experience. Telling stories of our experiences over time, in Spence's (1982) terms, allows the development of a *narrative thread* and it is this ongoing personal story that constitutes the core of our identity and sense of self. Thus, one's life story and one's identity may be understood as closely inter-twined. Perhaps it is even the case that one's life story *is* one's identity.

In terms of what we do – our behaviours and actions – Frank (2010: 157) observes that 'people act on the basis of stories they are caught up in ... reasons acquire their sense of rightness because they fit the stories that people think with'. Stories, he suggests, call on people to act in ways that are consistent with the story plot. Sustaining a particular personal story calls for actions that are a reasonable 'fit' with that story. Aligning oneself with a particular cultural nar-rative, too, calls for appropriate actions and behaviours. In McLeod's terms:

> The stories that, for the most part, construct our lives are 'out there', they exist before we are born and continue after we die. The task of being a person in a culture involves creating a satisfactory-enough alignment between individual experience and 'the story of which I find myself a part'.
>
> (McLeod, 1997: 27)

Narrative theory suggests that through a range of complex and often subcon-scious psychosocial processes, we all engage in negotiating the fit or tension between what we do (as agentic beings), what we say we do (through our per-sonal stories) and what our culture calls us to do (through publicly available nar-ratives). Frank (2010: 14–15) suggests that 'stories and narratives are resources for people, and they conduct people, as a conductor conducts an orchestra; they set a tempo, indicate emphases, and instigate performance options'. Here, cultur-ally available narratives become 'resources' that encourage and support par-ticular actions, identities and lives. At the same time, the absence of narrative resources within a particular cultural context is likely to limit or constrain par-ticular actions, identities and lives.

> People's access to narrative resources depends on their social location: what stories are told where they live and work, which stories do they take ser-iously or not, and especially what stories they exchange as tokens of mem-bership, with jokes being the most frequent among these.
>
> (Frank, 2010: 13)

When it comes to building identity and opening up or closing down life possibil-ities, social location matters and cultural context has real effects. It is this under-standing that is key to the research we describe in this book. We ask: what narrative resources are available within the culture and subcultures of high-level sport? What stories are routinely told? Which stories are silenced? What kinds of stories serve as tokens of membership? What stories lead to alienation or exclusion? Ultimately, we ask: what are the consequences of these stories and narratives for individual lives?

Witnessing sportspeople's life stories

In Chapter 3 we share a story about the 14-year research journey that provides the basis for this book. This story provides further detail on the four levels of study we draw upon:

1 Kitrina's lived experience of 17 years (1980–1997) of elite and professional golf, 12 of which were spent playing on the Ladies European Tour. This personal experience has been explored through auto-ethnographic studies published elsewhere (Douglas, 2009, 2012, 2013, 2014).

2 Kitrina's personal experience of elite sport culture was developed, deepened and theorised through a doctoral study (Douglas, 2004) and further research (Carless and Douglas, 2009; Douglas and Carless, 2006a, 2008a, 2008b, 2009a, 2009b, 2012a, 2012b; Sparkes and Douglas, 2007) conducted after she withdrew from professional sport. In this work, through her insider status Kitrina was able to negotiate access to women professionals on the Ladies European Tour, conducting multiple life story interviews with eight women over a six-year period.

3 We conducted a research project that comprised a series of focus groups and life story interviews with 21 elite and professional athletes (11 female, ten male, between 18 and 44 years of age) on UKSport's elite sport programme (Carless and Douglas, 2012, 2013a, 2013b; Douglas and Carless, 2006b). Participants were drawn from track and field athletics, rowing, rugby union, swimming, cricket, judo, canoeing, hockey and netball. Initially, a series of five focus groups (lasting between 90 and 180 minutes) were arranged and conducted for those individuals who were able to make one of these times and locations. Subsequently, five one-to-one interviews (between 90 and 180 minutes) were conducted at a time and place which suited each individual who was unable to attend a focus group.

4 Finally, we have sustained an engagement over 14 years in observing, witnessing, reflecting and analysing public and private stories of life in elite and professional sport. At times, it is this engagement in sportspeople's stories through *life* – as opposed to through particular research projects – that has led us to the insights, interpretations and conclusions that we share in this book. We have actively sought to engage athletes and sportspeople, coaches, parents, governing officials, students and practitioners with this research by presenting our findings and documenting the responses of others in a cyclical process in order to strengthen and test emerging knowledge. The material we present in this book has been shared in lectures, seminars,

workshops, talks and coaching sessions as well as during informal meetings and conversations (see e.g. Carless and Douglas, 2011; Douglas and Carless, 2008a, 2008b, 2009b; Sparkes and Douglas, 2007).

All the audio-recorded 'formal' interviews and focus groups we conducted fall in line with the narrative life story approach described above in that we sought a biographical, historical and cultural context for each athlete's current life situation and experiences. We do not favour the use of structured interview schedules which can limit or constrain open dialogue. Instead we use a more conversational approach, which typically begins by asking participants to recount their early experiences in sport. From this starting place each participant is then asked to describe how they went from there to 'where you are now'. As such, each athlete was invited to provide a personal story of their life journey, allowing a degree of autonomy over what events, people and issues were voiced, as well as how the story plot was progressed. As a result, individual participants led the conversation at different times to most effectively recount moments from their life story.

During data collection, we assumed different but complementary roles. Kitrina conducted all the in-depth interviews and led the focus groups, striving to adopt an open and accepting stance to enable participants to share stories of their experience in a supportive atmosphere. While gaining trust and establishing rapport is important in all research, interviewing elites poses some particular problems as, being well known publicly and used to giving media interviews, they may give 'rehearsed' responses and/or withhold information which they do not wish to be made public (see Hertze and Imber, 1995; Pensgaard and Duda, 2002). By drawing on and sharing her experiences in elite sport, Kitrina was called on to show that she trusted participants with her stories and was then able to offer empathy and show solidarity with participants. But she was also able to test and challenge athletes' stories, seeking alternative explanations, and provoking participants to examine their own motives, interests and explanations.

It seemed to us that Kitrina's insider status helped improve openness and trust as a two-way process in the researcher–participant relationship, and we believe this helped participants feel sufficiently secure to be candid in the stories they shared, increased the depth of conversation and understanding, and provided an alternative lens for athletes to look at their lives. The candid and taboo nature of some of the stories suggests that trust and rapport was established, sometimes in a relatively short period of time. This outcome suggests that Kitrina was respected by participants as an 'insider' to sport culture and also suggests that during the focus groups other athletes also played an important part in directing and supporting deeper, more self-aware conversations.

During the focus groups David fulfilled a different role. Having no personal experience of professional sport, he remained for the most part 'in the background' to the point that participants were often surprised when he eventually spoke. His role was to note key issues which emerged during often animated conversation and to ask clarifying or contrast questions to check emerging understandings. It was also important, given that focus groups provide a unique lens to explore athletes' shared stories of their lives, to present key issues back to participants to invite confirmation, clarification and/or modification. David's status as an outsider balanced Kitrina's insider status, bringing a different perspective or horizon to the focus groups as well as to subsequent analysis and interpretation.

In social and psychological research we have noticed an increasing tendency to focus ever more closely on *the data*. Sometimes this focus excludes other potential sources of insight and understanding. In qualitative research, 'the data' are very often the words that the participants have spoken into an audio recorder. While we support and advocate for the importance of ensuring that interpretations and conclusions are grounded in the experiences of real people's lives, for three reasons we resist excluding insights or understandings that are not 'captured' in the form of an audio recording.

First, individuals may not be explicitly aware of participating in the kinds of social, cultural and psychological processes we are interested in. We all, as human beings, participate in social, cultural and psychological 'dances' without necessarily appreciating that we are doing so. This is one reason why stories are useful: they can reveal processes that the teller may not be able to identify and describe through other forms. Second, even when we *are* aware of these processes, we may not be able to put them into words. At these times, the use of other senses (see Sparkes, 2009) may help uncover valuable insights. Third, it is sometimes inappropriate to record a conversation or exchange with a participant, perhaps because the subject matter is extremely sensitive. At these times, it is our memory and field notes of what a participant said or embodied that provoke new understanding.

On this basis, it is important to point out that the interpretations and conclusions we offer throughout this book are *not* based upon or derived solely from the 'data' that have been recorded during formal interviews and focus groups. Instead, our interpretations and conclusions have been arrived at through our immersion in an entire 14-year research process. *Our interpretations and conclusions come from a particular 'way of being' (as sport researchers and human beings) as much as they have come from a particular 'way of analysing'.*

The nature of this 'way of being' is impossible to pin down but is, we hope, demonstrated and evoked in Chapter 3. It is, we believe, the illusive 'more' of which Wolcott (2002) speaks in the epigraph of this chapter. It involves us in gradually arriving at understandings through reflecting in a broad sense on Kitrina's experience and through 'being with' participants over a period of several years. While our understandings may be grounded in the data, they do not necessarily derive from the data. Our work as researchers requires us to move backwards and forwards between our emerging understandings – in whatever form they take and from wherever they may come – and the 'data' of recorded participant stories. Throughout the book, we draw on these recorded 'data' to provide examples and illustrations (in a participant's own words) of the more general points, processes or consequences we suggest. Because we attribute a particular example to a particular participant does not imply that others did not also experience similar events, processes or consequences. Usually, the individual stories we share serve as representations of events, processes or consequences that were also significant for other participants.

Understanding and representing sportspeople's life stories

Given the volume of stories we have witnessed through this research journey, we have faced a major challenge in trying to find a way to understand and represent these stories in ways that are useful and informative. A critical aspect of this task has been *distillation:* we have needed to reduce, compress or focus the lessons these stories offer without misrepresenting, distorting or oversimplifying participants' experiences. This has not been easy. Narrative approaches, broadly speaking, have emerged as the most appropriate approach for us. In Margot Ely's words:

> The aim of some research is a complex linguistic analysis of chunks of [a participant's] actual language. However, that is not the aim of narrative research and its presentation. In narrative work, [a participant's] voice must be communicated with just enough of her own color, cadence, and usage to 'show' her to the readers, all the while taking care so that her voice cannot be used to stereotype and/or denigrate her.
>
> (Ely, 2007: 573)

Over the past decade we have worked towards and attempted to refine some narrative ways of working that fit our own unique context, needs, abilities, resources and purposes. These approaches, together, have best enabled us to strike the balance to which Ely alludes: a balance between distilling and distorting. This involves a quest for a complex and at times messy truth that may not be amenable to a straightforward telling:

> The truth we seek to tell cannot be equated with fidelity to 'the facts' alone; and, insofar as our own aim is to be faithful to the living, breathing reality of those we study, it will be imperative to summon all the artfulness we possibly can.
>
> (Freeman, 2007: 135)

To respond to this challenge, at times we draw upon a more explicitly *analytical* approach to unpack, critically examine and reflect upon a particular story. This is sometimes necessary because, as McLeod (1997: 112) reminds us, 'a story can be heard or read in different ways. The story carries meaning that the reader or hearer must work to unpack. In everyday life, the stories we tell each other are unpacked to a very limited extent.' We want, at times, to get behind the 'everyday' acceptance of particular stories to reveal (for example) the assumptions and value systems that underlie them. To do so, more traditional forms of narrative analysis (see Lieblich *et al.*, 1998; Crossley, 2000; Riessman, 2008) are appropriate.

At other times, we steer towards a radically different *storytelling* approach through which we resist 'taking a story apart' to preserve instead, perhaps, its emotionality, openness, impact, power or ambiguity. This equates to the 'artful' or arts-based approaches of which some social scientists speak (e.g. Freeman, 2007; Eisner, 2008). We utilise these approaches with various aims and purposes, but often these involve some combination of providing a holistic understanding of an individual, creating a sense of empathy, stimulating local and particular knowledge, blurring the self–other divide (between reader and storyteller), stimulating embodied understanding or providing an accessible account.

Recently, Frank (2010) has provided a conceptualisation of *dialogical narrative research* that fits well the methodologies we have worked with and towards over the past 14 years:

> Dialogical narrative analysis begins with how stories give people a sense of who they are. Then it addresses how stories connect: how affiliations, groups, and communities form because people know the same stories and make sense of these stories in the same way; these stories make people's actions and choices recognizable to each other. Dialogical narrative analysis considers how stories make human lives good by providing ideals, imagining hopes, providing models of resistance to injustices, and feeding imaginations of how life be not only different but better.
>
> (Frank, 2010: 159)

Frank (2010: 128) suggests that the first aim of dialogical research is not to analyse people's stories, 'but to witness them and to connect them'. Connections may be made between: (1) multiple participants' stories; (2) participants' stories and institutional or organisational narratives; or (3) individuals' lived realities and social policies. At different times throughout the book we strive to make all these forms of connection apparent within the specific context of elite and professional sport. Sometimes we try to achieve this through storytelling; at other times more sustained story analysis is necessary.

Central to all dialogical research however is placing different stories alongside one another. This hallmark is a constant throughout the book. Placing different stories side by side necessarily demonstrates a degree of multiplicity – it shows that while one story may be dominant, alternatives do exist. In this sense, '*two* stories are the beginning of *thinking*, as opposed to being caught up in one story. *Two* stories instigate dialogue.... *Two* stories are necessary for thinking because each opens up a critical distance from the evocative intensity of the other' (Frank, 2010: 152). By representing a carefully chosen selection of the stories we have lived, witnessed or glimpsed through sustained immersion and engagement with elite and professional sport, we hope to stimulate thinking, reflection and – above all – dialogue around the realities and consequences of stories in high-level sport.

3   Our research journey

In all sorts of ways, which we are only just starting to recognise without apology, the documentation of our own experiences and life stories are excellent starting points for research and are productive points to return to again and again.

(Plummer, 2001: 34)

Like many social scientists we recognise that there are political dimensions to our research, power imbalances that seem impossible to appease, and moral or ethical dilemmas that bring choices we might rather avoid. One dilemma we face, for example, is how to reduce the difference and distance we create by writing about ourselves, in the traditional way, as 'researchers' and those we research as 'participants'. To reveal these kinds of issues we must find ways to become reflexive researchers who, as Plummer suggests, locate themselves in the research process and document their own experiences throughout the research journey. However, the research in this book is not about us. But it does involve us. Therefore we have a responsibility, as best we are able, to present ourselves *alongside* our participants because this is the reality of how social research unfolds: we do research *with* participants, not *on* them.

Nowhere is reflexivity more important than when it comes to methodology. Plummer (2001: 205) writes that 'Studies have often been written as if they had been executed by machines: not a hint of the ethical, political and personal problems which routinely confront the human researcher.' We strive for greater transparency: we are not machines and do not wish to present ourselves as such; our studies are not mechanistic and we do not wish to present them as such. While Chapter 2 provides *one* account of the methods we used and developed in this work, there is much about our ways of working that is omitted as a result of the *form* as well as the content of that chapter. Elliot Eisner (2008: 5) reminds us that 'not only does knowledge come in different forms, the forms of its creation differ'. We can generate knowledge about methodology, too, in different ways and through different forms of representation.

The challenge is *how* to access and communicate these other forms of knowing. This challenge, we find, is particularly acute when it comes to bringing transparency to aspects of ourselves, which are particularly difficult (for us) to see. Oscar Wilde is known for saying that giving a man a mask allows him to tell you the truth. There is something about the act of hiding one part of the self that allows another part of the self to be revealed. We adopt a similar strategy in this chapter to provide a sense of how we have gone about conducting the research that underpins this book. Much like we offer our participants a cloak of anonymity to support a different telling of *their* life story, in this chapter we give ourselves a kind of 'mask' that allows us to write from a different position, with an eye to a different kind of story.

In what follows, we present a story about two researchers named Tom and Jessie. Their lives are based on our own. The scenes in the story offer a backstage view of our methods by focusing on some key moments and a selection of research relationships. They provide insights into how our research has progressed, contextualising the chapters that follow. It is impossible to *tell you* with certainty how our biographical positioning affected our findings and interpretations. We can however *show you* a selection of moments so that you may make your own informed assessment. The experiences we recount are too rich and complex to be described or summarised in a traditional way, such as a bullet point list or a how-to-do-research guide. Therefore we utilise a storytelling strategy on the basis of Frank's (2010: 37) observation that 'The value of stories is to offer sufficient clarity without betraying the complexity of life-in-flux'. By telling stories, we necessarily focus on a few illustrative moments – our entire research journey would require an entire book! We therefore remind you that different tellings of all social encounters are possible and there are always more stories that could be told. That said, the stories we *do* tell here provide, we hope, an accessible and engaging behind-the-scenes look at our research journey. We offer it to draw attention to the kinds of tangled webs that typically remain outside the remit of research methods textbooks and methods sections in journal articles.

Changing cultures

'You haven't been educated,' her sister said, 'not properly, not formally. You won't be able to do a degree, they won't let you in, you'll have to do an access course first.' They were having a post-Sunday-lunch-dish-washing-conversation and Jessie was feeling rather unsettled inside and slightly put down by the tone of her sister's comments. It was unusual for her sister to take such a stance, to assert her superiority, but then again, this was her area, she had a degree, she was a lecturer, she worked at a university; she should know. There was a degree of authority to her comments.

Nathan, Jessie's partner, saw things a little differently. He had suggested that she might enjoy doing a degree in the winter while recovering from a minor injury. She had hurt her neck on the tenth hole of the English Open and her physio had suggested she give golf a rest for a bit. Jessie thought the degree was a good idea. 'In my experience universities want mature students,' Nathan said. 'Go and have a chat with them, that's what I did.'

'Who's in charge of the sport science course?' Jessie asked at the porter's lodge.

'That would be Dr Black,' a man at the back of the room said. Then, looking up at a large board, 'she's in 211 Marks building, over there.'

Jessie wandered off and found the office. Dr Black wasn't in, nor it seemed was anyone else. She wandered back to the porter's lodge and spoke again to the friendly porter. 'She's not in, any other ideas?' Across the counter the porter continued filing mail into pigeonholes.

'Well that's her car,' he said pointing to a red Porsche. He carried on filing. 'She'll not go anywhere without that.'

Jessie decided to 'stake-out' the car in the belief that sooner or later Dr Black would turn up. She was, in fact, quite happy to sit in the sunshine for two hours on the edge of the curb, entertaining herself by watching the comings and goings of a university. She'd never been to a university before, never looked at a prospectus, never attended an open day and, as for a Russell group, or any other group, she was blissfully ignorant. She'd chosen this university simply because it was the closest to her home. Actually, she'd confused Exeter, which was an hour away, with Taunton, which is a 20-minute journey. She was merrily driving to Taunton when she realised that the place she wanted to go to was another 40 miles on. That *faux pas* made her laugh. But the sport science degree was what interested her because this one at least included sport psychology and other performance-related subjects. Thus the distance, to her, was rather irrelevant. And anyway, she was used to driving to London and Liverpool for golf lessons, both were three hours away. She was used to travelling the world to earn a living. She talked all of this through with herself as if talking to a friend in the car. *'The choices I've made in life aren't based on how difficult the obstacles or how long the journey. Rather, they all seemed to boil down to one little question: do I want to do it?'* She nodded to herself.

The indicators on the Porsche blinked with a *beep beep*. Jessie stood up and wandered round to the other side of the car where a woman was already burrowing into the belly of the vehicle through a half-open driver's door. 'Excuse me, are you Dr Black?' Jessie asked.

The woman backed out, a little startled, still holding an armful of books, and straightened herself. 'Yes?' she said.

'I'd like to get on the exercise and sport science degree course,' Jessie announced, 'and I'm told you may be the person who can make that happen?' Two weeks later she walked into her first undergraduate lecture.

It was a module called *Body, Identity and Achievement* and was part of the sociology component of the degree. Jessie didn't really expect to like sociology – from the little she knew of sociologists they seemed a funny bunch, slightly bohemian. Nothing out of the ordinary happened in the first two weeks; they just discussed what socialisation and enculturation meant. It didn't seem that relevant. Then there was a film about college basketball in the USA, injury, exploitation and the hopes of one young black lad. It was good, she enjoyed it, and the discussions had been interesting. But it wasn't what she called challenging, not personally challenging, that is. This week, though, the lecture really got her thinking. The lecturer suggested that 'she' – and of course all the other students – had different selves. She sat there thinking he was mistaken: to begin with, that is. *'I'm the same me wherever I am'*, she said to herself, listening to an unfolding internal argument. But there was something unsettling about what he had to say nonetheless. She started replaying scenarios in her head to test his theories out. She thought about when she played in a pro-am and had to 'act' in a certain way because of what was expected. She thought about the stories she told the press, and the things she chose not to tell them: 'Oh yes I think I can win this week', she said to a reporter, knowing full well that she was totally unconfident about winning and hadn't even thought about it. Slowly, the evidence was mounting up and she didn't like everything she saw.

Statistics, SPSS, biomechanics, physiology and metabolic calculations were things she'd never done. 'This is quite easy,' announced Dr Mike Lewis, 'it's just simple A-level maths that you've all done.' *'Great,'* she responded in her head, *'I didn't do A-level maths! So it isn't so easy for me.'*

When she got home Jessie pulled out the *Yellow Pages* and searched for maths tutors. She chose one at random, gave him a quick call and paid for a couple of sessions. Dr Lewis was right – it was simple enough. Then, she practised the equations for an hour every morning. Even so, she was a little surprised to gain the third highest mark in the exams. None of these subjects required her to think too deeply, however; they weren't challenging of her personal philosophy or way of understanding the world, nor were they morally perplexing in the way that *Body, Identity and Achievement* had been. It seemed the more those lectures went on the more challenging they became and the more drawn in she had become. It seemed that this subject cut to the heart of questions she had about life in sport, her behaviour as a sportswoman, the tensions she'd experienced in certain contexts.

Jessie expected to find sport psychology interesting – it was what she was there for. And parts of it were: she was a child in a candy store, sitting in the library reading research about putting and heart rate deceleration. Professor Proover then set some readings on career transition and athletic identity. Jessie had now become used to checking the findings against her internal catalogue of scenes and it began to concern her that her life didn't fit with a lot of the research she was reading. *'Am I the only one?'* she wondered, *'or am I deluding myself?'*

She turned another page and read: 'the professional athlete has, and must have, such a narrow focus on winning it is impossible for him (or her) to be much else.' *'What?'* she said, loud enough to turn the heads of those sitting nearby. *'Well thank you very much! I can't be much else!'* She was annoyed that these researchers could so flippantly finalise *her* – but at the same time she felt ill-equipped to talk back. Feeling frustrated, she shut the journal and walked out of the library. The sociology lecturer was in conversation with a group of students outside the entrance; he smiled as she walked past. 'You still here?' he joked. 'Thought you'd have flown off when the weather turned cold!'

Jessie got a very high mark for her undergraduate thesis; she was rather chuffed. She learnt she really liked doing research, designing the survey, recruiting participants, measuring heart rates, and she didn't even mind inputting the data into SPSS. The problem only began to raise its ugly head when she decided to publish the findings and present them at a conference. She became very uneasy about how she was talking about her participants, increasingly sounding like those researchers who she had criticised. '*You see,*' she pointed out to herself, '*this is how it happens.*' She began to see how the language she was adopting as a social scientist placed a barrier between her and her participants. She began to notice that she was beginning to be the 'know-it-all' expert, whereas her participants, on the page, appeared less informed, and sometimes even ignorant or stupid.

Jessie had a habit of speaking for and against herself in an inner court that only she was party to, as if on trial. '*I didn't mean to,*' she pleaded to her inner council. '*I didn't know I could put myself in the study, and I didn't know how to, no one showed me, we didn't learn that. If I included myself they said it would contaminate the findings. I was trying to be this detached observer.*' Her inner prosecutor was having none of it. '*You seem quite happy to be critical of other researchers and their findings, not so happy to find out your methods are just like theirs? A little hypocritical wouldn't you say? And what about the feminist research you've been reading? They don't use those terms!*' She realised that if she had included herself in her undergraduate research the findings would be different. She felt that if she had sat down and chatted with her fellow professionals the findings would be different. She realised there was a truth in her findings but she also realised that something important was missing. Even though the audience at the *World Scientific Congress of Golf* were really supportive of the findings, and talked about ways to give them greater statistical power, she began to feel less chuffed about it all. As she began thinking about a Ph.D., she was determined not to make the same mistakes.

Starting postgraduate research

'Who the fuck cares?' was all he said, but it pulled the rug right from under her feet. She landed with a bang, flat on her ass. Jessie didn't think she'd been doing so badly, describing her research – she was registered for an M.Phil., seeking confirmation for Ph.D. status – and this was her first presentation to what they called 'research group'. It was her first public encounter with other staff, academics and research students in the department and perhaps her first taste of 'being brought down to size'. The 'Who the fuck cares?' question came from a young man sat at the back of the room, leaning back and balancing on two legs of his chair, relaxed, suntanned, wearing shorts and an open shirt, the breeze from a nearby window lightly brushing his hair. Of course, Tom didn't actually use the 'F-word', but he asked the question as if he did, perhaps adapting his language before his professors. His 'So what?' 'Who cares?' missile, arrow, call it what you will, however, didn't seem to be aimed at encouragement or support. It seemed as if it was meant to flatten, disarm and destroy.

Jessie wondered what he saw that needed to be crushed. What arrogance did he spot?

What self-aggrandised ideas was he not going to be party to? She wondered: '*why did my presentation invite such rebuke?*' Of course, when she considered it, he had a point. Why should anyone care about a bunch of overpaid, highly cosseted, hugely socially esteemed female golfers? Why should public money be spent on investigating the health of this privileged group? But she also wondered why he didn't see any of the fragility, the vulnerability, the oh-so-many cracks. Couldn't he see that her 'performance' was just professional, the one topic she had experience of, or that she was struggling to find meaning and make theoretical sense before a bunch of very well-educated academics, in an unfamiliar space? Was she ignorant? A drop-out? A wave of insecurity rose – perhaps all those jokes were true: she was just a 'thick jock' and shouldn't even be there.

Jessie felt as if she was being pushed into something she didn't really want to do. Everyone in academia seemed to believe that because she was a tournament winner – a leading professional for over a decade – she had 'access' that no other researcher would have. Her adviser – just like those at undergraduate level – wanted to send her back. So, back she went, again. She'd remained a member of the tour even though she no longer played. But she was more than *just* a member: her 'all-time ranking' still allowed her to play in events that many poorer ranked tour players would kill to play in. But she wasn't going to play, didn't want to play and didn't really want to go. She was going because she could see their point: she *could* step over the ropes that Todd Crosset, in his award-winning ethnography, could not. He had only been allowed, like everyone else, to wander outside the ropes, and perhaps to wander outside some experiences, to gather only falling crumbs. He'd said that women professional golfers were 'outsiders in the clubhouse'. But for Jessie, he – the ethnographer – was the outsider; he could never step inside the ropes, into a world she had known so well.

The flight over had been relatively trouble-free, but still she felt apprehensive. It wasn't flying that had made her tense, or the thought of queues at customs, obnoxious immigration officials or overpriced taxis. It was, she reckoned, that she had walked away from this world and everyone in it in 1996, and now she was walking back, unannounced. Now, she needed them. And she didn't like it. Of course, many of the players were used to answering her calls, to play in a pro-am, help her raise money for some charity. Jessie likewise, when she was playing, supported their charity days, events, led the weekly fellowship meeting, organised gigs, served on the players' council and Board of Directors. On paper, she was still part of the tour – she'd 'earned' a right to be there. She'd given a lot. But whatever she had done it didn't make her feel secure, at ease, or look forward to going back.

Jessie stood momentarily in a cloud of dust as the taxi sped away. Now what? '*Bag the big names,*' she told herself, '*be focused.*' She'd come to this particular event because they all played in this event. '*Big names – ha!*' She thought. Well, that's how they were referred to in the newspapers and by the sponsors. Of course, many of them had very little names: Kim Smart, Anna Toms, Beth Frank. They were BIG in terms of their ability to dominate the women's game: big earners, big hitters, big egos, and they drew BIG crowds. No sponsor would contemplate putting on a BIG event without them. Jessie was resigned to the mission: get the best female golfers in the world to agree to take part in the research. As she wandered through the clubhouse she was amazed by the warmth of greeting from many women she hadn't seen for years.

'Jessie, how lovely to see you!' Kandy said, as she wandered on to the putting green, roped off and inaccessible to others. Jessie told Kandy about the research, asked if she would take part. Graciously, Kandy said, 'Of course, let me write down my number, give me a call at the West Coast event and we can do it there.' It was a lovely conversation but in the process Jessie realised she knew nothing about Kandy and had never actually talked to her, even though they had played together numerous times over the past 14 years. Then she refocused. '*One bagged*', she said to herself and wandered on.

'Are you OK?' she asked Anna after a few exchanges in the corridor outside the locker room. Of course, Anna *wasn't OK*. She was stumbling over her words and had tears in her eyes. 'What's up?'

Anna began to unload in public, on view in the corridor outside the locker room. It seemed that despite them not having spoken for at least four years they picked up where we left off. 'Ah, my mum's here this week and we've had words, I had a go at her, and. . . .' A stream of tears was unleashed. 'I didn't mean what I said!' Anna wiped her tears with her huge golf towel. 'I've had a crap year and. . . .'

'*Whoa!*' Jessie thought, uneasy with the story Anna was starting to tell. As a researcher this was exactly the type of story she wanted to 'capture' in an interview, not a random conversation by the locker room. Her next thought was, '*Jessie, get a grip, Anna's upset, why are you thinking about data collection, you should be saying something supportive!*'

'What did you say to your mum? Jessie asked gently, letting go of her agenda and interests, trying to support and listen. Silently she returned to the role of a caring sister, offering: 'I'm sorry to hear that' and 'don't be too hard on yourself'. She stood beside her: 'I know', and then offered, 'Look, you're obviously going out to play now, why don't we talk about this later?'

Eventually, having arranged a time and place to chat privately, Anna got around to asking, 'What are you doing here?'

Jessie now felt uncomfortable owning up to her motives, but still found herself saying, 'Well, you know what we've been talking about – that's sort of what I'm here for, to do research. I want you to take part in my research.'

Participant–researcher relationships

At the bottom of your garden you have a well which is full of nutrient-enriched drinking water. It's been collecting there for a while. Possibly it was filled by the

rain in the spring; then again, perhaps it was the winter storms that were responsible. Or, maybe, you and your garden are just lucky that it's an area with a high
water-table. So, you're not really bothered about the well, its just there among
the brambles at the bottom of the garden. But if asked, would you draw some
water for a thirsty traveller? And what would you say to someone in need at the
end of the telephone line? Would you be moved hearing their tears, hearing *their*
world had crumbled, *their* status had been undermined, *their* skills suddenly
departed, they were feeling alone, lost, exposed? They've been told, by those
around them, that you are the one who has the best chance of helping them, of
restoring their equilibrium, of getting them *back on track*.

Jessie was surprised to hear from Georgi: she didn't even know Georgi had
her home phone number; she must have got it from one of the others, but here
she was, in tears and asking for help. She found herself saying, 'Of course, come
round', and three days later after a transatlantic flight Georgi walked in through
her front door, putter under her arm and sat, like many others, on her sofa. It
wasn't exactly awkward, but, it wasn't exactly relaxed. She hadn't seen Georgi
for, what was it, at least four years? Jessie had just dropped out of women's golf
and enrolled in a sport science degree, the tour carried on, it didn't need her, and
Georgi had been playing on the LPGA tour. That was the gist of it; their lives
had gone in different directions.

Before the meeting Jessie was rather ambivalent about Georgi and if pushed
would probably have said she didn't like her very much. Georgi hung out with a
group of players and caddies who spent their down time gambling, playing
cricket, football, snooker and who knows what else. They were a little clique and
rather *lad-ish*. While Jessie was on tour she didn't have much to do with them.
They weren't unfriendly towards Jessie, and vice versa; they just had different
interests.

Of course, Jessie had played with Georgi – a lot. She remembered that Georgi
had hit some of the classiest pitch shots she had ever seen in the final day's play
of the Open when Jessie was in contention. Georgi blew her away. And then she
remembered she did the same in return at another big event where they were
paired together and Jessie had won. It had been neck and neck all week, a tight
course, big prize money, and on the final day, on the second hole, they both hit
their tee shots through the green, their balls nestled like eggs in a basket in the
rough. Jessie went first and chipped her shot so close that she just had to tap it
into the hole. Georgi's chip wasn't so close; she missed the putt and a one-shot
gap opened up between them. After that, Jess had been impossible to catch and
she extended her lead by holing putt after solid putt over the next 16 holes,
looking like she would never make a mistake. Of course, she didn't *feel* that way
– she always felt the others had so much more than she did, they all hit it further,
they could reach holes in two that it took her three shots to reach. So she just
focused on hitting it down the middle, hitting it as best she could, doing what
she did well. Taking the putter back, keeping her putting stroke tuned in, much
like a radio keeping the signal strong, and staying focused on that feel, that
rhythm, that pendulum. She knew the *feel* she wanted in her hands, she knew

how she wanted the ball to come off the clubface, she knew how she wanted it to roll and she knew why.

After that win Jessie was impressed with what Georgi had said to the press. They'd repeated it back to her, as they often did. It was the same week another player had said it would be 'bad for the tournament' if Jessie won because she was so boring. Georgi disagreed and said so. Sitting opposite Georgi now, something buried deep in Jessie's being was rekindled. Now, several years later, that act counted. '*Funny how we all remember the little things*', Jessie thought to herself. It also provoked memories of the way Hannah, as she walked past her on the putting green, had said, 'about time too' and smiled after there had been a one-year gap between the two wins Jessie had in her first year on tour, and the next win in her third year. *They*, that is, other players, appeared to notice these things, even if they didn't talk about them. They knew what the press had written – how people write you off when you are not winning as Jessie had found, in her second year on tour. Those few words from one of the all-time best players on tour spoke volumes. *Solidarity*. She came back to the present.

'So,' Jessie asked, 'what's happening?' Georgi seemed to find it difficult to describe what had *actually* happened and so they talked about *that* before doing anything else. On paper it wasn't a big deal: Georgi just missed a few short putts, live on TV, in a very big-money event, and shot a high score. Finally, after a lot of talking, and after Jessie shared some of her own behind-the-scenes insights, Jessie asked Georgi to take some putts on the carpet.

'*Ah!*' Jessie thought in a kind of enlightened way – she hadn't seen such an awful putting movement in ages and was hard pressed not to laugh. It was like watching an octopus run the 100-metre sprint. Crazy! She wondered what was going on in this player's neural network; how could something go so horribly wrong, how could something that can be so beautiful become so ugly? Of course, she didn't say that to Georgi, so she probably appeared more confident and professional then she felt. Then, after six putts Jessie just began at the beginning. Simply, slowly and reassuringly, with a gentle mix of humour, firmness, knowledge and sense, she began to talk about putting. An onlooker might have said she was going 'back to basics' as she took six balls in her hand.

'This is what I think is important,' she said, 'this is what I'm looking for.' Then she just took her arm back, bent forward and released the first ball on to the carpet. It landed and ran smoothly forward as her arm followed through slowly once her fingers had let go. She carried on releasing each of the six balls from her hand and as she did so she drew Georgi's attention to the speed of release, the direction, the smoothness of the roll, the rhythm in the move. Then she asked Georgi to copy what she had done, to take a ball in her right hand and roll the ball down the carpet. As she did this, Jessie asked Georgi to think about the feel of the tempo, the rhythm of the movement, to close her eyes and release a ball. After six balls had been released Jessie brought them back again, another six were dispatched, and another, until the movement was smooth and rhythmical. Then Jessie gave Georgi her putter and asked her to remember the tempo and feel she had just been creating and to do the same with her putter. Jessie knelt down on the ground and stopped Georgi's putter head going too far back, or too far forward, and slowly she worked with this multiple winning tour player until her swing began to look more repetitive and smooth. Almost like magic, a good putting stroke began to emerge and, though it still needed some more work, if you were watching you'd have said: '*its coming.*'

For over a decade, Jessie would practise her putting for three hours every day, sometimes on the carpet, sometimes on the course, sometimes on a practise putting green, sometimes with her headphones on, sometimes while watching a film on TV. It could be meditative, competitive, sensual, rhythmically, beautiful, boring, fatiguing, musical, thought provoking, philosophical or fun. Standing with Georgi, she drew on every moment of it in order to condense what she knew and to help this woman. By the time a couple of hours were over Georgi was gaining firsthand knowledge of what the other professionals had said to her about Jessie. She was now less upset, more upbeat, more informed, more rhythmical, more aware, more technically sound, and extremely grateful.

Georgi pulled out her chequebook, ready to pay. But you see, there was a problem – well, two, actually. The first was simple for Jessie to explain: you don't take money from family. Georgi was a sister pro, they were on the same side, she had been brought in to offer help and she gave freely. Payment wasn't expected. She learned this from the first coaches who taught her and from seeing other tour players help each other. But of course the world of coaching was changing: more and more coaches were seeing tour players as lucrative income sources – 'cash cows'. While that was true, she still didn't want to take money from players with whom she had grown up. But there was more to it than that, something she couldn't explain to Georgi.

Jessie knew it was also something to do with how she wanted to see herself – as not being able to be 'bought' like groceries. She believed what she did was quite special and unusual, and she believed a cheque devalued what it was she had done. She didn't want her skills to be purchasable, not so easily. She didn't want what they had achieved for Georgi – *together* – to be part of the consumer economy. She wasn't looking for national acknowledgement either, although it was good that Georgi *had* credited her when she won again. Jessie didn't really want to get more of this type of work, although she knew if she wasn't careful it would come. Perhaps she wanted control of the situation, perhaps it was her way of keeping something to herself; she wasn't sure, but she considered the possibilities.

Looking back over their encounters with some distance between them, she felt pleased that she had been able to test herself 'as a coach' with someone of Georgi's calibre. She had the skills and wisdom to help Georgi win again. She could do it, and do it well. But there was something else important to her, and it really only emerged after she asked Georgi to take part in the research. During one interview, Georgi said: 'I know I am a psychopath, but my whole outlook has totally changed, maybe working with you ... I think to myself, I come away thinking, bloody hell, I didn't know that, I hadn't looked at it like that at all. I just look at this huge big picture that scares the life out of me really and didn't really know what to do about it. So that was fascinating. So thank you for that.'

Berni was used to travelling to Jessie's flat from her home – it took several hours, but there was the radio, music and snacks to munch on to pass the time. What would they work on today? What was there to report? These thoughts too provided a distraction from the long drive. It was a familiar pattern: she parked by the tennis courts, wandered up the hill, negotiated the intercom and corridors, then finally, the door was opened, she was welcomed in and they smiled and hugged.

Berni took the lead, walking through to a large room filled with sofas, exotic cushions, a window seat and an expansive blue sky bursting through a large window. On the top floor of this converted nautical school light flooded the room, but Berni wasn't interested in the vista across the Bristol Channel or the Welsh hills in the distance. She wasn't interested in where the brightly coloured cargo ships came from or if the containers stacked high on the deck would topple off in a storm. She didn't concern herself with why the coal boat needed five tugs to bring it in. She was there to work. She wanted to improve her performance. She wanted help with her putting, with her mental game. She was there to cipher what knowledge she could from someone whom she'd seen 'deliver the goods'. She perched herself on the window seat, back to the view, accepted coffee and cake, and only occasionally stole a glance out of the window. So, they chatted about her game, her family, her health, her hopes, her schedule, her progress, her performance, her putting, her faith, her life – as usual. They worked on her putting. She got input for her practice, thinking, schedule, approach, attitude, faith, technique, relationships.

On this visit, Jessie also told her about some research she was hoping to do. 'I wondered if you'd be willing to take part?' Jessie asked after outlining the study.

'Will it help you to help me to improve my performance?' Berni asked. 'Anything that helps you help me, I'm up for.'

Interviews and witnessing stories

Jessie really didn't like to be restricted by an interview schedule but it was required. So too, was the 'cost–benefit ratio' she'd been 'recommended' to follow. She was rather dubious but recognised her inexperience – she'd need to allow others to guide her. All she had to do was, at some appropriate time during the interview, to ask her participants to identify the costs of playing the tour, then the benefits, and then give a score to each. Simple. She did it with Annabel, and it seemed to be OK. She did it with Leanne. Not particularly insightful but no problems. Today Georgi was coming down.

When fixing a date and venue Georgi insisted, 'I'll come to you', as she had for coaching, and Jessie didn't protest too much, recognising that Georgi seemed comfortable talking there. She arrived in a flash new two-seater sports car with the hood down. She sprawled, Nero-like, over the sofa.

'I need to go through this ethics form with you and get you to sign these consent forms', Jessie said, somewhat embarrassed by all the forms, as if they were somehow more ethical than she would be.

'Bloody hell!' Georgi remarked. 'Yeah, yeah, yeah.' Finally, they got to the interview.

'I get it from my Dad,' Georgi was saying, just as her telephone rang. 'Oh, I need to take this,' it was her manager. 'Sorry, I just need to call my caddie now.'

Jessie sat patiently, watching, listening to this end of the phone calls. Then she tried to pick up the conversation. Georgi was fine with talking about her first memories, and then the journey to where she was now. Then came the cost–benefit ranking. 'Christ!' Georgi said, nearly spitting her orange juice over the sofa as Jessie tried, once again, to ask her to consider the costs of playing the tour. 'You *want* me to have a cost don't you?' Georgi laughed again and leaned forward. 'Well I'm not going to! I'm actually very happy. There *are* no costs! There we go.' She slumped back into the sofa again and spread her arms out sideways. Voila! *'So now what do I do?'* thought Jessie.

Have you ever sat and watched a dark cloud move on a wind-free day? You may have noticed the way it hangs and envelopes the sky and descends in patches around you. You don't actually see this happening as much as feel it. Meteorologists of course will point to the barometric pressure, but you'll notice the grey sky, you'll feel the dampness in the air, the chill, the clamminess of your skin perhaps. Jessie felt all of this when interviewing Berni – wherever she turned there was no light. And now, as a researcher – not a coach, helper or supporter – she felt obliged to ask a question which she knew, intuitively, might cause the cloud to burst. She didn't particularly want to stand in the eye of the storm, but she asked it anyway: 'Can you help me understand what you mean?'

'Bastard!' she heard Tom say in her head as lightning cracked across the sky and Berni began to cry.

'I feel my life is worthless,' Berni said, 'as if it didn't matter if I'd been born.' The recorder was working, she had the 'evidence', but she didn't like doing it. Jessie sat, detached, over the other side of the room, noting it all down, like she was supposed to, in her little book. What she wanted to do was give Berni a hug and talk about those times when she too was left out, felt rejected. But she didn't.

'There's too much of you in this interview,' Alan, one of the other senior academics in the department, had said after kindly reading one of her early transcripts to offer feedback. 'You want them to speak, not you. But look', his finger pointed *bump, bump, bump*, on the transcript where he suggested she was talking too much. So she had stopped. The problem however was that her inner council weren't very happy.

Tom wandered in, dropped his gym gear in the corner, took his sandwiches from the top drawer of his desk and sat down on the low sofa. All that time Jessie was staring into space. 'What is it?' he asked, trying to distract her thoughts. He'd come to know her quite well over the past few months since she'd asked him to be part of her 'research team' and since they began sharing an office. As he tucked into the first mouthful of a huge sandwich he thought back to their first few weeks discussing her interviews. It was quite an eye-opener and was in fact way more interesting than he had thought it would be. Tom was also coming to the conclusion that the mental health of the participants in his research – who were categorised as 'seriously mentally ill' – seemed better than the mental health of some of Jessie's participants who were supposed to be the ones for which everything was going well.

As he looked across their office at her now he was also reminded of their first few weeks in this office, sorting desks, cleaning it up, and the day Jessie had put her head round the door sheepishly and said, 'Tom?' He'd been checking the weekend surf forecast and wondered why she didn't come into the office.

'Yes?' he'd answered, wondering what was coming next.

Without entering the room she'd asked, 'Would it be OK if I put some pictures on the wall?'

'Sure,' he'd said, glad it was nothing more serious, and 'have you something in mind?' Silly question. She stepped back to allow an enormous framed pastel of a desert scene make an entrance. 'Wow! This is great!' he said, as Jessie brought in two more.

There had been very little space for postgrads in the department. Like many departments, they were bursting at the seams and doctoral students were well down the priority list. Nobody wanted this L-shaped dungeon room with bars on a tiny window in the bowels of the building. But, at the time, Jessie didn't have desk space upstairs and Tom liked the thought of escaping the constant chatter of the Greek students who worked at a different decibel range than he did. So they moved down and made the little room theirs. The pictures had been a welcome addition alongside the comfortable seats, subdued lighting, filter coffee machine and Jessie's constant supply of homemade muffins. Tom found that the tranquil space they had created made it possible to talk about their research in a way that had been impossible upstairs. It seemed they shared an aesthetic awareness that couldn't be quantified.

'Have you noticed,' Tom had said to Jessie one afternoon, 'how many professors and students are coming down to visit? They like how we've made this.'

'It's an audience with Tom!' she'd joked.

While Tom had been lost in these visions, Jessie still hadn't spoken. 'Jess! What is it?' he pestered. She turned, as if only just seeing him, then registered what he had asked. She looked straight at him.

'Well,' she started, 'when I was on tour if someone had sent me a 40-page transcript of a conversation I don't think I would have been bothered to read it.'

Tom finished a mouthful of humus sandwich, as she held up a sealed envelope, stamped, addressed and ready to go. 'And?'

'This ethics stuff, sending participants a copy of the interview, what does it accomplish? It's 40 pages long for goodness sakes! What am I doing other than ticking someone else's box? They don't want this! This fits with *our* way of doing things – not how tour pros want feedback or to agree what is an accurate record.'

Tom took another mouthful, and then, like Jessie, began to consider how his participants might respond to their interview transcripts, or his field notes being given to them to read. 'So, what would you have responded to,' he asked, 'if you were still playing the tour?'

'That's just it, I don't know, I'd probably be happy to help and do the interviews, but I probably wouldn't want to be pestered after that. This is a whole lot more for them all to take on. This feels like a farce, a sham, and has nothing to do with how we write about them in our case studies or report. *That's* what they need to see – not *this*.'

Understanding stories

'There you are!' Tom said popping his head over the partition in the open-plan area. 'What are you up to?' The noise of a horse chomping somewhere distracted him, until he realised it was Tammy, one of the other students, eating a raw carrot. Tom stifled his laughter. The department move had meant they were now in a spanking new, highly visible open-plan work space – all hard corners and efficiency.

'I'm trying to analyse Berni with NUD*ist software', Jessie replied, looking up, crossing her eyes and sticking her tongue out.

Tom came round, pulled up a chair and looked at the screen. 'So how does it analyse your data?' The chomping of carrots faded into the background of his thoughts.

'Well,' Jessie stopped pulling funny faces, 'it *doesn't* analyse your data,' she couldn't help but let her eyes roll to the top of her head as she said, 'obviously!' before carrying on: 'You decide which words or bits of a sentence you want to categorise, you give those bits a tag or name and then you add that extract to your node. It's just a management system. Look,' she pointed to a paragraph of text, highlighted three words with the cursor: 'these are linked with self-esteem.'

'Ah,' Tom said. 'Have you been through the whole interview doing that?'

'Yep,' Jessie replied, 'word by word, line by line, paragraph by paragraph, question by question.' Jessie relaxed back into her chair, thinking about the 10,000 words she had been micro-managing.

'You think it's any good?' Tom thought it looked like it was taking a long time but wasn't really sure what she'd get out of it.

'Well, I'm reserving judgement,' she said, trying to capture for Tom in a sentence what she was learning through this very lengthy process. 'I'm just trying everything in the Miles and Huberman book, and any other book really. I don't have enough experience to know what would be best.'

'Ah, the scatter gun approach!' Tom teased pushing his wheelie chair away from the desk and completing a 360-degree spin.

'Yes something like that,' Jess laughed.

'To be honest, I don't know, it may be that I'm incompetent, or not doing it right, but I seem to get more out of listening to the interviews and adding margin comments to the transcripts and then talking through with you and Stella about our reflections.' Then Jess had another thought. 'I tell you what though,' she swivelled her chair towards Tom but her eyes wandered off somewhere in a cloud of thoughts while her mouth gave utterance to her internal reflections. 'What this process does is...' she paused. 'It like, makes me learn the lines, kinda like, like drama, when I'm learning lines. Doing this makes me remember everything, the words and phrases, the flow of conversation. I sometimes even feel physically like how I see them, the things we talked about, how they each sounded, I feel it. And then the categories are like keys in my head, they open up understandings, you know the ah-ha moments. They link with each other or with other things we've been reading about.'

Tom smiled, and repeated what Jessie had said to him in his head in a way in which it made sense to him: *Participants' words are keys, they open up our understanding about life and experiences.* 'Hmmm. I like it,' he said. 'Lets go for a coffee and talk some more.'

Sharing findings

'You OK?' Tom asked in a perceptive kind of way, noting how much she had taken on and the opportunity she and Stella had given him to present his work. It was billed as a *Student Mixed Methods Conference*. Stella and Jessie were running it together, bringing in speakers who they thought would help their research. Stella, who was using mixed methods, asked Professor Mark Claridge, and Jessie, looking for someone who knew about sport and qualitative research, asked Professor Hugh Morton-Knightley. Jessie couldn't help but want *everything* to be right – food, running order, speakers, an opportunity to talk about their own research, the room, seating, the programme. But that meant she was stretched and didn't have time to practise her presentation. She was aware that everyone else had. She was upset about that, Tom could tell.

'I'm fine, its just, everyone has been practising and I haven't, I'm not ready to do this.' There was no way round that though; the time had come.

The morning sessions went well. Professor Claridge spoke about exactly what Stella had hoped, then Professor Morton-Knightley talked about different ways of representing research, such as stories. One rather critical student commented, 'But it's not *natural* to write like that!' Tom and Jessie made eye contact – how was the professor going to answer that one? They faced these types of condescending comments every day – they were doing 'soft' stuff, 'qually' research.

The professor wasn't fazed. 'Its not *natural* to write in the third person!' he reminded her. 'You've been trained to do that! Why else do you think we have the 400-page *APA Publication Manual*?' It sounded as if he was saying, 'so don't kid yourself, honey!' He carried on. 'Do you think its natural to write: "the subject's anthropometric measurements were recorded..."? No! You *learn* to write that way.' It was like Jessie and Tom had reinforcements.

The morning was great but went too quickly. Then it was time for the four students – Tom, Jessie, Marcos and Stella – to present their work. They sat in a row facing the audience. Tom was first; he'd been experimenting with the story of one of his participants. Jessie introduced him, but, rather than standing up to speak, Tom hitched his chair up by its seat, moved four paces forward, slammed the chair down and just began. 'It's a fear of a fear,' he said. He seemed to catch everyone by surprise – Jessie was impressed. Sitting behind Tom she had the perfect view of the audience. She watched their eyes, their bodies, their gaze, their lack of movement while he was speaking. It seemed as if 50 people were collectively holding their breath the entire time he told the story, frightened to move or exhale in case the spell was broken or they missed a word or vital ingredient. At the end there was a communal exhalation. People sat back in their seats. There was a moment's silence, then huge applause. 'How did you do that?' 'Wow, that was amazing!' 'I never realised, is that your story?' Bang, bang, bang. Everyone had a question.

Jessie was up next. She decided to read out four poems she was working on that had been taken from an interview. Like Tom's story, people seemed to respond differently to how they had in the other presentations. It wasn't major differences – people just seemed to watch more intently, listen more closely and not move about so much. Neither Jessie nor Tom had ever done anything like this before and they felt different too.

'So what does Leanne think about the poems?' Professor Morton-Knightley asked. Then, perhaps sparing Jessie the embarrassment of admitting before 50 people that she hadn't asked her, he simply suggested, 'It would be really good for you to read them to her, find out what she thinks.' That thought filled Jessie with dread: '*telephone Leanne, read her the poems and ask her what she thinks?*' She was also amazed that she hadn't even thought to do that, to share what she'd been writing. But, what she couldn't escape was the feeling that feeding back, in that way, was really important. She felt like, yes, now we are getting somewhere.

Never disturb a man and his Guinness – he has to take a sip, lick the crème from his top lip, put the glass down slowly and just sit. This may be for a minute or two, or perhaps half an hour may pass in contemplation, occasional sips, cool to the lips and soothing to the mind. And so it was. Perhaps the day was sinking in, perhaps it was the alcohol, perhaps the tobacco-laden atmosphere or the dark interior of the aptly named *Vaults* pub. Something was soothing in contrast to what had been a good but rather intense, confusing, challenging and highly charged afternoon. An afternoon presenting their work in a way that took them far beyond anything they were expecting in terms of understanding their participants, their 'data', their selves and how other people might respond to research. A psychologist, therapist or narratologist may have noted that they were each, in their own way, trawling through life's experiences to make sense of and name what they believed had just occurred. That they were sorting through other rememberings to see if past experiences added insight. They were sifting through remembered academic literature, radio discussions, presentations, books, encounters, interviews, experiences and body sensations, all lodged somewhere in their vast interior, now being set each alongside the other. These unseen tasks took all their available capacity and reserves. And so while from the outside it may have looked as if they were being unsociable, or perhaps too tired to talk, they were doing something really important in terms of linking the presentations with their ongoing research and understanding.

After some time it was Tom who spoke first. 'Would you like another?' he asked, before tilting his head back and allowing the last remnants of the black soup to drain from his glass.

'Let me get them', Jessie said, standing, ready to buy the next round.

Tom put his hand on her arm. 'No, sit, let me.' Tom was slightly numb, exhausted and didn't really understand why performing the story made present-ing such a totally different experience to a power point presentation where he might read an extract of the participants' words. But it did. As he made his way to the bar he wondered why he was experiencing this in his body, this sense of heaviness, humility, responsibility. All he did was read a story.

'Hellooooo!' came the voice on the phone – it was alive, bright, and slightly joking.

'Hey Leanne, it's Jessie.' Jessie tried to sound upbeat too, and like she hadn't left it so long since their last conversation before calling again. She wished she didn't have to ask Leanne to listen to what she had written about her, and she wished that she hadn't decided to write Leanne's case study as a series of poems. She felt lost for words, even though before making the telephone call she had carefully written down her own script: what to say, what to cover, an explana-tion, all there in her own handwritten scribbles.

They began talking about sport and ruminating on the latest news, then side-tracked into how difficult it was for women coaches and the struggles female athletes have. 'I don't think it's so sexist in other sports,' Leanne surmised. 'Do you think it's always been this bad?'

'Well, at the Olympics,' Jessie began, 'Barron de Coubertin said women were there to place a garland around the heads of the men winners.'

'Ah, but they're so prickly those garlands, don't you find Jessie? I've stopped wearing mine.'

Jessie tried to be sensible. 'And at the turn of the century GPs were advising women not to run because they said their wombs would fall out!'

'Mine would!' Leanne joked, 'and I'm sure I saw yours in Munich somewhere!'

It was difficult to have a serious conversation because Leanne kept telling jokes. Eventually Jessie began to talk about her research, and the case she'd been writing about Leanne, and then the poems; then she jumped in: 'Would you mind, could I read one to you?'

Leanne wasn't bogged down with whatever Jessie was struggling with and just said, 'of course' in a rather offhand way. Then there was silence.

Jessie didn't expect the moment to arrive so quickly, so she began with the shortest poem: 'I think we are all actresses, I think you have to be. It's a big stage, you go on to perform. ...' Jessie came to the end of the poem and still there was silence. 'Hullo, Leanne, are you still there?' Perhaps they had been disconnected?

'Yes, I am, I am. I don't know what to say – that is exactly how I felt – that's incredible.' Jessie was both excited that Leanne sounded positive, and hugely relieved, as if a burden had been lifted. She asked if she could read another. 'That's amazing,' Leanne kept saying. 'I can't believe you've captured that from interviewing me. Can you send them to me? It's so funny, I never really recognised it, no one ever asked how I was, it was all about my golf. How did you score? Where did you finish? No one ever asked how I was.'

At the end of their conversation Jessie had learned something new about feeding back to participants: she realised that sending an interview transcript really didn't achieve much compared to this. She also learned something about the relationships among women on tour and about poetic and creative representations, about herself and about how demanding qualitative research could be. She was exhausted by the process. 'One done, seven to go.'

'Hello, Jessie?' the male voice asked at the other end of the phone.

'Yes,' came Jessie's reply.

'It's Mark Right here.' He was a sport psychologist Jessie and Tom had met a few months earlier at a coaching conference.

'Oh, hi Mike', Jessie replied, wondering what it was he was after this time.

The presentation Jessie and Tom had given at the conference had been a difficult one. Up until that point she hadn't really been aware of just how provocative their research was. Before their presentation they'd sat through two other internationally acclaimed practitioners' talks about their work. The first began with a slide showing the comedian John Cleese, as the character Basil Fawlty, a hotel owner renowned for his idiosyncratic and ludicrous behaviour, glaring at his wife Sibyl. Alongside the photo was the caption: 'Athletes have never been very good at following instructions!' The audience made the link between the characters on the show and athletes' refusal to do as they were told – laughter erupted around the room. Most people seemed to think this was really funny: *'Oh yes! Athletes never do as they are told!'* As Jessie surveyed the scene it seemed that she was the only athlete there. She didn't find it funny and thought, *'I'm not there to do as I'm told!'* The second speaker didn't do any better. He talked at length about his personal investment in 'his' athletes and then recounted a story about reading an interview with a gold medal-winning athlete he'd worked with. The athlete didn't credit this sport psychologist for his success – the athlete was clearly mistaken. *'How can we trust them?'*

Feeling rather out of step with everyone else there, Tom and Jessie presented their research which included Leanne's poems and her throwing events. As soon as their presentation was over two officials from the English Golf Union cornered her.

'Right!' said the large-bosomed woman, 'who was that player?'

'We have a right to know!' a man accompanying her demanded.

'This is terrible for golf!' the woman continued, pen and paper at the ready.

'I'm very sorry,' Jessie said, without any emotion, 'but we can't possibly divulge that.'

'You have to!' said the woman, slamming her hand on the table. 'We can't have golfers who cheat playing in tournaments!' She moved closer to Jessie, her huge bulk threatening.

'Well, that goes against the anonymity we've promised our participants', Jessie said, standing her ground, glad of her height even if she didn't have the width.

'Well, was she English?' the official snapped. 'We don't care if she's not English.'

Jessie was lost thinking back to that moment, and didn't really listen until Mark got to saying:

'John and I are writing a book and we'd like you to take part.' So this was what it was about? 'What we'd like you to do is write about how you got to the top and then we'll analyse it,' he said.

'I see,' Jessie said, running through in her mind how *they* might analyse *her* life. She wondered what was the matter with *her* analysing it. She wasn't sure whether it was because it was two men, or because they didn't ask her to analyse it, or because they were earning money out of her, or that Mark's co-author didn't seem to be remotely humble or person-centred at the conference. Whatever it was she had a bad feeling about it. 'Ah, don't think I can do that. Thanks anyway.' And that was that.

Her inner council didn't miss a trick though. *'So you're happy to analyse others' lives but not so happy to have your own life analysed then?'* She told herself she'd sleep on that one, but yes, there *was* a problem with some researchers and some writing. But she didn't feel ready to publish her experiences, not yet, although she was writing everything down, knowing one day the time would be right.

Postdoctoral research

Tom liked to be organised. He also liked to be well planned and so he probably went over the focus group details a few too many times, but that way he didn't make mistakes or say the wrong thing or seem uninformed. He would take notes, keep an eye on the tape-recorders, write verbatim comments that might be critical to feedback at the end, and lead the summary discussion. Jessie would lead the focus group and ask the questions as she had done with the golf study because she was the athlete. That term always made Tom laugh when he applied it to golfers – in his mind, when he thought of a golfer he had a vision of a slightly balding, middle-aged man wearing silly clothes and with a sagging belly. He didn't know where Jessie fitted into his vision but it still made him laugh.

Tom was always slightly on edge working with Jessie. In some ways, he thought, she was a typical sportsperson – over-confident, self-assured and never takes no for an answer. If he said, 'the shop is closed' because it said *closed* on the door, she would try to open the door just to check. 'Look, its open!' she'd say, and walk in. If the waiter said the restaurant was full, she'd say, 'Aw! Can't you squeeze us in?' It was like being around royalty, she seemed to expect life to be full of open doors, to always have a parking place reserved for her right outside. He called her 'your ladyship' when he wanted to tease her. She was too optimistic, too pushy, drove too fast for his liking and too close, in his opinion, to the car in front. She also had a habit of embarrassing him by abandoning her car, with him in it, just to pop into a shop. But he also liked that she'd take chances, had the confidence to go for things, follow hunches, try things, even when they seemed doomed to fail. It was because of her that they got the work with the PGA, and the book writing, and it was because of her writing to these other organisations that they got the funding to do this research. So he tried to accept her unconventional ways of working and go with the flow. But it meant he was always more on edge than when he was on his own.

And so he found himself pacing up and down waiting for the first athlete to arrive for their first focus group, running through in his mind how the day would unfold, lining up a contingency for when something went wrong, covering every single base. He didn't really feel he was trying to take control of everything, but he may have, if he could have seen himself. He was impressed by the size and shape of biceps on the first athlete to arrive. He didn't need to say anything; he just smiled at Jessie, who raised her eyebrows in response. After shaking their hands, the athlete headed straight over to the table of refreshments and, picking up a plate of sandwiches, said, 'well, here's my lunch, what are the rest of you going to eat?' Abby was her name and she was very funny, witty, bright and quick. She made Tom smile; he liked her. And he was one up on his bet with Jessie: *she was* wearing sports kit.

'I might of guessed I'd find you at the trough!' said a tall man walking in through the door, clad in a cotton jacket, jeans and leather shoes. Jessie smiled to herself: *one all*.

'Matty baby!' Abby said through a mouth full of a baguette, spraying rocket and crumbs in every direction. 'What do expect from a rower?' They hugged and Matt took a muffin from the table. 'I had no idea you'd be here!' Abby continued.

'I knew *you'd* be up for anything with food!' Matt joked, taking a bite of the muffin.

'Fancy one of these?' she asked, moving the sandwich plate in tempting circles under his nose.

'Crickey, these are bit good aren't they?' Matt took a sandwich in his other hand but waited until the muffin was gone before starting on something piled high with mozzarella and red pepper.

'Do you remember those awful soggy pastry things?' They started reminiscing over Olympic receptions, the food, the farce, the fronts – it provided an excellent place for Tom and Jessie to begin, listening to these athletes talking about their behind-the-scenes experiences. They might not have looked as if they were listening, but everything that was said was being filed meticulously away.

'Oh yeah! And all the equestrian team were huddled in the corner drinking gin!' Matt laughed.

'And smoking god knows how many Marlborough's!' Abby added. 'I have huge respect for *their horses* though. They're the athletes – not the jockeys!'

At that moment a third, well-dressed, high-heeled athlete arrived. Before Jessie could welcome her she'd already spotted familiar faces. 'Abby, Matt, how are you?' They all hugged and a new conversation was spawned. This one was about officials, selection, uniform and coaches, current policy and funding. It was all fascinating but not quite what they were there to do. Tom nodded over to Jessie and followed it by making a circular motion with his finger. He wanted to get the focus group going. Jessie took the hint.

'OK guys,' she put on her announcer's voice, a little louder than the conversation but not too loud to break it. 'Would it be all right to get started?'

It was easy for Tom to play the role of observer – the initial talking was down to Jessie; he took notes, so he always felt slightly detached from the event. When he looked at Jessie, she was the opposite. She was totally physically engaged. He noted the way she took her time introducing the study and answered all their questions. He noted how she continually made eye contact with each member of the group and invited each athlete to tell *their* story. He laughed at the way she protected the time each person was given by holding back the tide of other athletes who were eager to surge forward with their stories. He learned as he watched how she used her own experiences or observations of athletes she'd played golf with or had done research with to play devil's advocate. She would test if an individual was acquiescing, or agreeing too readily, or giving them a 'pat' answer. He had to stop himself laughing out loud a couple of times as she pressed someone, just to make sure of what they were saying.

He remembered their first interviews together, down in Cornwall interviewing women over the age of 65 about their exercise habits. He recalled how, even though he wanted to wrap up the interview believing they'd got what they came for, Jessie would just hold out her hand, or touch his knee under the table, signalling to him they should be still for a few moments more, let this woman speak, have her say, however long it took. He remembered he'd been a little annoyed at first knowing an extra hour interviewing would mean eight hours more transcribing for him. But he'd learned that every extra hour was an extra hour invested in learning, listening, becoming immersed in the smells, tastes and visions of another person's world. Without that immersion, he knew the songs he'd written wouldn't have come to be, not without sitting, letting go and allowing someone else's world to penetrate his own. Of course this young, fit, healthy bunch of Olympic athletes were very different to the old women. Still, Jessie knitted together a tapestry and drew their stories like threads until the moment came when Tom was asked to reveal a picture, something they could agree upon, something that represented what it was that they'd said about life in sport.

Tom thought this group were into competitive talking, cramming as much of their lives as they could into a two-hour focus group. Their speaking in double time left few spaces for Jessie and was going to be a nightmare to transcribe. Tom was glad that this time he wasn't going to be doing that task. While they may have been competing to tell their stories minutes earlier, they were all respectful of Tom once he began, each one nodding, 'yes, yes, that's right, yes' or 'wow! yeah!' They seemed amazed that someone could pay such close attention to the details of their stories, the colour of their lives, the ebb and flow of their experiences. Tom and Jessie had barely clung on to the reins of the conversation, but now Tom spoke slowly, clearly and professionally. He gave each athlete in turn an opportunity to respond, to reconsider and to reflect. And then, with a quick nod towards Jessie, he was done.

Jessie knew she had Luke's business card somewhere. She never threw anything like that away, always expecting it to come in handy one day. But in which assortment of papers might it be hiding? As she sifted through four in-trays in her green room cupboard her mind went back. The process helped her situate what other markers there were that would help her locate Luke's contact details. Ah, that was right, she'd been buying a pair of running shoes, it was about eight months earlier. If you want to buy good running shoes the place to go is *Sprint*. It's the type of place where running shoes aren't a fashion accessory – an Aladdin's cave bursting with kit of every description. But it's no megastore, just a small terraced house.

Jessie had pushed through two guys discussing over-pronation and heel-strikes in the doorway, into a small room jam-packed with clothing and on to the back room brimming full of shoes. The vista was shoes on feet, shoes on the floor, shoes on the rack, shoes on the wall, shoes in boxes, shoes half out of boxes, shoes strewn here and there alongside runners at very stage of the purchasing process discussing size, shape, cushioning, the latest research and the fit. As always it was a hubbub of activity and a rather nice place to watch people.

The picture came back as Jessie sifted through odd bits of paper, a conference poster, an old to-do list, an article torn from a newspaper and a postcard from a friend. '*Yes, this is the type of pile where I'll find it*', she thought.

Jessie never wanted to talk about shoes before she'd sized up the price and had to twist her head sideways to read some of the price tags. Having been used to *being paid* to wear a brand of sports shoe her eyes grew wide noting how much some of them cost when you actually had to buy them. '*Wow! I don't want to take out a mortgage for a pair of trainers!*' she thought. Although she didn't ever put herself in the 'serious' runner category she would run every day, so it wasn't unusual for her to clock up 40 to 50 miles each week. She wanted a decent pair of shoes but *that* was out of her league. She hated feeling pressurised by sales assistants so she tried not to make eye contact until she felt secure about what she wanted.

She was just checking out some cheaper options when someone behind shouted, 'Jessie!'

She turned to see a face moving towards her – a young athlete whom she'd met at a weekend retreat a few years before. 'Luke?' She smiled back.

'I thought it was you', he said, but before he could finish someone walked between them handing Luke three boxes.

'Could you nip these downstairs when you've a moment Luke?'

'Will do', Luke said, accepting the boxes and then turning his gaze back to Jessie; he smiled. 'Its great to see you! How long ago was it? Two years ago, 18 months, something like that. How have you been? What have you been up to?'

She remembered how vital and full of energy Luke had looked, bristling with life and really funny. That memory was held in a frame in her mind as the shop's business card came into view with his telephone number handwritten across the top. She held the card between her hands as if it were gold, feeling he would be an ideal addition for their research: male, early career, high profile, successful, European Junior champion, track and field. And they had spoken before, broken the ice, so to speak. As she looked at the card it struck her how little she knew about him, but she was curious to learn more.

4 The performance narrative

I couldn't be successful without it being the most important thing in my life. I don't think that you can possibly be successful without it being the most important thing.

(Georgi)

In this chapter we present and explore what we consider to be the dominant narrative type in sport: the *performance narrative*. We describe this narrative as *dominant* for two reasons. First, because it is the most common type of story we hear elite athletes tell. Second, because it corresponds to the master narrative (discussed in Chapter 1) that underlies the majority of public portrayals of athletes.

In this narrative type, performance-related concerns infuse all areas of the storyteller's life. It is a story of single-minded dedication to sport performance that justifies, and even demands, the exclusion or relegation of all other areas of life and self. Performance stories provide illustrations of how and why, for some athletes at least, 'sport is life and life is sport'. Performance stories align with, extol, communicate and reinscribe the culturally dominant values and beliefs of elite sport. Typically, the storyteller assumes that all athletes *must* be the same when it comes to adherence to these values and beliefs. Performance stories often reveal the fragile nature of self-worth when it is dependent on sport performance, and show how a glorified self and exclusive athletic identity become problematic during performance fluctuations or when the storyteller contemplates withdrawal from sport. Retirement or career-ending injury are typically storied with a degree of fear and as a time of impending loss. Critically, as we will see as the book progresses, performance stories – sooner or later – tend to end badly for the teller.

We begin the chapter by offering an illustrative performance story – in the words of Georgi, a multiple tournament-winning professional golfer – to give a flavour of how a performance story looks and feels. We have chosen to use Georgi's story, as it portrays particularly clearly many of the characteristics of the 'ideal-type' performance narrative. Next, we offer a summary of the plot of the performance narrative before exploring in more detail its defining characteristics. In doing so, we draw on narrative theory to signpost the meaning and potential significance of the performance narrative type for those individuals whose personal stories follow its plot.

A performance story

I just love sport, any sport. I just like competition – I suppose to see how good you can actually be, so you can stretch yourself. I need to stretch myself to see how capable I am. I need competition – that's what it is, that's what you chose to go into. At the end of the day there is a trophy and there is a cheque, and another notch in how many wins you have had. A lot of it is about winning.

I mean, to be honest – this is hard to say without sounding arrogant – I think whatever sport I'd have chosen I would have been good at it. I was extremely coordinated. I could do every sport that I tried. I wouldn't compare myself to other children of my age because they'd never make the comparison. I impressed myself, if you like, right from a very young age. And I think my parents would say the same.

I started playing golf with my family. Dad played, and my brother, and we were just on the golf course. We played everything together believe it or not. We played a lot of tennis, badminton, football. I don't think I ever loved it. It was just one of those things that I knew I was supposed to do – because there was never a great love or affection for it. I remember my brother when he was 16 – he used to play 54 holes a day – him and his mates. They *loved* it. No chance, you know, I just did it because I was quite good at it and I was always going to turn pro. I mean at 13 I knew I would turn pro. Not because I loved it – I just knew I would be good at it. I can't say I love golf. No, I don't love golf. But I love the feelings it can give you, those separate moments in time. I don't get a kick out of going out and playing, I love tournament golf. Turning professional was natural progression – I'd won most things as an amateur by the time I turned pro.

I think most of it, sporting ability, would extend from my Dad. He was very good at most things. I think my stubborn streak comes from him. Dad's got such a will to win, even when he plays golf. Christ! It's unbelievable! Oh my god! It's absolute. And whenever I play with him he wants to beat me so much. I don't care! I just want to compete against professionals in tournaments. I suppose because you want to be the best and being the best is not about beating my brother and my Dad. That wouldn't give me any satisfaction at all. I'm quite happy to play against them but there is no better feeling than being the best that week. It doesn't matter where you are, which country you are playing in, whether it is the States or over here, if you win that event you are the best player there that particular day.

I don't think I can describe those feelings, after it's done, after the presentation. Nine times out of ten I walk into like the ladies' toilets or whatever, after it's over, I usually punch the air and jump about and usually some words come out that you wouldn't use in public. And that is sheer and utter satisfaction. It's hard to explain. It's just being on a high without any aids basically – not that I'd know about that actually 'cos I haven't tried any. And really it doesn't matter how you achieve that, whether you play great or not. But if you can do it performing to the best of your ability and wipe the field away as well, that's just a little bit extra special, isn't it?

I think if I'm really honest, if I've come back from a tournament and I've won, I feel very strong, very strong and very proud, so it probably makes me feel better about myself. One of the nicest feelings I've had is after I've been on *A Question of Sport*[1] and if that episode is shown on a Friday, and this has happened a couple of times, I go out on a Saturday night into town with few mates or a few of the boys and I'm stood up there getting a couple of drinks and you can see the blokes looking, thinking, 'I know you don't I?' That's an ego thing and it's great – I would be a liar if I said any different. That I love!

When I missed those cuts I felt dreadful about myself. I was letting everybody down and myself. I had no self-esteem. Everything just went, totally. I was distraught. What do you do? You know, you feel lower and lower about yourself. It was just a nightmare. Huge. I think I just lost all my confidence in one round of golf. That last day I was out with two of the top players and shot over 80 and was distraught, obviously. Totally and utterly distraught. Didn't know what was going on. I shot 69, 68, 70, 85 – figure that one out! Oh, god, I lost about eight balls in the water. I was appalling. Awful. I wasn't actually openly sobbing but I was crying because I was so embarrassed. Christ! I think, actually, that one round of golf knocked the stuffing out of me for a long time.

But, I think that is just the nature of the beast – you are competitive and you want to achieve. You want to be successful. I don't believe you can have a bloody awful day at the office or on a golf course or on a tennis court and just come off and be exactly the person everybody wants you to be – to me that's not natural. Maybe people don't care about it enough if they can just forget about it. There's no doubt when I say that golf is the person, it has to affect us. You know it does! I see other people on tour playing badly – they are miserable bastards, hard work to get on with. You don't even have to talk to them but you can feel the atmosphere, the energy when you walk into a room. You know whether someone is having a good time or a bad time even if you didn't know their score. You immediately think: 'Oh dear!' And I'm sure – unless they are a remarkable person – in every sport it's the same. Probably in life in general.

As a professional golfer, golf is always on my mind. Even when I'm having a week off I've got to hit some balls. I wouldn't call myself moody but I know most of my friends call me moody. So if I take the general consensus, I suppose, yeah, I am quite a moody person. But I don't think I'm moody for no reason. I say that the person and the job and the person and the golf go together. I couldn't be successful without it being the most important thing in my life. Let's put it this way: the top players on the tour, regardless of who they are seeing – whether it is a man or a woman or whatever – their golf will always come first. You take Sonia – take her partner, whoever it is, away from Sonia the golfer and basically her partner would go out the window before Sonia's golf would. Annika – David would go I think before her golf. That is the most important thing to them at this moment in time. Might change down the road but I think the golf will always come before a relationship. And those are the things I measure it on basically. What can be more important? My golf is more important than anything. If I was in a relationship I would have to say to whoever that was, this is huge – it is not a job. It's much more than that. It's not just a career. I think that for all of us, it becomes our whole life. Because I don't think that you can possibly be success-ful without it being the most important thing.

I mean last night, it was half past six and I thought I better go and hit some pitch shots. Now, it was a lovely night, I should have cut the grass, I wanted to be by the pool to be perfectly honest. But no, I will go. That's what I mean. It really does have to be important for me to give up you know sitting out by the pool with a drink in my hand to go and hit some pitch shots. Oh Christ! Get a fucking life! You know, please! 35 years of age! But I can't imagine a better feeling than coming back next week having won the Italian Open. That's what I want to feel and I'm prepared to do everything I am capable of doing to get that feeling. Am I prepared to injure my body to go and win a tournament? It would appear so. You know, this [points to injury] is from years of punishment. I suppose I'll just have to learn to play with it.

Sometimes I think I'm very lucky to do what I do. Apart from the times when someone says, 'God, you're very lucky to do what you do!' And then you turn round and say: 'Hang on a minute!' Its true isn't it? *I'm* allowed to think I'm lucky, but *you* aren't allowed to say that, okay? 'God you are so lucky!' they go. And we are supposed to go: 'Yeah, I was born and they gave me this golf club and I was brilliant and then I turned pro, never did a thing. Fantastic. I'm so lucky!' That annoys me, I've got to be honest, when people think you're lucky – because they don't actually put anything together. They seem to think that you did sod-all to get yourself there. That one fascinates me. And the other thing – people don't think you work, do they? You have a few months off and even my friends and people I know very, very well seem to think I'm on holiday these last three months! They go: 'You're on holiday!' 'No! No! No! No, I'm injured! Flippin' hell!' And they go: 'I know you're injured but you're not doing any-thing, are you?' And you go: 'No, but I'm not on holiday! I would be playing if I wasn't injured. But if I played golf it will hurt and the only way to get better is to rest.' And unless they can see you physically hobbling around, then you can't be injured, so you're just a bit of a layabout really. I've never understood that.

Before I finish playing I would like to win 20 tournaments on this tour so I've got seven to go and I think I should be quite capable of doing that. I play because I love competing. I love the competition. I love the thought of being the winner at the end of the week. And, to be perfectly honest, if I do everything I'm capable of doing work-wise, then I don't see how I could fail. And so I won't fail and so it won't change how I feel about myself because I will be doing everything in my capability. If I did everything in my capability and I still wasn't successful … I don't see how that can happen. If I work hard enough I *will* be successful.

Retiring – that is a frightening thought for me to be honest. I don't know what necessarily I'm going to do and, you know, you don't want it to come to an end. Right now I feel it would be like losing a limb, 'cos I haven't achieved what I want to achieve. I couldn't imagine not playing. And its something, you know, I've done it for what, 13, 14 years and it's something I am used to doing and I'd then have to do something else and that would be a big step. I'm not ready to give that up at all. It's a huge part of my life, massive.

The performance plot

Although the specific details of different individuals' performance stories vary according to their life circumstances, all performance stories broadly follow an identifiable plot. It is this plot that defines the general progression and evolution of performance stories over time. In performance stories the plot is oriented towards achieving specific goals, namely performance outcomes such as winning and/or being the best. The ultimate dream or destination in the story is the podium, the medal, the cheque or the trophy. Progression towards this destination is likely to involve not only triumphs and successes but also setbacks, hurdles, obstacles and difficulties. However, these challenges may typically be overcome through hard work, discipline and sacrifice over time.

Within the performance plot, as a young or not yet 'expert' athlete, you need to demonstrate that you have potential in terms of, for example, temperament and talent. Certain allowances are made (i.e. you are excused certain things) while you are learning the craft. Expectations of appropriate behaviour, attitude and performance may be softened. But there is a day of reckoning. At this time, expectations of behaviour and performance outcomes become more hard and fast. Now is the time to deliver. By this time, others (such as coaches, physiotherapists, sport scientists, etc.) have been drafted in to work on you and for you. As a consequence, you are expected to – over time – fulfil your potential by winning. To retain your position in terms of attention and investment, you are obliged to prioritise performance outcomes, demonstrate particular culturally sanctioned behaviours in line with this focus, while publicly endorsing and retelling performance stories. You will judge your career – and perhaps life – on the basis of your achievements in sport, often through comparison with other athletes. The outcome of your judgement will likely fluctuate over time, affecting your feelings of self-worth.

Within the performance plot, certain characteristics are evident, as illustrated by Georgi's story above. Together, they define the performance narrative type, highlighting some of the consequences and implications of this type of story. Below, we explore these characteristics in detail.

An outcome focus: winning or being the best

The primary or exclusive focus of performance stories is performance outcomes – winning or being the best. It is an *outcome-focused* narrative. Descriptions of the *process* of playing sport – for example, for enjoyment, mastery or social reasons – are either absent or side-lined in favour of achieving particular outcomes. Process is only important to the extent that it influences or leads to performance outcomes.

Part and parcel of this focus is a sense of *needing* competition and the belief that competition is what sport is all about. This is apparent in Georgi's story when she says, 'I just like competition – I suppose to see how good you can actually be, so you can stretch yourself. I need to stretch myself to see how capable I am. I need competition.' For her, 'At the end of the day there is a trophy and there is a cheque, and another notch in how many wins you've had. A lot of it is about winning.' As an indication or perhaps result of this focus, she describes how 'I don't get a kick out of going out and playing, I love tournament golf'. For performance storytellers, sport would be largely meaningless if it didn't include opportunities to win or demonstrate superiority through competitive events.

A strong prioritisation of winning or beating others was evident in several participants' accounts. For example:

> [I]t's more the winning that I've liked. I've gone through sports and tried to find one where I could be better than other people and just found that this was the one that I could hack. I could get better than other people at quite a high level. So it wasn't that I was particularly passionate about the activity – it was a vehicle that I could beat other people and, yeah, just get better than other people ... I think it's just, succeeding, like, winning, knowing that you are better than everyone else.

> I wanted to win everything. I wanted to win every tournament I tee'd up in. I just thought if you are going to start winning tournaments you automatically become a better player. It wasn't the thing I was trying to do – I just wanted to go out and win. It wasn't particularly the money. I liked the fact that I proved something to those that said I couldn't and I wasn't good enough. I've always been a bit hard-headed that way and it was mostly all about that. I hate getting told that I am wrong and I hate getting told that I can't do something. It just rattles me and I just want to pull everything out of myself. And I felt that I had to prove something, just felt I had to really go deep inside myself and pull something extra out.... When I won that first tournament it was like putting a notch in my gun, you know. And I thought, well, I have to get some more notches. But becoming a better player had never entered my head. It was: I wanted to win more.

In the first extract from a male rower, the need to win, to be the best, is articulated as sufficiently strong that it dictates the individual's involvement sport: he has chosen to participate in rowing *specifically* because it offers the best opportunity for him to satisfy the demands of a performance story. In the second extract, the first win 'proved' something to those who doubted and, in this female golfer's words, 'put a notch in my gun'. She is very clear that she didn't want to become a better player, just accumulate 'more notches' and 'win more'.

We are coming to the view that, in the long term, the desired outcome of performance stories (of winning or being the best) is a *mythical* destination. Any win or demonstration of superiority appears destined to be temporary and transient, lasting, at best, only until the next event or the next contender comes along. For many athletes, sustained winning or being widely recognised as 'the best' is a statistical impossibility – simply, only a very few can achieve this. Even for those few who *do* achieve this, athletes' life stories suggest that it is somehow not enough, there is always somewhere further, always something more that is required. At some level of comparison, the individual is still seen to be lacking.

Relegation of other areas of life

A consequence of the prioritisation of performance outcomes is the relegation or minimisation of other areas of life. In performance stories, other aspects of life, if they're storied at all, are storied as subservient to performance. Sport performance is storied as more important. For example, in Georgi's words: 'I couldn't be successful without it being the most important thing in my life. My golf is more important than anything.'

Personal relationships – particularly with a partner – are typically considered as important to many people in general society. Yet in performance stories even intimate personal relationships are storied as of secondary importance. Georgi, for example, said: 'If I was in a relationship I would have to say to whoever that was, this is huge – it is not a job. It's much more than that.' Other athletes too described putting relationships behind performance concerns, at times to the extent that relationships were sacrificed or ended because they were believed to adversely affect performance. In the following extracts a female golfer and a male runner offer their reflections on relationships:

> I was engaged at the time, and was going to get married. So I was worried about that aspect. I thought, 'if I am away ... he's not going to like it'. That was my first reaction: 'What's he going to think?' The other thing was: 'Am I good enough?' A few members at my home club said, 'What are you doing?' sort of thing and I think that really drove me. They didn't think I was good enough – that's what got me going. And basically I thought: 'I'll show you buggers!' I did win my first tournament in my first year. As it happened, the old ball and chain did give me an ultimatum: 'It's me or golf.' So I said: 'Sorry, it's golf.' So that was it. I went from there.

> You kind of get to a point where you have to ask the question where is this going? You know, someone living in Plymouth and someone living in Sheffield. What's the priority? What needs to be done? And when we broke up I just felt that ... I needed to be the athlete ... what would be the point being

in Sheffield training and someone influencing me so far away that I couldn't do anything about? So we kind of finished.

While descriptions of relationships (sometimes in positive terms) may be present, a defining characteristic of performance stories is that relationships are storied in the context of helping or hindering performance. For example, we have heard young athletes reflect on whether or not staying in a relationship with their boyfriend or girlfriend will help or hinder their performance, suggesting, as did one cricketer, 'I suppose if I wanted to be with someone and *it didn't affect my game* then I'd do it.' One sporting cliché along these lines goes: *it might be good to have a partner, for stability, to relax you, to help your performance, but only until that partner starts to make demands that get in the way of training and performance.*

In public, athletes often refer in winning speeches and interviews to relationships with significant others. Many times, athletes describe the importance of the support they have experienced through these relationships, perhaps from their family members, coach or fans. We do not mean to suggest that these stories portray relationships as unimportant, but rather that the relationships are storied in terms of their contribution to the athlete's journey towards sporting success. In other words, the relationship is valued not for its intrinsic worth, but because it has helped the athlete to perform.

In the following extract a professional golfer talks about her partner's need for her to excel, and the pressure this contributed:

> It's like, you remember Marcus? We were together for 11 years and he was always [saying], 'Oh, the life you have is very tough and yes, I understand you want to be independent, of course. If you are good and win, for me it's okay if you are away,' that was his point of view. 'But if you are *not* playing well, and you *don't* have results and have to be away so many weeks a year, it's not good for me.'

Here, the compensation this woman's partner gains *if she wins* leads to an acceptance of her being away. However, if she is *not* winning, being away is *not* acceptable to him. Besides revealing some troubling gender politics, this excerpt also reveals how others – partners, coaches and family members – also often rely on performance stories as a narrative map that shapes their expectations.

Other performance stories describe anything from minor adjustments to radical changes to life circumstances in the pursuit of improved performance. We have heard accounts of athletes giving up employment, abandoning education or leaving the family home for a performance centre. One Paralympic swimmer, for example, described moving around the country to follow his coach:

> I moved around the country trying to find the right coach ... I just kept moving around trying to find someone who could communicate with me....

It took me a long while to find somebody like that and once I found him I stayed with him and moved houses when he moved jobs because that was important to me.

While we do not wish to judge individuals' behaviours, we do wish to high-light a seemingly inevitable consequence of storying performance outcomes as paramount: all other aspects of life risk being minimised, suppressed, given up, excluded or relegated. This point leads to a further characteristic of many performance stories which is the *sacrifice* of certain avenues of human experi-ence in the belief that this is necessary to stand a chance of reaching the highest level. Within the performance narrative it is not merely that certain aspects of human life (that others value highly) are routinely sacrificed, but that these sacrifices are storied as *necessary* in the pursuit of optimum performance.

Fragile and contingent sense of self

Georgi's story fits much sport psychology literature and received wisdom which suggests that in order to be successful an athlete must be single-minded in focus and must resist or relegate other facets of life (e.g. Brewer *et al.*, 1993; Holt and Dunn, 2004; Warriner and Lavallee, 2008; Werthner and Orlick, 1986). So total is the focus on sport performance that the person and the job become insepar-able. As Georgi puts it, 'the person and the job and the person and the golf go together'. Another golfer described herself as like a stick of rock you might buy at the seaside which, when you cut it open, has the word 'golfer' written all the way through. For these individuals, when performance is going well the person is going well. In this sense, performance stories portray the teller as a person with a strong or exclusive athletic identity (Brewer *et al.*, 1993). Thus, a further characteristic of the performance narrative is that sense of self – or identity – is wholly tied up with sport.

More than this, though, sense of self is closely tied not only to being *an* athlete, but being a *successful* athlete. Under the terms of the performance nar-rative, as we have noted above, success equates to achieving performance out-comes such as winning or being the best. Therefore the sense of self evident in performance stories is wound up with – and intimately connected to – winning. From this perspective, the self that is created through performance stories – an identity that is built around winning or being the best – is often a *glorified* or *aggrandized* self (Adler and Adler, 1989).

In performance stories, winning is typically storied as fulfilling one's sense of self as a person. In McLeod's (1997) terms, there is a close alignment or fit between the athlete's experiences (winning) and the script of their personal (per-formance) story. As a result, there is likely to be a sense of relative harmony or 'rightness' as lived experience matches the sense of self articulated through the story. Georgi's story portrays this process in action, particularly when she says, 'if I've come back from a tournament and I've won I feel very strong, very strong and very proud so it probably makes me feel better about myself.' It is also evident, along with the sense of a glorified or aggrandised self, in the following account from another professional golfer:

> It wasn't particularly the golf, it was the competition, I wanted caps, I wanted titles, I wanted recognition. It makes you feel differently about yourself. Achievements give you confidence. Also, how other people perceive you and treat you literally changed just because I won a title and so when you feel people are in awe of you it is kind of nice at first.

In contrast, losing (or anything less than winning) is typically experienced as damaging to sense of self. This is evident in Georgi's description of missing cuts (i.e. failing to qualify for the third round of a tournament): 'When I missed those cuts I felt dreadful about myself. I was letting everybody down and myself. I had no self-esteem. Everything just went, totally. I was distraught.' At times like these, concrete, lived experience (of not winning) *does not* align with the performance plot. The individual's performance story is – for a moment at least – derailed. The story no longer fits the concrete events of the individual's life. In performance stories, then, losing is typically described as involving some loss of sense of self, perhaps accompanied by feelings of shame. Georgi said: 'I wasn't actually openly sobbing but I was crying because I was so embarrassed.' In extreme examples, the individual's story portrays a broken self, accompanied by strong feelings of disorientation and disappointment with the self, verging on trauma. At times, as we will see in Chapters 9 and 10, the implications of this collapse of self can be catastrophic for the individual's well-being.

As Georgi's story suggests, tellers of performance tales often experience oscillations between a positive sense of self-worth and a partial or complete loss of sense of self. The change from a seemingly secure sense of self to a collapse of identity can occur within a single competition. Another golfer, for example, described her sense of self as a 'yo-yo' that corresponded directly with whether or not she performed well in the most recent tournament. In the words of another female golfer:

> With sport, you tend to be on an imaginary roller-coaster. When I play well, you're less tense and just ride on a wave of doing well. Other times, because I have done well, I can't seem to cope with not doing well. I find it very difficult to laugh on the golf course. I'm a miserable, miserable cow on the golf course. Miserable if I didn't play how I wanted to. Really in horrible bad moods all day. You know how I played by the look on my face.

For those individuals who live according to the performance script, sense of self is on the line every time they compete. Each time these individuals step into the competitive arena – the course, court, field, track or pool – their self-worth is put into question until it can be resolved by a satisfactory performance outcome. The question of whether or not sense of self survives intact depends on the extent to which their concrete lived experience of performance outcomes aligns with the plot of the performance story. Any time the achievement of performance outcomes is called into question (for example, by injury, poor form or when contemplating retirement) the desired narrative trajectory of the person's story is threatened. What the individual expects for herself and from her life becomes contingent upon whether or not performance can be sustained. Because performance outcomes are to a greater or lesser extent uncontrollable (because they depend in part at least on factors outside the individual), sense of self in performance stories is both *contingent* and *fragile*.

A monological, linear narrative

In the light of recent narrative theory, we suggest that two characteristics are evident in performance stories. As we will see in Chapter 9, these characteristics hold potential significance for long-term identity, development, mental health and well-being.

First, we have come to understand the performance narrative as *monological*. For Hermans (2006: 152), a monological narrative is:

> distinguished by a strong but rigid hierarchy of self-positions with one or a few positions dominating the repertoire.... There may be multiple experiences but all of these are interpreted according to unchanging self-positions ... persons who are in a monological state construct an internally consistent story, but one so rigid that it would resist any evolution.

In performance stories, the single self-position that dominates the repertoire is that of athlete. All events and experiences described are recounted from this self-position. In other words, the role of 'athlete' is storied not only *above* all other possible identities, roles and selves, but at times to their *exclusion*.

Second, we consider the performance narrative to be *linear* because it follows a specific trajectory towards a single destination (i.e. winning in competitive sport). Performance tales suggest that this destination is the only one that matters and that it can only be achieved in this way. Other routes and destinations are simply not as important. For Douglas Ezzy (2000: 616), 'linear narratives emphasise individuality and agency. They assume that people can control their lives and down play the significance of other people and of environmental constraints on their actions.' These points broadly fit with our experience of individual athletes' performance stories as well as the master narrative in public portrayals of elite sport. In both, the athlete is the protagonist – or central character – within the story that is ultimately storied as responsible for the outcomes achieved or not achieved. Here, the realisation of positive performance outcomes is often storied as personally controllable rather than as a result of external chance occurrences.

Totalitarian, normalising and naturalising

When speaking about their personal experience, tellers of performance stories often reveal a belief that the expectations, assumptions and values they hold are universal. Put another way, they articulate the view that the terms of the performance narrative apply to *all* sportspeople. We have noticed how, in describing their own experiences, tellers of performance tales subtly or explicitly speak for and about others. Georgi's story provides several examples of this. One example comes when she describes the effects of an 'awful day':

> I don't believe you can have a bloody awful day at the office or on a golf course or on a tennis court and just come off and be exactly the person everybody wants you to be – to me that's not natural. Maybe people don't care about it enough if they can just forget about it.

Here, Georgi ascribes a judgement on others as inadequate or unsuitable for high-level sport, on the basis of her own beliefs. A similar suspicion is evident in the words of another professional golfer: 'I never believed people who say that they don't dream about winning tournaments.'

Georgi goes on to say: 'I think that for all of us, it becomes our whole life. Because I don't think that you can possibly be successful without it being the most important thing.' This excerpt provides an illustration of how a dominant narrative can come to represent others' lives. At this point, Georgi changes from making self-statements about her *own* life to make a generalisation about the lives of *all* women golfers. At times like these, performance storytellers don't just speak for themselves, but assume they are speaking for everybody in sport. Georgi names other top players, speaking for them when she says they would sacrifice their partner before their golf. By doing so, tellers of performance tales impose their values, beliefs or way of being upon all other athletes in a totalitarian manner. The cliché goes something like this: *we are all this way and we must be in order to be successful.* In stating this totalitarian belief – that the performance narrative is the only route to success – Georgi reinscribes the dominant narrative of elite sport.

Through this process, performance stories *normalise* and *naturalise* (Nelson, 2001) particular behaviours as necessary for performance. Georgi's story, for example, naturalises her high-level involvement in golf and adoption of a performance story when she says, 'I was always going to turn pro. I mean at 13 I knew I would turn pro. Not because I loved it, I just knew I would be good at it.' For her, 'turning professional was natural progression'. Here, Georgi hides all the other factors involved in her progression by suggesting that she was *born* to be a professional golfer. Similarly, Georgi's story normalises her behaviours and responses as part and parcel of the quest to attain optimum performance when she says, 'I think that was just the nature of the beast – you are competitive and you want to achieve. You want to be successful.' Through these kinds of accounts, performance narratives soften potential tensions and problematic moral concerns by naturalising actions as being necessary for success and therefore justifiable under the story's prioritisation of the pursuit of optimum performance. By so doing, potentially damaging or oppressive practices may be normalised on the basis that they are – supposedly – necessary for optimum performance. The moral implications of these actions are side-lined or ignored.

The work of performance enhancement

Under the terms of the performance narrative, performance enhancement is both *desirable* and *controllable*. It is desirable because it is a primary way in which performance outcomes may be improved – it is, potentially, a route towards wins. It is controllable in that within performance stories the athlete is often portrayed as a 'machine' that is amenable to specific techniques or interventions designed expressly to improve performance. These interventions range from (on the surface at least) relatively safe and harmless behavioural adjustments (such as sleep, rest, minor dietary modifications) right through to potentially damaging practices (such as abusive training programmes, use of steroids and other harmful substances, and extreme dietary regimes). Within the terms of an ideal-type performance story, any or all of these practices has the potential to be portrayed as normal and natural in the pursuit of maximal performance.

Georgi provides one example within golf when she says:

> I can't imagine a better feeling than coming back next week having won the Italian Open. That's what I want to feel and I am prepared to do everything I am capable of doing to get that feeling. Am I prepared to injure my body to go and win a tournament? It would appear so. You know, this [points to injury] is from years of punishment.

This example provides a flavour of how, if performance is the overriding goal, it becomes logical and rational to accept or tolerate injury, harm, abuse or other damage to health (see Madill and Hopper, 2007). Under different conditions, of course, these same actions may be storied as illogical and irrational. For us, this point is important and may pave the way towards improved understanding of the personal and cultural pressures that may operate on athletes to consider, adopt or reject a variety of performance enhancement interventions.

Linked to a commitment to enhance performance is a further characteristic of the performance narrative where sport is storied as *work*. Notably absent from most performance stories are accounts of sport as play, fun or ludic activity. Instead, sport is serious. It requires discipline, commitment, intense effort, persistence and tenacity. For some of the women golfers we interviewed, golf was most definitely *not* fun, but *work*. The two were storied as incompatible. This is evident in the words of one professional golfer who emphasises the importance – for herself as a professional – of the outcome of winning money:

KITRINA: *Your bottom line is the money?*

DEBBIE: Yeah, of course it is. You don't go out there for fun, do you?

KITRINA: *Do you judge whether you are successful or not by how much money you earn?*

DEBBIE: Hmmm, yeah. Oh, sorry, of course it is. *You* know! *You* won eight times! What's the matter with you? Of course it's for the money.

In her story, Georgi takes the metaphor further: for her, sport is, in fact, much *more* than a job. The job of work is applying oneself to activities, tasks and practices that are designed to enhance performance outcomes. Again, it is not the process that is important, other than the extent to which focusing upon it will lead to improved outcomes. In other words, the process is not enough in itself – it depends on achieving certain outcomes for it to be afforded space within one's personal story.

Georgi's portrayal of practice and training as work illuminates a connection with motivation. While communicating a strong work ethic, Georgi's story aligns the incentive and commitment behind her motivation to 'hit some pitch shots' when she'd rather be 'sitting out by the pool with a drink in my hand' with her belief that performing well in golf is the most important thing. For her, this belief allows her to resist other activities that she might prefer to engage with in order to sustain her training.

Life after sport

A particular tone of account when contemplating life after sport is a final hallmark of performance stories. Whether through retirement, career-threatening injury or de-selection, performance storytellers typically narrate life after sport in negative terms. A sense of this is hinted at when Georgi contemplates retiring from golf:

> Retiring, that is a frightening thought for me to be honest. I don't know what necessarily I am going to do and, you know, you don't want it to come to an end. Right now I feel it would be like losing a limb, 'cos I haven't achieved what I want to achieve. I couldn't imagine not playing.

To us, the tone of this account signals worries for the time ahead and is a cause for concern that we explore further in Chapters 9 and 10.

One often-heard refrain in sport is asking athletes (perhaps by coaches, managers, fans or media commentators) to 'give me everything' or 'give us 110 per cent'. Under the terms of the performance narrative, athletes are expected – at times demanded – to give everything to their sport, their training and their career. It is perhaps this feature, more than any other, that most clearly highlights the dangers of exclusive performance stories. What happens when that person fails to fulfil their potential or stops winning? One young cricketer reflected on this question:

I suppose there's people now in the first team who, if I do well this year, it will finish their career. Obviously, they're not gonna want me to come in and take the place where they've been for the last ten years. But that's just part and parcel of sport really – there's no way round that. If I'm young and I'm doing well then I play, you know. If I'm doing better than the person who's already in there, then that's what happens isn't it?

Here, there is not even any consideration that there may be an alternative, a different or a better way. Like other tellers of performance tales, this young man believes 'that's what happens' and that it is 'part and parcel of sport'. For those players who have been excelling for the past ten years, the same fate awaits. There is a good likelihood that they will be 'disposed of' – dropped, side-lined or forgotten. At that point, attention usually shifts to the next contender. The question of where that leaves the individual who has been 'disposed of' is less likely to be considered in mainstream sport culture.

Note

1 *A Question of Sport* is a long running prime-time BBC television quiz show which features guest appearances by well-known sportspeople.

5 The discovery narrative

I want to know about food, about wine, about wood, about gardening, about outdoors, about everything. I think everything is very interesting in life. I think it's so fantastic to discover.

(Kandy)

The performance narrative, discussed in Chapter 4, is the dominant type of story we hear within the culture of elite and professional sport. It is a story form articulated in the personal stories of some sportspeople in our research that resonates with public portrayals of elite athletes. The power of performance stories such as Georgi's, when combined with the emphasis on public portrayals, may lead us to conclude that the performance narrative is the *only* way of life open to high-level sportspeople. But is this the case? In the face of the dominance of performance stories, you could be forgiven for thinking so. Yet our research has shown us that alternative narrative types – different ways of storying life in sport – exist within the culture of elite and professional sport. Often, however, these stories exist in the margins, silenced or hidden from mainstream public view.

The first alternative type of story is the *discovery narrative*, which is the antithesis of the performance narrative. This is a story of exploration and discovery, over and above performance outcomes. The discovery storyteller recounts achieving success without prioritising sport ahead of all other areas of life, and describes the very life that the performance teller believes must be sacrificed to achieve success. In discovery stories, the teller presents a diverse and multifaceted self, describing a life full of people, places and experiences, using sport as a conduit to facilitate these experiences. Signs of an exclusive athletic identity and glorified self are notably absent. Self-worth is not dependent on sport achievement but, rather, is related to negotiating, sustaining and valuing multiple roles and activities. In contrast to the performance narrative, withdrawal from sport is storied more as an opportunity for new exploration and discovery than a time of loss.

We begin by sharing a discovery story told by a multiple tournament-winning professional golfer we call Kandy. Kandy's story offers a radically different perspective to Georgi's, and we have chosen to include it here, as it brings many of the differences between the two narrative types sharply into focus. We summarise its plot before identifying the characteristics of the ideal-type discovery narrative. By doing so, we highlight the differences between performance and discovery narratives.

A discovery story

I started golf because my mother started playing golf. She was born overseas and she moved here with her husband after they were married, to an area with lot of golf courses. And she was crazy about golf! To begin with I played tennis, athletics and swimming. I started to swim when I was three years old and I started to play golf when I was seven; I didn't like golf because I thought it was boring. I was the only girl, I was tiny and I had no friends. All my friends were at the swimming pool or, the athletics, running. Then the boys were already about ten, 11 years old, so they were older and they used to bully me. Oh yes! They were terrible. I was the tiny one, the only girl, and there may well have been six or seven boys telling me to pick up the ball, do this, do that, you know. I didn't like it. And every Wednesday afternoon I had three hours of golf classes with those boys and I was very alone in the middle of those kids.

Then, on Saturday and Sunday, if you didn't have your handicap, you couldn't go out on the course. The rules were that you needed to be ten. So I had to caddy for my Mum and the trolley was bigger than me! And I was tired and I thought it was boring and my Mum said, 'That's the way you are going to learn.' So I had to concentrate and mark her card. And I hated golf. I didn't like golf. I didn't want to play but I had to play because at that time you couldn't say to your Mum, 'I don't want to play.'

I had a very strict education and a good education in the sense that my mother said: 'You have to be good.' And I'd say, 'Why?' And she'd say: 'You have to be good.' Then, 'You have to be honest.' And I'd say, 'Why do you have to be honest?' You know, those kinds of simple and silly things, but very important in life. 'You have to work, you have to study, you have to be yourself. You're clever, so use your brain.' She was very disciplined, very straight and very simple. She had no education but started to work when she was 12 years old. Her father was a butcher and she had to ride the butcher's bicycle and do the deliveries. Then she went into the fashion industry and became a self-made woman. So with me she decided I had to be something good in life – everything she couldn't do. She aimed high, because she had nothing behind her, and said, 'Everything I didn't have you will have.' So I had education, I had studies and I had the opportunity to be good at golf.

Then, when I was ten years old, I could go out and play and I was growing up of course, so I was getting stronger, starting to hit the ball a little bit longer, I could play the competition and I started to win. When I started to beat the boys that was more fun. It was my revenge. Oh yes! Because I had a bad time with those kids it was my personal revenge. And I said, 'Yes, you beat me, but now *I* am winning!' I was very proud to have my revenge. But then I stopped swimming. My mother decided that swimming was not enough good for me – she didn't like the entourage. She said, 'When you reach 20 you'll have to retire if you swim.' Oh, I didn't like it! I was very sad because all my friends were at the swimming pool so I had none for ten years and it was very hard for me. In the golfing circle people were very old, they were all about 25 to 50 and I was 12, 13, so for me they were old and they were always talking about the kids, the supermarket, and I had no interest in it at all. Finally, I was picked for a regional golf squad and I thought, '*Oh! I'll meet young people!*' And so it was a little bit like swimming where we would go to different cities by bus with all my friends.

When I was a child my mother was always saying, 'Kandy, she doesn't know how to walk!' I was always running. I love to run. I am very active. That's why I love to cycle, always. Every kind of something you could do outside – I hated being inside. I love to be in the air, to be outside, to swim in the sea, in those big waves. After 45 minutes fighting against tall waves you come out on the beach and you are completely exhausted, and you lie down in the sunshine, and you're sunbathing after a big effort and you're just like, '*Ahhhhh!*' You know the feeling? This is *so* good.

You go to school by bicycle, then hit balls, study, dinner, bed. And you caddy on Sunday. It's always the same! So when you escape it's fun. It's exciting. It's different. It's discovery. So when I quit swimming I was very disappointed but then when I was picked I thought, '*Oh, that's the same as swimming so that's fine.*' And I discovered a new world and we had fun. Of course we had the people behind us saying: 'You have to go to bed! You have to do this!' Yeah. We were staying in a kind of dormitory with lights out at 9 o'clock. But as soon as the teacher was gone we'd go to the boys' dorm, smoking, laughing, chipping and putting. And we broke a window. And the smoke alarm went off! And then you are punished of course. Once we escaped because we wanted to see how far the pub was and of course it was far away and there was no bus, so we had to walk and the police came. But you are so excited about doing something bad because you are told, always, 'You have to be good.' Inside yourself there is something saying, 'You have to try.' You know, 'Once, I want to be bad.' And it's a kind of excitement, and this excitement is stronger than the good feelings you have in your head. Well – the 'good' things they taught you.

So in my mind it wasn't important to be the first or the second or the third. The important thing was to have a good time. When I was an amateur and I started to be good and to win – about 15, 16, 17 – it was good, but it was not that important. It was nice because you go away for a week or for four days, you are in another world, it's a trip. It's like '*Oh that's nice!*' So you are going to see new people, discover new towns, new foods, the hotel, you know, a different bed. Everything is very exciting. If I was working in golf and I was good at golf, I could have the opportunity to discover more, and to discover was interesting for me. So, because I wanted to discover, in my mind it was logical that I had to work at golf, to be good. I was outside, which was nice for me, and it makes me discover. Winning, yes, it was important, but it was not the only thing. It was not: I have to win, only winning, winning. No. I spent a lot of time playing.

So winning was a personal satisfaction like I did my homework, I have a good note, okay? For me what was important was that golf was the conduit to be in different worlds.

I was in the States – I had a scholarship. I met my husband and then I went back from America when I was 19 and said to my Mum, 'I don't want to study any more, I want to go to Denmark, I want to work there and I want to marry.' Oh, it was like a disaster! Everything she thought for me was best, suddenly everything was broken. It was not what I was supposed to do. But I said I don't mind, I am 19, and I took the suitcase and my car and I drove to Copenhagen and I just left. I said I'm sorry but I am the owner of my life. I used to ring her twice a week you know, but I decided to make my life. I wanted to be the boss. For me, independence is the key. And if you like to be independent they can say heaven is on the left and I don't care a shit – I go right because *I* am the one to decide, and if I am wrong, bad luck. I'm like that. I think that to learn you have to be wrong a lot of times – even if you suffer a lot. And it hurts a lot of times because you make a lot of mistakes and it hurts. But from there you learn.

Then I decided I had to be a mother because I always thought for me to have a child was very important. Turning professional was a job and that job was because I had my daughter. I had to pay a lot of money to my husband for my divorce and you know when you are alone and you have a child as well it is expensive. That is the part of my life that was maybe the hardest one at the beginning. My daughter was small and it is very tough to go away, nights were very hard when you are back alone at the hotel and you know that you've got a child at home. The first two or three years – really, really tough. You are alone, crying, depressed, thinking 'Fucking golf!' and 'Fucking everything!' Then there is a time after you've cried – you need to be like that, you need to cry, to express everything – then, you think yes, but you are here and you are the one and you have to do it and you are strong enough: do it. Shut up and do it. Yes. Just like this. You go out on the course and you hit that ball and you do it.

Maybe if I was on my own and had no baby I would have done another job or something else. But I was good at golf. I could earn a lot of money and I was 27 and I had a daughter of 3 years old – deal with it! So I turned pro. Golf was important because it was a job, money. It was not for my own pleasure. It was the best I could do. No one ever asked about my daughter or how I was coping. The media only wanted good news. My problems did not interest them at all.

The day I played badly, or the tournaments I played badly, it was not like, I am not good enough or I am bad. No, I have less money. It was part of the job. For me it was, 'Well, I am a pro.' If you are a butcher you have to cut meat. I know people were expecting, the press, people, but in my mind golf was not a priority. 'You have to play well because they expect and have an image.' No. Golf was important because it was money and education for my daughter. I never felt better because I won a tournament. I felt fantastic when I had my baby – the best moment in my life was when I gave birth.

In my life, golf was always a conduit. If I said, 'What do you feel you are?' probably I feel mother, wife, myself. I am Kandy and a part of me is mother.

I know I am a mother but I have time in my day that I don't feel I am a mother. Then when I am with my daughter I am a mother. I am still Kandy, but as a mother. And then, with my boyfriend, I am 'the wife'. I am still Kandy but my conduct is different because I can give to my daughter nothing to do with the love I can give to my boyfriend. It is completely different.

So I started to enjoy that kind of life. First the life not the golf – the opportunity to travel, meet new people, food, clothing, because when you travel you wear a different type of clothing, and I love to observe and think, '*Oh this is nice*' or '*I don't like that*' or '*I never saw that. This is interesting*'. Like wood, for example. Old types of furniture in wood I love. But you need to be interested. You have people and they are not interested, they don't care, they are just, like, 'it doesn't matter'. I want to know about food, about wine, about wood, about gardening, about outdoors, about everything. Even if I don't like to drive I like to know about cars and bicycles. I think everything is very interesting in life. I think it's so fantastic to discover. You know more when you are 40 than when you were 20, but every day you can learn or discover something and have different feelings and impressions, and I feel it is fun in life to do that.

I think probably everything in life has a time. But when you go away for three, four, five weeks in a row and you have dinner the last day before you go and your friends are saying, 'We're going to Egypt in three days on a boat that will be fantastic holiday' and you're thinking, '*I'll be on that golf course, in that hotel, in that shitty place*'. That's what I think I missed. And I think you need to do those other things because it makes you balanced as a person. You need to share, you need to smile, you need to laugh, you need to have a good time with people you love. Sometimes you feel, '*Oh I can't do it. It's tough because I would like to be over there and I'm not,*' but you think, '*When I finish, when I retire, I'll do it!*'

A lot of players think: '*What shall I do later on?*' I don't have that problem. When I finish and I retire I will play golf for my pleasure but I won't work in golf. I want to learn to play the guitar. I want to learn Russian. I want to learn to restore antiques because I love wood, the smell, colour; I love it. I love gardening. I'll have a big garden. I want a dog. I want to go and bicycle with my dog and I want to do many things and I want to travel. And my boyfriend is the same. We want to travel and discover the countries we don't know because we don't know the food, we don't know…. It's like: '*Oh my goodness! I want to have time to do all these things.*'

The discovery plot

The plot of the discovery narrative revolves around exploration of the full and multidimensional possibilities of life. There is no single destination; rather, a multiplicity of potential journeys that become available through the storyteller's openness to new experiences. Surprise, excitement, joy and passionate immersion in the present moment recur across the story trajectory, from youth to old age. Through diverse experiences over time the storyteller tells of personal growth, development and change that she perceives as continuing indefinitely into the future. Performance outcomes are not the focus, but simply one aspect of life among many. Should winning be referred to at all, it is most likely on the basis of opening up or facilitating new opportunities and experiences. Retirement is typically narrated in positive terms, as an opportunity for ongoing discovery and new experiences. Retirement is storied as neither loss nor end-point.

Within the discovery plot, as a young athlete, you are likely to experience a love and passion for the embodied experience of movement. Your engagement in sport will probably be based on enjoyment of, and immersion in, the present moment. As time goes by, you might come to see sport as a vehicle that can open doors for new opportunities and life experiences. Throughout your life (not 'career'), you are likely to remain focused on discovering, exploring and playing, rather than training, competing and winning. If and when others try to insist you prioritise performance outcomes, a degree of tension or conflict is likely to result. You may abandon your discovery story, to follow instead the plot of a performance narrative, which will likely lead to tensions in other areas of your life outside sport. Alternatively, you may choose to continue your discovery life story, despite the tensions you experience within sport culture. Should you become successful at the highest level, your personal discovery story is likely to be shared only outside sport culture – or in private, among trusted confidants – as a result of a lifetime's experience of others in sport ignoring, ridiculing, opposing or silencing your story.

These general tenets of the discovery plot are evident in Kandy's story above. Together, they help define this narrative type, highlighting the consequences and tensions that result from adhering to this story. Below, we describe the key characteristics of the ideal-type discovery narrative in detail.

A process focus

A first characteristic of discovery stories is a focus on *process* in contrast to the performance narrative's overriding orientation towards *outcomes*. This distinction is apparent in Kandy's story from her earliest memories. For example, Kandy describes her immersion in an embodied physicality while in the sea:

> I love to ... swim in the sea, in those big waves. After 45 minutes fighting against tall waves you come out on the beach and you are completely exhausted, and you lie down in the sunshine, and you're sunbathing after a big effort and you're just like, '*Ahhhhh!*' You know the feeling? This is *so* good.

What is good is not beating someone else – swimming faster or further than her peers – but rather the total experience of being in a wild and exhausting sea. A focus on process over outcome is again evident when she says, 'When I was a kid in my mind it was not important to be the first or the second or the third. The important thing was to have a good time.' As Kandy's story unfolds, these initial building blocks are sustained and developed as, while never suggesting winning is irrelevant, she continues to describe other experiences as equally or more important.

This process emphasis is demonstrated in Kandy's story as a turn around of personal aims, motivation and purpose. Whereas performance storytellers typic-ally see performance outcomes as the point of sport and therefore the primary or sole incentive to invest themselves, discovery tellers see the opportunity to explore, discover and experience a full life as the point of sport. For them, the incentive to work to enhance their performance is because by becoming a better player further opportunities for exploration and discovery arise. Kandy makes her orientation clear when she says, 'So, because I wanted to discover, in my mind it was logical that I had to work at golf, to be good. I was outside, which was nice for me, and it makes me discover.' Eloquently, she summed up her position in this way: 'For me what was important was that golf was the conduit to be in different worlds.'

Thus, whereas in the performance narrative winning is associated with dem-onstrating physical prowess and gaining social esteem, winning has purely func-tional associations within the discovery narrative. Winning is a route to other things, such as new opportunities and experiences. It is neither glamorous nor exciting. At times in Kandy's story, for example, winning is simply about earning the necessary money to support her daughter. Any glamour and excite-ment stem from the opportunities to discover and experience life that are offered through playing sport to a high level. For discovery tellers, it is typically these experiences – rather than wins, titles, world records, championships or trophies – that motivate their investments in sport.

Excitement, play and immersion

Closely connected to – perhaps inseparable from – accounts of exploration and discovery is a palpable sense of excitement and joy that result through these experiences. This is evident in Kandy's earliest memories, for example, when she said: 'I love to be outside. I love to swim in the sea. I love to run. I am very active. That's why I love to bicycle, always. Every kind of something you could do outside.' It remains evident in her accounts of her early life in golf, when she described going to play in tournaments as a young woman: 'You are going to see new people, discover new towns, new foods, the hotel, you know, a different bed. Everything is very exciting.'

It was also evident in the stories of some of the other athletes whom we inter-viewed; for example, this international rugby union player when he described his immersion, exploration and discovery in learning a new skill:

> I remember someone doing a screw kick, you know one of those wonderful torpedo kicks and I thought, '*Hmm, I can't do that. Why can't I do that?*' So I just thought, right, that's something that they can do that I can't do. Maybe if I add that to my repertoire that will help. And I can remember finding that

very difficult because nobody actually taught me, but just practising, practising, practising until I eventually began to work out how to do that consistently. We actually had a very good coach but he was the first team coach
and I wasn't in the first team, the other guys weren't really, I suppose, able
to teach something as specific as that. So it was just repeated observation of
what happens to the ball and then just manipulating your foot – the height,
the angle of the ball, and just messing around and copying. You watched
internationals, you watched the Welsh fly half, I remember him being a fantastic screw kicker of the ball, you know a fantastic torpedo kicker, he was
the sort of classic Welsh fly half who left his leg hanging there for days after
sending this thing spiralling off.

There is a sense, then, in discovery stories of the teller embracing life in its
fullest sense, experiencing joy from all the little things in life, as well as the big
things. For some, this may be directly to do with sport, as in the preceding
excerpt as well as in this account from a Paralympic swimmer:

For me, it's the closest thing you can get to actually flying because on land
you can only move in two dimensions – unless you jump and then you're
momentarily in three dimensions, not truly in three dimensions. But when
you're swimming you really can move within this cuboidal space…. When
I get a good training session it still feels brilliant. I think what it is, it's the
ability to get hold of something that you can't get hold of. The water's got
this sort of incredibly kind of illusive nature and if you fill up a sink of water
and put your hand into it you can't get it but when you swim through it it's
solid like a wall. And you know the harder you hit it the harder it will hit
you back and it's got this permanent dynamism – it's never the same twice.
And I think that's what I really like about it – all its strange kinds of vortices
and things.

For others, like Kandy, the activities that are embraced with excitement and
immersion are only tangentially connected to sport. In both cases, excitement,
immersion and joy do not depend solely or primarily on *results* (i.e. on achieving an externally referenced performance outcome), but on engaging with the
opportunities for discovery, exploration and excitement in the processes of the
moment, often through embodied movement.

As a professional sportsperson, Kandy did not suggest that winning was
unimportant. Instead, in her words, 'Winning, yes, it was important, but it was
not the only thing. It was not, I have to win, only winning, winning. No. I spent
a lot of time playing.' By using the word *playing* here, Kandy's story trans-
gresses another tenet of performance stories where sport – and training in particular – tends to be storied as *work*. While previous research (Therberge, 1977,
1980) as well as, at times, the sports press have portrayed life for a woman
golfer on tour as hard and compare it to the life of a nomad who lives out of a
suitcase, Kandy describes her life as a professional as exciting and fun. For

example, she enthusiastically describes the new food, new places and new people that she experiences and meets through travelling to play golf. Also evident in these descriptions of life is a sense of playfulness. Her story does not make it sound as though she experiences a hard, disciplined working life in sport, as Georgi's performance story does in places. Instead, discovery stories tend to exhibit and expand at times a 'childlike' quality. They portray a sense of awe at the possibilities of life, playfulness with a variety of possible roles and activities, and immersion in the process of living out – or exploring – these roles and activities.

However, even when practising their craft – and perhaps seeing it as work in that it is a way to earn a living – discovery stories are likely to suggest that it doesn't *have* to be 'hard' and 'disciplined' just because its work. The words of another tournament golfer illustrate:

> It was just a nice sport to go and play. I used to just cycle after school to the golf club and play golf until dark, cycle home, go to sleep, get up, go to school, cycle to the golf club, play golf and live up at the golf club in the summer holidays. I just enjoyed it. It's just being outside.... The golf course is my office. The practise ground is my office. Rather than four walls, a ceiling and a floor, looking at a computer all day. So I feel very lucky, very privileged to have done that. It is nice to go up in the evenings to have a practise for two or three hours. It keeps you occupied. It's healthy. It's great.

Critically, though, discovery stories, such as Kandy's, do not romanticise success. Nor does her story refer to innate talent, fate or temperament as responsible for her success. Instead, she likens playing professional golf to being a butcher who must cut meat. Two points are worth making regarding this section of Kandy's story. The first is that, for discovery tellers too, elite or professional sport sometimes feels like work. Discovery stories may, as Kandy's story does, narrate aspects of life in sport in quite mundane or matter-of-fact terms. Here, the daily routine of practise can sometimes be a repetitive routine. However, for discovery tellers this need not eliminate from these tasks embodied experiences of joy, excitement and playfulness. Whereas performance stories typically portray the work of performance enhancement as serious business and the most important task of day-to-day life, discovery stories are more likely to portray similar activities as potentially joyful and merely one aspect of daily life.

The second point is that likening life in professional sport to a butcher who cuts meat is perhaps as far away as it is possible to get from the glamour of the performance narrative which instead speaks of the excitement and buzz of being noticed as a high-level athlete. It is not that Kandy is unable to feel excitement, but rather that excitement does not stem from the spoils of elite sport. These outcomes, while highly valued within the culture of sport, are not highly valued within discovery stories. Instead, for discovery tellers, excitement comes from other, more highly valued activities. For Kandy, these are activities and experiences such as trying new foods, meeting new people, visiting new places, exploring new activities and, ultimately, having a baby. While not all women value having a baby, within a culture where winning a trophy is so highly cherished, Kandy's story – of winning trophies but valuing giving birth more highly – acts like a trump card.

Openness and growth

Accompanying the diversity of experience inherent in a discovery story is the sense of a teller who is open to life's contingencies. For us, Kandy's story does not portray a life lived in the service of a particular predefined outcome, but instead a person who is open to whatever life possibilities may arise over time, provided that they allow for further exploration and discovery. Whereas performance stories lean towards a desire to control, define and focus lifestyle in the service of performance outcomes, discovery stories tend towards opening up possibilities, crossing boundaries and traversing new territories. Discovery life stories narrate a series of 'delicious moments', and reveal an openness to serendipity, chance and the unexpected in life. The ideal-type performance narrative removes these kinds of events – that are typically storied as 'distractions' – to strive instead for an exclusive and predetermined focus. In contrast, the ideal-type discovery narrative welcomes, embraces and incorporates whatever may be gained or experienced from any situation in life, remaining open to the opportunities of the moment.

Personal change, growth or development as a result of the explorations that are storied is a further hallmark of the discovery narrative. Kandy's story is typical of the discovery narrative in that it communicates a sense of life as an ongoing journey that takes in different places, peoples and events. This is evident in Kandy's story when she articulates her plans for her future life after professional golf. Here, she lists an array of new activities, each of which is likely to lead to or require some degree of personal change.

As an inevitable consequence of the journeys recounted in discovery stories, life changes and new roles and responsibilities arise or are called for. The teller is called – or *interpellated* (Frank, 2004) – to act and respond in ways that suit those changed life circumstances. This is particularly evident in Kandy's story as she describes the ways her life changed in the wake of becoming a mother. Motherhood was something Kandy wanted to experience as part of her own life journey, yet this experience – and the subsequent embodied presence of her daughter – brought with it responsibilities that affected the kinds of discoveries and explorations she could make in the future. For discovery storytellers who demonstrate a moral acuity and commitment, as Kandy does, exploration is never a 'free lunch'. Instead, realities of the present and possibilities for the future are shaped by the discoveries of the past. In discovery stories, personal change, growth or development is, perhaps, inevitable.

Separation of self and sport

A striking difference exists between the discovery and performance narratives in terms of the sense of self that is constructed and communicated through the stories. As we noted in Chapter 4, in the performance narrative self and sport go together: when performance is going well the person is going well. There are typically signs of an exclusive athletic identity in that the teller identifies primarily with the sporting role. Likewise, there are often signs of a glorified and aggrandised self, which depends on the achievement of – and social recognition for – particular performance outcomes. As an illustration of the discovery narrative, Kandy's story shows that, in professional golf, the person and the job do not *have* to go together. In Kandy's words: 'The day I played badly, or the tournaments I played badly, it was not like, I am not good enough or I am bad. No … I never felt better because I won a tournament.'

From Kandy's story we learn that what is assumed within the performance narrative to be the case for *all* elite sportspeople does not in fact apply to everyone who plays at the elite or professional level. We learn, for example, that a woman in elite sport can describe her self-worth in terms that are not related to achievement in golf, and that bad golf scores need not reflect negatively upon self-esteem. We also learn that a need for discovery can take precedence over a need to perform in golf regardless of the expectations of close relatives, the media, the golfing world and popular Western culture. Underlying these differences, we suggest, is a broad and multidimensional sense of self that is created through – and demonstrated by – the kinds of stories that comprise the discovery narrative.

Rather than recounting a monological and linear life story as Geogi does, Kandy articulates a *dialogical* life story. Lysaker and Lysaker (2006: 59) write that dialogical models of the self 'conceptualize the self and its many narratives as the products of ongoing conversations both within the individual and between individuals'. For these authors, 'coherent self-awareness does not come from a solitary single voice or seamless viewpoint, but emerges out of a collective of complementary, competing and contradictory voices or self-positions' (Lysaker and Lysaker, 2002: 209). In Hermans' (2006: 149–150) terms, 'the dialogical self functions as a "society of mind" … with tensions, conflicts, and contradictions as intrinsic features of a (healthy functioning) self'. We suggest that the discovery narrative is dialogical in that its different stories originate from multiple self-positions and roles that enable diverse identities and interests to be sustained.

We also consider that discovery stories typically exemplify a healthy, functioning, dialogical self. Kandy storied her life from multiple perspectives or self-positions such as an explorer, a traveller, a daughter, a 'wife' and a mother. These self-positions were presented as fluid and shifting according to her roles, responsibilities and activities at that moment. It is evident that maintenance of more than one self-position is a prerequisite for dialogue between different self-positions. Establishing and maintaining diverse self-positions allowed Kandy to engage in ongoing dialogues with herself and others. Through these processes, we suggest, Kandy developed and maintained a broad, multidimensional sense of self that allowed a sense of personal depth, coherent self-awareness and authenticity. This multidimensional sense of self contrasts markedly with the singular athletic identity that typifies performance stories.

Narrative tensions

When we use the term 'narrative tensions' we are referring to those times when the story an individual tells is at odds with either the material conditions of their daily life, or the plot of the dominant narrative. In other words, if we expect to hear a performance story and an athlete tells us a discovery story, a degree of tension will result. Tensions are evident in more or less all stories to some degree as the story rubs up against opposing narratives. Discovery stories are no exception. Within the discovery narrative, tensions are most likely when the teller is confronted with others who espouse the performance narrative. When an individual who stories life around the contours of the discovery narrative comes up against an individual or culture that adheres to the performance script then problems are likely.

These issues are apparent in Kandy's story at two moments. The first is when Kandy recounts her decision to marry and drop out of university. In her words:

I was 19 and I said to my Mum, 'I don't want to study anymore, I want to go to Denmark, I want to work there and I want to marry.' Oh it was like a disaster! Everything she thought for me was best, suddenly everything was broken. It was not what I was supposed to do.

At this moment, Kandy's discovery story – which values exploration, travel, experiencing new relationships – runs up against her mother's expectation that Kandy adhere to a different story: the performance narrative. Kandy's mother expected Kandy to prioritise her golf career through continuing her scholarship in America. But Kandy wanted to set out on a new journey of discovery that put exploration, travel and new relationships ahead of sport.

A second example occurs through the pain and doubt Kandy experiences when leaving her daughter to travel to tournaments. While tensions are evident here between her own discovery narrative and a culturally prominent narrative around motherhood and caring for one's child, further tensions are evident for Kandy as a result of her feeling that she cannot talk about this aspect of her life because others are not interested. As she put it: 'No one ever asked about my daughter or how I was coping. The media only wanted good news. My problems did not interest them at all.' Her emotions are felt in silence and isolation because she perceives that the press and the public only want to hear stories about her golf performance. Her success stories are welcome whereas her relational stories are not. In our view, this situation arises, in part at least, because the media usually adhere to the master narrative we described in Chapter 1. It is only stories of her golf achievements that the media seem to want – the 'golfer' self-position within her life and story is all they appear interested in. While we occasionally see articles about other aspects of athletes' lives in *lifestyle*-type supplements, the 'serious' coverage of sport almost invariably focuses on sport performance. As a result, the other self-positions that Kandy sustains within her personal life story are largely removed from public portrayals.

A third example of how these tensions arise is portrayed in the following account from another tournament golfer:

> I never really set goals or anything. Never. When I started to play there was never all this mental side to golf, that I knew about anyway. Because you haven't set goals you just feel within yourself: *Yes, I've had a good day. Yes, I've had a good week.* Or *No, I've had a bad day. No, I've had a bad year.* It's just within. I suppose my life is always, I am never outgoing or anything, if I feel I've done well, I know I've done well, and so that's within me. I don't sort of shout it from the rooftops or anything. It becomes a bit different when you get a sponsor involved, which I never really did at the early stages. *They* want to sort of see you get results. Suddenly there is more pressure when you've got a sponsor and you've got to answer to somebody and go in at the end of the year and say, 'This is what I've done. Is it good enough? Would you help me again next year?'

Here, this golfer reflects on her lack of goals and how she allowed her internal guidance system to provide feedback about how she is performing. Significantly, 'others' in sport culture – in this case a sponsor – required performance stories. The sponsor wants a different kind of result to the athlete. Tensions arise, therefore, not because the athlete is dissatisfied with her performance but rather because she is pressured to align her story with cultural expectations. By *not* shouting about it 'from the rooftops' but feeling it 'within yourself', this story-teller protects her values from others. But, as a consequence, this type of story remains silent in sport culture.

These examples provide insights into some of the scenarios where narrative tensions are likely to arise when a discovery storyteller is faced with the dominant performance narrative. The two narrative types are built around quite different values, orientations and plots – when they come face to face a degree of tension or conflict is likely. Kandy had the strength of will to follow her own story – other discovery tellers might not. These individuals will risk abandoning their personal life story (or elements of it) in favour of a socially desired (but inauthentic) performance story.

A further important narrative tension is also evident between Kandy's discovery story and Georgi's performance story. Paradoxically, Kandy stories the very 'life' that Georgi says she had to sacrifice to be successful. Life, for Kandy, is exploring her self and the world in a broad sense – as a traveller, a woman, a mother and a partner. Yet Georgi describes the need to sacrifice these experiences in order to become successful in golf. While the performance script requires giving up or relegating other dimensions of life, discovery stories portray excitement, joy and immersion in those very dimensions. In this sense, discovery storytellers, if they achieve at the highest level as Kandy did, pose a direct challenge and threat to the performance narrative and its proponents. Discovery storytellers provide the living proof that the terms of the performance narrative are not the only way to be a successful elite or professional sportsperson.

Notably, there are few if any narrative tensions associated with retirement or withdrawal from sport in discovery stories. In keeping with the values that have been consistent throughout her career, instead of mourning the end of a life in professional golf, Kandy focuses on new opportunities to discover. It is the opportunity to *discover* new experiences that discovery storytellers value – and this opportunity will not be discontinued in retirement. In this sense, there is a high degree of past, present and future coherence within the discovery narrative. As narrative maps, discovery stories provide an alternative to the dominant narrative in professional sport and therefore offers a possible path for those who have a desire to discover the experiences of a full and rich life alongside striving for success in sport.

6   The relational narrative

At the time I played for my Dad. I played my heart out for my Dad. It's for him.
(Leanne)

So far we have presented, in Chapter 4, what we see as the dominant narrative type in elite and professional sport – the performance narrative – and, in Chapter 5, its antithesis: the discovery narrative. We have suggested that the existence of discovery-oriented life stories among successful elite sportspeople proves the falsity of the belief that prioritising winning ahead of all other aspects of life is the only way to achieve success. Through our research, we have also identified a third narrative type that provides a further alternative way to story one's life in sport. Like discovery stories, this type of story exists within the margins of elite and professional sport, most often silenced or hidden from public view.

We call the second alternative the *relational* narrative type, a story of complex interdependent connection between two or more people in which sport performance is a by-product. Although it could be said that all stories are relational in that they exist in relationship to others, we use the term to highlight that, in the relational narrative type, it is accounts of relationships with others that anchor the story plot. For the teller of this type of story, *being with* another person or persons is more important than performance outcomes such as tournament successes and trophies. Altruistic rather than ego motivation permeates the story plot as the storyteller places the perceived needs of others alongside or above the needs of the self. Therefore the relational storyteller does not only exist *with* another, but also *for* another. Like the discovery narrative, the relational narrative explicitly challenges the assumptions of the performance narrative because these storytellers achieve success at the highest level in sport *without* subscribing to the values and behaviours scripted in the performance narrative.

We begin by sharing one illustration of a relational story, as told by a multiple tournament-winning professional golfer we call Leanne. Leanne's story directly challenges Georgi's performance story but also differs structurally from Kandy's discovery story. After sharing Leanne's story, we articulate the plot and characteristics of the ideal-type relational narrative.

A relational story

I can't remember ever not being able to play golf. Being able, yes, but not necessarily wanting to. I always imagined me to be a golfer – a professional golfer –
but I probably wanted a fairy godmother to come along and go '*Ping!*' to cast a
spell and then I would *be* successful. I didn't want to do the hard work.

My dad was a keen golfer and it seemed the most natural thing for me to do.
Dad was out playing golf and I wanted to do what Dad did. So I got a little club
cut down – I'd have been about four – and I remember being dead chuffed managing to play three holes and then six holes, then nine holes. I just liked being
with my Dad and I liked that thrill of hitting a ball. It's hard to explain. You get
just such a sense of achievement from the way the ball feels on your clubface,
how it feels on your hand. It's difficult to describe.

Because you want that feeling all the time, if you don't get it, it's the reverse,
like this love-hate relationship. When you're playing well you just love the game
and when you're playing badly it's like the end of the world. That's what I hated
about it. I couldn't accept bad shots. I would get really angry with myself
because I hadn't performed – felt as though I could kill somebody or do something. That's how I felt. I hadn't done the right thing and on a few occasions I
broke clubs, particularly putters. I disliked hitting bad shots, big time, and in
teaching kids now I notice that they have this thing, they expect all their shots to
be good. I was like that. And it's not the case. But no, I had a wicked temper and
my Dad was always sending me home.

Then when I was about ten a lady at the club says to my Dad, 'This national
event is on,' a girls' event and 'wouldn't it be an ideal opportunity for Leanne,
to see if she likes playing competitions?' So I went down and played but I didn't
like it. I didn't like the pre-course nerves, and was sick I was just so nervous. I
have no idea why. I wish I knew really. I mean, I was like that for years. And I
remember in the first round I beat a girl called Jan Drake, now I don't know why
I remember that name but I do, and it made the press because I was only ten and
I had won something like seven and six. So the following day I was playing
against one of the Welsh internationals and got beat eight and six. But that didn't
matter – I was out of the tournament and delighted to go home. I didn't have to
worry any more.

I remember getting to the stage where I would go to a tournament and get
myself all worked up and start crying. One time, we were staying in a caravan of
all places, and my mum took me back to the caravan and said: 'Leanne this has
got to stop. I am not putting up with this every tournament we go to. You play or
you don't – but if you don't play this time you don't play ever.' So I had to
straighten my face and I played. But I still didn't like it. I didn't like even
playing competitions at my home club when I was little. I hated it. If somebody
said 'tournament's cancelled' I would have been delighted. But once I was on
the course I was fine. I actually was like that as an adult.

Well, I don't think I've ever told this to anyone but since this isn't me – this is
anonymous – I threw a few games. Not as a pro, only as an amateur. In Bangkok,

in the semi-finals or quarter-finals of the World Cup. I remember standing on the sixteenth tee one-up, but I didn't want to be there. I thought: *'There's better things to do than being on a golf course, I'm in Thailand for goodness sake.'* And I thought, *'Oooh now!'* Have you ever? Now you've probably never done this – but do you know it's actually more difficult to deliberately hit a bad shot without making it look as if you've hit a bad shot? I thought: *'I'll hit it in the trees.'* So I hit it in the trees but it came back out! How typical is that? Eventually I got to the eighteenth and we're all square and I had about a ten-foot putt to half the match and I thought: *'I'll, just try and'*, you know, *'hit it too hard'*, which was deliberate and it lipped out. But the relief was fantastic. I knew if, I don't know, it's just the pressure. I just didn't want it any more. And that was when I was 16 – I just didn't want the pressure. It was the pressure of winning.

Someone was telling me recently, and I didn't realise, over a period of five years I won 30 national championships. So at that point I'd played in a lot of finals and I never lost the finals. And it was almost as if the more finals I play and win, in these matches, I'm going to lose one and then I'm going to be totally devastated. So I'd rather lose in the first round than get to the final and lose. I don't know, I think because I never lost and I never wanted to lose, almost as if I'm not going to put too much pressure on myself. Let's *not* win. If you get the chance to win, then fair enough, but let's not try too hard. That's what it sounds like, isn't it? Yeah, I think I wanted to be happy. And I think I was, yeah.

I can't remember ever coming off a golf course and wanting to punch the air – that was never me. I always felt, 'Right, good job, done it.' Everybody else got excited around me, like my Dad. My Mum actually had to go away; she couldn't even watch the semi-finals. She had to go away she was so nervous for me. It was just I was *expected* to win. I remember the first time I ever won a national title, about two or three weeks before the tournament, it was the middle of the winter, I knew I was going to win and I didn't sleep at night I was so excited about the Championship. I really believed that nobody could beat me. I was confident, really confident, you know.

I think my father wanted me to play golf. But you see, having said that, I think our family were very close but we don't really talk and I was always under the impression that they wanted me to play golf. And it's far from the truth. As long as I was happy, they were happy. But at the time I played for my Dad. I played my heart out for my Dad. It's for him. Dad and I were really close. Similar to you and your Dad I would have said. There was a bond. It doesn't mean to say that you didn't love your mother – it was just that you bonded more with him.

And people often ask: 'What did he give you back in return for you playing golf?' And I say: 'It was nothing other than the fact that I had pleased him and his pleasure was enough for me.' He wasn't the sort of guy who, you know, I got a handshake and a pat on the back: 'Well done.' And that was me winning the National Title: 'Well done, not bad, not bad.' That's what I got – just a little pat on the back and a 'not bad'. But I could tell he was proud. And that made me feel good.

Even if I didn't do well he would be there. He was never the sort of guy who'd say: 'Right then!' or 'Sit down!' in an angry way. He never shouted at me and I never displeased him where golf was concerned. But, he was, even if I hadn't won, you know, if he saw me play and do something perhaps I shouldn't have done we would have that moment of 'yeah we've won', sort of thing and then later he'd say: 'You know, I saw you had a little mistake there. Let's see if we can improve on that.' He wasn't a great golfer himself, but he had a great golfing mind and that's the most important thing. So when he died, well, for a while I completely lost the plot, as you know. I just felt, all of a sudden, I couldn't just do it for me. I had never done it for me.

My great friend Patrick Johansson, when my Dad died, he was great, 'cos I told him how I was feeling – that I just hated being on the golf course – and he insisted that there was 'Leanne the person' and 'Leanne the golfer'. All you've got to do when you go to the golf course is you take 'Leanne the golfer' and put your golf-er's head on. So that's what I tried to do and that worked for about two years. I was much more businesslike with golf. I thought: '*Okay I might not really want to be here but this is what I do, this is how I earn a living, it's fine. I've got to do it prop-erly.*' But that only lasted for a while you know. I just didn't want to be on the golf course at the end of the day. I realised that the huge drive – for all of my golf career – was my Dad. No one ever asked how I was – it was all about my golf. 'How did you score?' 'Where did you finish?' No one ever asked how I was.

Things got harder and I wasn't advised enough. Looking back now my golf swing was progressively getting worse and nobody else was helping me like my Dad had. If I had known then what I know now about my golf swing and what I was doing with it I think I would have lasted a lot longer as a player. So techni-cally I was getting weaker and psychologically I was just giving up. Emotionally I had had enough.

I remember when it first started. I'm sure it was in Denmark and I was getting this early bus every blooming morning, half-six bus, and I holed a putt on the eighteenth in the second round to make the cut. And Tammy and Fiona were going: 'Well done Leanne!' You know, it was really a time when I really needed to miss a cut and I had never missed a cut – or I can't remember ever missing a cut. Now I was on that golf course and I cried – and this is not like me at all – for about two holes I couldn't see the ball for tears and I came off that course and just threw my clubs in the storage and got on the bus, went back, and went to my bed. I just felt like I couldn't – I didn't know where it was coming from. I still don't know what happened that day – the anger, frustration and anger, for no real apparent reason other than the fact that I didn't want to be there.

I would hit a shot and it wouldn't even necessarily be a bad shot, but for some reason there was something inside me, like it was just a wave swelling up inside of me, this anger. And the only way I could get rid of this anger was to hold a golf club in my left hand and punch the club with my right hand. Hence the reason why that knuckle is still a little bit high. It was almost as though I had to punish myself for being there. It was just this incredible anger and I wasn't even playing bad but I was somewhere I didn't want to be.

Prior to that tournament I really was seriously considering quitting. I couldn't, I couldn't even, I couldn't play for myself. Never have been able to. I think we are all actors and actresses and I think you have to be. It's just like a big stage. You've got to go on there and you've got to perform. Having said that, when I was in a happier state that was part and parcel of it, being in control, playing the part. You don't want to be there and you've got to play the part. But it starts to beat you – that's what it felt like. Then you're thrown away. And then I thought, *'Well I'm an adult, I don't have to do this, I don't have anybody to answer to any more. You know, I can stop.'* So that's how I came to the decision to retire, because at that point I really didn't know what I was going to do. We were in Germany I think and the first thing I said to Tammy was: 'I really can't take this.' And she said: 'Don't keep putting yourself through this.'

To be perfectly honest I was never that bothered about the money – simply because of course I always had it. I played well enough to earn a living, so that didn't worry me. It was a huge benefit when you won a tournament, let's face it, but again it was more of a sense of achievement as opposed to kind of – I remember coming away from a tournament we played at St Cloud and I didn't have a particularly good tournament but I'd set myself a goal because I was fairly bad, down the field. And I reached the goal in the last round and I came away from that tournament feeling as if I'd won it.

I think, pretty much in everything I do, I don't like the unknown. I'm always frightened of what might happen. I wish I was more like you. When you got to a venue you would work and then you had the guts to hire a car and get away to see things. I never had the guts. I'm still like that. I'm happy just to stay put. You're not and I would love to have been more, 'let's go and see what's happening!' Not be frightened to get out of this place. I don't know what I was frightened about – just not knowing what's round the corner.

I think about where I have been at certain times in my life, and I really didn't want to play any more golf and I think it almost cost me my sanity to be honest. It got that severe. And one of the things I was worried about was what my family and my friends would think of me if I gave it up. I worried and worried and worried about what other people would think.

If I don't get approval from certain people, it makes me feel – say, for example, I wanted to do something and they said, 'Oh no, I don't know about that', I wouldn't do it. I'm very easily swayed by people. I have to admit there were a couple of major decisions that I made which were not what they wanted – like getting the house for a start. I mean that was: 'Oh, no, I don't think you should do that.' But I really wanted to. I needed a break from home. You always said I should have done that ages ago but I wasn't ready. You thought I was ready. Everybody else was: 'Come on Leanne! Get a move on! You've got to get out!' But I used to be comfortable there. And then, well, I just was looking at my life, thinking, *'Gosh I'm 32!'* I needed my independence. I really did.

The relational plot

The plot of relational stories revolves around creating, experiencing and sustaining relationships with others. Unlike performance stories, there is no single destination in the relational plot. Rather, like discovery stories, a multiplicity of potential journeys is possible. Critically, however, the story is driven forward by the storyteller's desire to – above all else – experience life *with and for* another person or persons. The events recounted in the story are framed by and through relationships. Some relational stories (such as Leanne's) are seeded in childhood, remaining constant throughout the life course. Here, valued relationships define the trajectory of the teller's life story from childhood to old age. Others (such as those portrayed in Chapter 10) begin later in life, replacing a story type that no longer works for the teller, that no longer fits changed life circumstances. Like discovery stories, performance outcomes are not a focus of relational stories. Should winning be referred to at all, it is most likely to be as a by-product that benefits or provides enjoyment for others, rather than leading to a direct personal emotional benefit. Retirement or withdrawal from sport may be narrated in either positive or negative terms, depending on whether or not valued relationships are likely to be sustained or lost as a result of transition.

Within the relational plot, you are likely to have become involved in sport as a young person through relationships with others, often parents and/or siblings. While we have found this feature to be common to many life stories in sport, a distinguishing feature of the relational plot is that your ongoing engagement in sport will continue to revolve around playing, competitively or otherwise, with friends or family members. This will be true throughout your elite and professional participation. Your story will prioritise descriptions of being immersed in the present moment with or for significant others, rather than accounts of desired performance outcomes for yourself in the future. Throughout your life (not 'career'), sport will remain a meaningful and valued component only to the extent that it allows, supports and facilitates relationships. If and when others try to insist you prioritise performance outcomes over and above relationships, tension and conflict are likely to result. If you come to perform at the highest level, your personal relational story is likely to remain mute within sport culture as a result of repeated ridicule, opposition or silencing by others in elite sport culture. If you choose to share your relational story at all, it will either be from a place that is some considerable distance from sport culture (such as several years after retirement) or among your most trusted confidants.

Several characteristics of the relational plot are evident in Leanne's story, which we use to help articulate the ideal-type relational narrative below. Leanne's story reminds us that we must listen closely to discern the narrative plot that underlies complex and sometimes messy life stories. Certainly, Leanne's story brings in other threads that aren't experienced by all relational tellers. So, although Leanne's story raises issues that some may consider challenging or problematic, we have chosen to use it here because it is a powerful example of a relational story. Later in the book we delve deeper into the possibilities and problems of relational narratives, as well as providing further examples of relational stories that may be interpreted as less problematic than Leanne's.

A process focus: being *with* and *for*

From Leanne's story, we learn that it is possible to succeed (in performance terms) at the highest level in golf with a primary focus on another person. For Leanne, golf is, and always has been, an activity through which she spends time with, and does things for, her father. The suggestion that money, glory and trophies cannot compare to a relationship is dynamite in a sporting world which promotes money, glory and trophies as the ultimate satisfaction and interests of the self as paramount. Yet this is exactly what Leanne suggests when she describes winning as 'just nothing other than the fact that I had pleased him and his pleasure was enough for me'.

Although it is not uncommon for athletes to seek social approval in return for their sport achievement, this orientation differs in two important ways from the relational narrative. First, Leanne identifies *being with* her father as important. This sense of valuing spending time with a family member through sport was common to many participants' stories of their early sport involvement. For example, a female judo player shared this story:

> From the age of zero to the age of probably 8, when my Dad was competing, our weekends were spent at scrambles – which is basically a field where people are going around on motorbikes.... And I've got so many memories of summer holidays where we'd drive out to a race some place in France and with the prize money my Dad won we'd then have a week's holiday and then move on to the next race. And that would probably happen for about three weeks until we had to go back to school or whatever. But the best bit of those weeks wasn't the holidays; it was the standing on the rostrum with my Dad. And in the pictures, you can actually see, I've looked at them, and you can see I'm standing up taller than my Dad! I'm not even up to his bum but I'm holding his trophies. I'd never really thought until what you [another focus group participant] were saying then, I really put the two together then, of this childhood and what on earth that could mean later on.... It was that kind of being really proud when you're stood there next to my Dad.

In a similar way to this example, Leanne's story makes clear that her father's interest in her golf allowed them, over a number of years, to spend quality time together. She is at pains to point out how his encouragement was gentle, how she 'never displeased him where golf was concerned' and how the time spent with her father was special for Leanne. In contrast to some psychological theorists who have seen attachment as negative, Ruthellen Josselson (1996) argues that a need for attachment continues to develop throughout life and is a sign of healthy rather than pathological development (see also Gilligan, 1993). For us, Leanne's golf participation preserved a closeness with and attachment to her father.

Second, Leanne suggests she played golf *for* her father, as if by doing so she was giving him a *gift*. Gift giving is culturally important and has been shown to create a relational connectedness between the giver and the receiver (Hyde, 1983). In this sense, Leanne's gift to her father (succeeding in golf) could be considered altruistic: 'His pleasure was enough for me.' Although Leanne says that giving to her father also 'made me feel good', her desire to give does not appear to be primarily self-focused. Instead, her descriptions are more akin to the women Carol Gilligan (1993) describes as experiencing their world *in a different voice*; focusing on care and connectedness over and above the masculine values of separation, individuation, hierarchy and competition. In doing so, we suggest that Leanne was 'offering self to others' needs' (Josselson, 1996: 8) through an empathic and attentive orientation towards another as opposed to a self-orientation.

Underlying descriptions of living with and for another person or persons is a further characteristic of relational stories that, generally speaking, emphasise *process* over *outcome*. In this sense, relational stories differ from performance stories, but have something in common with discovery stories. For relational tellers, the process of sustaining positive relationships will typically take precedence over achieving particular performance outcomes. Relational storytellers have the potential to satisfy the plot of their life story – meet their personal needs – without depending on an uncontrollable performance outcome. They do, however, depend on a reciprocal openness to, and engagement with, the relationship on the part of the other person. Unlike tellers of performance narratives, who 'use' someone (such as the coach) in order to improve performance outcomes, relational storytellers hope to manage their life and environment in ways that sustain and enrich their relationships.

Should (relational) process and (performance) outcome appear to the teller to be in harmony – i.e. *both* seen as possible – then particular performance outcomes may be achieved alongside sustaining the relationship/s. Should the two appear to be in opposition, performance storytellers are likely to act in ways that favour performance outcomes ahead of sustaining the relationship/s. This is evident in the words of an Olympic-level women's hockey player: 'I have to say that relationships have suffered because of my hockey. So if I hadn't been playing hockey then I still think maybe I would have still been with a certain person so I chose hockey really ultimately.' In contrast, the relational storyteller is likely to act in ways that favour the relationship over and above performance outcomes. This is evident in the following story shared by a young track and field athlete as he describes his decision to leave a centre of excellence to return home:

> I remember being back in [the centre] pretty much deciding that really I'd given everything to my athletics in probably the most single-minded way I could do.... I'd kind of broken up with [my girlfriend] and I didn't really speak to my Mum and Dad when I was there.... I didn't know anyone from

church, it was all pretty much everything was based around training – completely. And I just felt that really that's crazy, what happens when I'm not an athlete? I've got to start to look at where I'm going in the long term and then weave athletics into it.... I think the only way for me to do that is for me to get certain areas of my life sorted, in the sense that now I've moved [back home], got married, kind of established friends, got involved in the church quite a lot, and got friends within university, in training and church and stuff. I feel like I've really gone back to basics but in a way I've got back to me.

Separation of self and sport

Like the discovery narrative but unlike the performance narrative, relational stories generally portray and sustain a separation between sense of self and performance outcomes in sport. In contrast to Georgi, Leanne said: 'I can't remember ever coming off a golf course wanting to punch the air. That was never me.' Like Kandy, Leanne doesn't feel better about herself through winning a golf tournament. Here, Leanne's story is at odds with the dominant narrative which tends towards an exclusive athletic identity alongside a glorified and aggrandised sense of self. Performance tellers *do* describe feeling better about themselves through winning. So although self-worth, self-esteem and psychological well-being are likely to be affected by one's win/loss record under the terms of the performance narrative, there is no direct connection between these qualities and performance outcomes under the terms of the discovery and relational narratives.

For relational tellers, however, it is possible that performance outcomes may affect sense of self through the medium of a significant other or others. There is some sense of this occurring in Leanne's story. Leanne describes a sense of *relief* having come off the course after a good performance – her story does not articulate a sense of glory, self aggrandisement, excitement or pleasure through her success. Yet she suggests that *others* did experience this as a result of *her* performance: 'Everybody else got excited around me.' When she says, 'I was *expected* to win', Leanne's story suggests that others around her – including her parents – subscribed to performance values to a greater or lesser extent. This is evident too in Leanne's description of how 'I think my father expected me to turn pro' and 'I could tell he was proud' in the wake of tournament success.

We suggest that should significant others in a relational storyteller's life endorse the values of the performance narrative there is a fair chance that performance outcomes may exhibit an indirect effect on the athlete's sense of self and identity. In these instances we might expect a small improvement in sense of self when performance is going well, or a comparable decrease when performance is going badly. This change is likely to be in response to *others'* excitement and pleasure at the teller's success. The connection is unlikely, however, to be as clear and extreme as it is for performance tellers whose sense of self is often closely tied to their results.

A sense of relational processes in action is evident in the following two accounts. The first was shared by an Olympic rower as, post-retirement, she reflected on her sport career. The second was shared by a young professional rugby union player.

> People always ask me: 'What was it? Why did you want to win? Was it the accolades?' Because there's no money involved and, you know, I'd chosen a sport with a particularly low media profile. I wanted to be able to walk down the road and I wanted respect. But I didn't want respect from *anybody* on the street – I wanted respect from the people I would value their respect. So it was *my* people. So it was the people I had made that journey with, I wanted for them to say to me – the proudest thing would be for someone who I rowed with in my novices boat to say, 'Oh yeah! I rowed with Martina.'

> To be brutally honest, the thing I really enjoyed about rugby was just the physical contact. I had two younger brothers – wrestling all the time and stuff like that. I just really enjoyed the physical contact. And that's one main thing. The other thing is I've been lucky enough to play in some really good teams with some good boys and I've made some great friends and rugby is, you know, you have to look after each other on the pitch. You've got to know – when you're going out onto the pitch – that your mates, your team-mates, are going to back you up. So when you've got that and you're playing well it feels good, you know.

In the first extract, relational factors to do with respect from significant others are identified as central to the teller's satisfaction with her achievements in sport following retirement. In the second extract, being physically '*with* the boys' who are like brothers and being '*for*' one another is what is described as meaningful from playing rugby – as opposed to winning.

David's grandfather – Ernie Carless, a professional footballer for Plymouth Argyle and Cardiff City and cricketer for Glamorgan in the 1930s and 1940s – articulated a relational orientation that we do not often hear in contemporary sport culture. Walking through Cardiff four decades later, Ernie was stopped by several 'strangers' who wanted to say hello and share their memories of particular matches or moments from Ernie's playing career. Later, Ernie said that knowing he'd brought pleasure and enjoyment to these fans and spectators – who perhaps witnessed a home win or a Carless goal – was the most rewarding aspect of his life in sport. For us, this is one example of a relational story post-retirement that sounds sadly alien to the kinds of stories many of today's elite sportspeople tell in public which often seem to focus on the self rather than the other.

Previously, we described the performance narrative as a *monologue* (in that the life story is told from the singular role or self-position of 'athlete') and the discovery narrative as a *dialogue* (in that the life story is articulated from multiple self-positions). Such a straightforward distinction cannot be made regarding the relational narrative. We have arrived at the view that relational stories have the potential to be *either* monological *or* dialogical depending on the conditions surrounding the storytelling act.

Should a relational life story be told exclusively around *one* relationship, we would potentially consider it a monologue, for much the same reasons performance stories tend to be monological: because the life story is narrated from a single self-position or role. Under these conditions, a one-dimensional sense of self and identity becomes more likely. In focusing strongly on her relationship with her father, Leanne's story verges on becoming a monologue at times. Without reference to her relationship with her mother, Leanne's story could fairly be described as monological because her story would have been told from this single role or self-position (i.e. as her father's daughter). In the case of a monological relational story, we can see the potential or risk of harm or even abuse. Some might argue that Leanne's story contains signs of one or both of these elements. Leanne was very clear, however, that *her* father was never abusive. An important question, then, is: when a relational teller focuses exclusively on one relationship, is the possibility for manipulation or abuse opened up as a result of the teller's desire to sustain a positive relationship with the significant other? Could this desire lead them to accept or tolerate behaviours that put their own well-being at risk? We currently have no firm answers to these questions – they are questions that require further exploration.

Narrative tensions

Relational stories prioritise connection with others. Time spent in harmony with significant others is storied as valuable and desirable. The relational storyteller describes, in positive terms, routinely engaging in tasks, activities or events for the sake of others. In contrast, the dominant performance stories of elite sport typically value competing against others and promote the needs and desires of the self ahead of others. The entire language of performance is underpinned by accounts of interpersonal conflict through, for example, fight and war metaphors. Once these oppositional characteristics of the two narrative types are understood, it should come as little surprise that there is potential for significant narrative tension between performance and relational stories. In fact, the form of tension which relational storytellers are most likely to experience results from them – and their stories – running up against proponents of the performance narrative.

Leanne's story recounts three instances when her personal relational story came into direct conflict with the dominant performance narrative. First, she describes how, when she was ten years old, 'a lady at the club' suggested that a national event might be 'an ideal opportunity for Leanne'. Leanne went to the event and played but 'didn't like it'. Under the terms of the performance narrative, this move towards competition appears a normal and natural progression. Yet under the terms of the relational narrative, it signals a threatened fracture or devaluing of Leanne's relationship with her father. More specifically, by playing in a national event as a ten-year old, Leanne moves from playing golf with her father (which she enjoyed and was a key motivation for golf) to playing golf *apart* from her father. He is ushered to the side-lines. In the culture of elite sport, parents who are unqualified coaches are not considered to have the necessary skills to 'develop the potential of a young person'. Under the terms of the performance narrative script they are seen as 'problems'.

Second, it appears that something about the competitive act – the embodied experience of playing against others – was at odds with Leanne's relational way of being in the world, as articulated and sustained in her life story. She describes how at tournaments she experienced 'a wave swelling up inside of me' and that 'the only way I could get rid of this anger was I'd hold a golf club in my left hand and punch the club with my right – almost as though I had to punish myself for being there'. Here, it seems, the mismatch of performance and relational values created an unbearable tension for Leanne, which led to repeated episodes of anger and self-harm.

Finally, Leanne recounts how after her father died a 'close friend' tried to help her to continue to play professional golf:

> [H]e insisted that there was 'Leanne the person' and 'Leanne the golfer'. All you've got to do when you go to the golf course is you take the 'Leanne the golfer' and put your golfer's head on. So that's what I tried to do and that worked for about two years. I was much more businesslike with golf. I thought: *'Okay I might not really want to be here but this what I do, this is how I earn a living, it's fine. I've got to do it properly.'* But that only lasted for a while you know. I just didn't want to be on the golf course at the end of the day.

Leanne experienced repeated episodes of psychological tension to the point that she felt her mental health and well-being were under threat. We would suggest that the gulf between her personal story and the performance stories embodied by her friend (and others in the competitive arena) was simply too great. She had little alternative but to exit a culture that was so permeated by performance stories.

In all of these instances, narrative tensions arise when Leanne's personal stories are most at odds with the story of which she found herself a part: the performance narrative. The tension is portrayed by Leanne when she shares her inner feelings concerning the costs of playing in competitions and 'not wanting to be there' which led to self-harm and emotional suffering. Importantly, this tension arose not as an inevitable consequence of telling a relational life story, but as a result of a relational teller being channelled into a context in which the only acceptable story was the performance narrative.

Some of the mechanisms through which this 'channelling' can occur are hinted at in Leanne's story. She implicates 'everyone' – family, friends, the media – who asked only about her performance but never about her well-being. In her words: 'No one ever asked how I was, it was all about my golf. "How did you score?" "Where did you finish?" No one ever asked how I was.' We have heard similar stories from many elite and professional athletes, about how the majority of people – including, sometimes, family members or partners – routinely ask 'How did you do?' yet seem to forget to ask 'How are *you?*' While performance storytellers will likely find this line of interaction reasonable and perhaps unproblematic, for relational tellers prioritising questions about performance outcomes can represent a denial of what is most important to them: the closeness of their relationship.

Leanne's story suggests that, perhaps as a consequence of exclusively performance-oriented interactions sustained over many years, she came to the view that others only really valued her as a golfer, not as a person. As she put it: 'one of the things I was worried about was if I gave up what my family and my friends would think of me. I worried and worried and worried about what other people would think.' Might Leanne have arrived at a more positive position had her interactions with just *a few* people included a balance of other (i.e. non-performance-oriented) kinds of questions and conversations? Could Leanne have felt valued as a person – not just as a professional golfer – had *some* others articulated and enacted the relational script that anchored her own story? Would she have experienced less emotional suffering or self-harm episodes had her own relational stories and values been reflected by *a few* of the people around her? While it is impossible, of course, to answer these questions for sure, we suggest that the likely answer to each is *yes*.

Leanne's words suggest a realisation, after many years living within the culture of elite sport, that the path encapsulated by the dominant performance narrative fails to fit her own needs and desires. For Leanne, *not wanting to be there* brings an unresolved tension throughout every phase of her life in elite sport, until she leaves professional sport forever. Retirement is storied as relief – as an escape from performance values and a potential return to the relational values that underpin her life story. From the perspective of relational storytellers who are able to sustain valued relationships post-retirement, withdrawal from sport is likely to be relatively smooth and uneventful. From the perspective of those who are unable to sustain valued relationships post-retirement, withdrawal has the potential to be as challenging, harrowing and disorienting as it is for many tellers of performance tales.

7 Learning the story

Enculturation of young athletes[1]

You kind of became consumed in your athletics. You became at the end so into it that you couldn't see your perspective on other stuff ... I was quite, I always felt, I was quite laid back. But I don't think I was when I was at [the performance centre]. I was just really kind of channelled to wanting to just run faster.

(Luke)

In the previous three chapters we identified the hallmarks of the performance, discovery and relational narrative types. To provide illustrations of each type of narrative we shared first-person life stories taken from interviews with three professional sportswomen: Georgi, Kandy and Leanne. One reason we selected these particular stories was to show that even among similar-aged individuals from the same sport who were equally successful in terms of tournament wins, money and recognition, it is possible to narrate life in very different ways. That is to say, despite achieving similar landmarks of success in professional sport, each woman's story turned on a fundamentally different narrative axis.

In this chapter we consider how these different types of life story come into being. One way to shed light on this issue is by exploring in detail early life experiences and the processes of enculturation. In Crossley's (2000: 45–46) terms:

> our experience of self, others and the world more generally is inextricably tied up with our use and understanding of the linguistic and moral resources made available to us in the cultures we are brought up in. Narrative theories suggest that the primary way in which such meanings are transmitted is through our embeddedness, from the moment of birth, in familial and cultural stories.

Here, we are interested in the *narrative habitus* in which each person is immersed – the repertoire of stories offered within the environments, subcultures and relationships the individual inhabits. Some events, relationships and storytelling forms open up possibilities for narrating or claiming a particular identity, while others close down possibilities. It is this repertoire that 'sows the seeds' for a particular life story and a particular sense of self. If a monological life story and identity foreclosure is harmful, as is widely accepted (e.g. Freeman, 2010; Hermans, 2006; Lysaker and Lysaker, 2002), it seems important to root out where these seeds have been sown in early sport experiences.

Some of the questions we want to consider are: is it the case that we are *born* with a particular story or affinity? What processes lead to the *adoption* of one story as opposed to another? What are the *effects* of sustained exposure to the dominant performance narrative? How is it that some individuals have the tools to *resist* a dominant narrative? Where and what are the 'building blocks' that *enable* this resistance?

Narrative heritage

The formal aspects of enculturation – such as education, praising, rewarding – aren't difficult for many of us to bring to mind. In Chapter 5 Kandy used formal 'lessons' to map out a framework for the things she has come to value in life as an adult:

> I had a very strict education and a good education in the sense that my mother said: 'You have to be good.' And I'd say, 'Why?' And she'd say, 'You have to be good.' Then, 'You have to be honest.' And I'd say, 'Why do you have to be honest?' You know, those kinds of simple and silly things, but very important in life. 'You have to work, you have to study, you have to be yourself. You're clever, so use your brain.' ... So I had education, I had studies and I had the opportunity to be good in golf.

These backward-looking stories (about 'working, studying, using your brain') provide the building blocks for Kandy's forward-looking stories (about 'learning another language, travelling, discovering the world'). They are part of Kandy's narrative heritage.

Formal enculturation processes are of course only part of the story. More difficult to identify are the informal and subconscious aspects of our enculturation because these processes begin *before* birth as 'the pregnant woman and other family members call the baby-to-be into personhood' (Lindemann, 2009: 42). Mikhail Bakhtin provides some insights on this process:

> Everything that pertains to me enters my consciousness, beginning with my name, from the external world through the mouths of others (my mother, and so forth) with their intonation, in their emotional and value-assigning tonality. I realise myself initially through others: from them I receive words, forms, and tonalities for the formation of my initial idea of myself.
>
> (Bakhtin; cf. Frank, 2004: 45–46)

Along similar lines philosopher Alistair MacIntyre sheds further light on the way in which our identities are never completely our own, suggesting that we inherit expectations and obligations which provide each of us with a 'moral starting point'. He goes on to suggest:

> The story of my life is always embedded in those communities from which I derive my identity. I am born with a past; and to try to cut myself off from that past, in the individualist mode, is to deform my present relationship. The possession of an historical identity and the possession of a social identity coincide. What I am, therefore, is in key part what I inherit, a specific past that is present, to some degree in my present. I find myself part of history and that is generally to say, whether I like it or not, whether I recognise it or not, one of the bearers of a tradition.
>
> (MacIntyre, 1984: 205–206)

Of course, most of us don't think about what tradition we are bearers of, any more than a molecule of water considers its place in the flowing river. We perhaps only realise that we have taken on the values, moral standpoint or ideology of our culture, as Louis Althusser (1971) explains, when we find ourselves turning to face someone who has hailed us. 'Hey you!', the policeman shouts and as we turn round (or possibly run away) we enact the process of interpellation – performing those actions expected of us as citizens in our particular society. We act in response to the expectations of the apparatus (e.g. law, governing institutes) of the culture in which we are embedded. These insights provide the basis for understanding some of the unconscious knowing that we accrue – part historical, part tradition and part our own decision to act according to a way of being set out for us.

These unconscious epistemological and ontological truths are suggested when Georgi talks about her early life experiences:

> I think most of it, sporting ability, would extend from my Dad. He was very good at most things. I think my stubborn streak comes from him. Dad's got such a will to win, even when he plays golf. Christ! It's unbelievable! Oh my god! It's absolute.

Georgi doesn't imply (as Kandy did) that a parent *told* her to win, to be stubborn or to be like them. Yet, despite Georgi's father never verbalising what he values, she *knows* that her 'will to win' and 'stubborn streak' are inherited from him and she accepts this in a profound and life-shaping way.

Below, Kitrina shares four stories of moments from her own biography: playing in the garden, leaving school, a first golf trip to the USA and her first major championship win. These stories provide a more in-depth illustration of how sometimes subtle enculturation processes unfold from a young age to offer a narrative repertoire – a set of 'building blocks' – that is unique to each of us. When added together, these kinds of moments shape our future expectations, actions, decisions and developing identity.

Learning to be relational

When he watched, his body would seldom, if ever, be still. It twitched, to the right, then the left, his head following the play, unable not to mirror what he saw, the moves his body knew so well. He clasped the arms of the chair, body tense, tongue pressed and resting on the single front tooth, the one that remained when its neighbour was knocked out by a defender's elbow many years ago. Immersed, his eyes darted across the screen searching for the ball. The winger hit a lob towards the goal and he, balancing himself in tandem in the armchair, anticipated the ball's flight and flicked his left foot forward. 'What a goal!' the commentator screamed as John Toshack, Liverpool's tall attacker, slid along the wet grass smiling at the crowd. Lured long enough to stay for the final whistle his passion could be restrained no longer and turning back years and expectations it was his turn to play. 'Come on', he urged, disappearing through the patio doors.

He dribbled the waiting ball and niftily back-heeled it without breaking stride as he approached the goal, a white door, four feet wide, housed between two concrete pillars in a grey wall. Then, spinning round, he assumed, for a moment, a cat-like state, alert, ready to defend his white piece of wood. But she had already caught him off-guard, stealthily nutmegging this former pro by volleying the back-heeled ball straight between his legs. The door hinges shook, the lock screamed and the ball rebounded into the flowerbed.

'Referee!' he cried, but she was off on a lap of honour, ponytail wagging in the sun.

'Yeeeeeessss!', she cried out to the flora and fauna silently fearing their fate. 'The youngster does it again', she commentated while gathering the ball from beneath the fuchsias, begonias, lobelia and petunias, and, undaunted by a few falling petals, dribbled off towards the Cox Orange Pippin tree and back to take yet another stab at the narrow goal, this time the shot ricocheting of the goalie's arm. 'Ooooooooooh so near', she squealed running after the ball again.

'The youngster's on fire today,' he commentated. 'The goalie's having to work really hard.'

But, after a fifth goal rattled home the rules of this game dictated different roles be adopted, players automatically changed – without pause for comment or need for discussion the striker became the goalie and the goalie became the striker and with tables turned he ran round the garden squealing after his shots bombarded the white door and she took her turn shouting: 'REFEREE!'

Do you fancy an ice cream?

The lure was the ice cream. He had offered them ice creams on the way back from the golf range. She and her little sister eagerly accepted the invitation to ice cream and even hit a few shots. This offer, two days later, was a little different. 'Do you fancy leaving school and playing golf for a year?' her Dad asked, as if he was asking about ice creams again. She thought golf was boring, but school was pretty boring too ... and she had no burning desire to do anything in particular. 'If you don't like it you can do your A-levels', he reasoned. It all sounded so simple driving along in the car; it wasn't an intense conversation, it didn't even seem particularly important, it was just like he was asking *do you fancy chocolate or vanilla?*

'If you like it,' he continued, eyes not diverting from the road, 'but aren't very good, you do your A-levels, but you will have a game you can play for the rest of your life. Golf's played everywhere. If you like it,' he glanced over towards her shrugging his shoulders in the process, 'and you are good at it, no one can stop you. You see, you can always finish your education, at any age, but with sport,' there was a moment's pause, 'time is an issue, it's a little different.' He left his proposal hanging. The ball, so to speak, was in her court.

Of course, she didn't know anything about golf, other than it was boring. She liked the smell of the lamb's wool sweaters in the golf shop though – she quite fancied having one of those.

She didn't consider how her father's experiences might have influenced his proposal, how coming over on the boat from Ireland as a child, being stigmatised as an Irish immigrant in Bristol, the school mysteriously losing his exam results and refusing to give him his leaving certificate, may have made him less confident of the school system. Nor was she aware of how not being able to accept the contract to play football for the Arsenal football club when he was 17 because his father didn't believe in professional sport left a residue, a *what if* that could never be answered. She only saw the face of three options: no drawbacks, no pressure, only opportunities. So she shrugged her shoulders: why not?

While she and her father had been rather underwhelmed regarding the gravity of her decision to leave school at 17, without qualifications and without skills in the activity she was pursuing, her teachers weren't quite so at ease with the decision and announcement at the beginning of term.

'You're doing WHAT?' enquired her form teacher.

'I'm leaving school at Christmas to become a professional golfer', she said.

'Do you think you have reached the standard then? It's very difficult to make it in professional sport you know! Do you think you are good enough?'

'I don't know,' she replied in all honesty, but enjoying the drama, 'I haven't even played yet.'

Trust

He didn't look up from the paper, he just asked the question: 'Are you taking a Bible with you?'

In the excitement of what to pack for her first trip to America, a Bible hadn't figured on her list. So she took a moment to consider her options. A simple 'no' might look as if she didn't care, saying yes would be a lie, so she came up with: 'They're all too big, too heavy', hoping that would be an end to the matter. It wasn't.

'I'll buy you a travel one', he said from behind the broadsheet. Which he did, with the instructions to read a chapter every day, which she did.

In the dark bedroom she fumbled to find the bathroom doorknob, uneasy, ashamed, slightly tense, and at 5 a.m. still half asleep. Pausing to make sure she hadn't disturbed the sleep of her roommates Annie and Tanya she turned the handle in slow motion while holding her breath. Her skin acknowledged the coolness of the sterile room, but it was only once the door was softly closed and locked tight that she put the light on, the toilet seat down and commenced reading.

She wondered why reading this book was such a problem in front of her two friends. She wondered why she was driven to read, even though her father didn't check up on her or ever ask her about it. She began where he suggested, namely the search for wisdom and understanding, the proverbs of renowned philosopher, Solomon: *He who refreshes others will be refreshed. A kind-hearted woman gains respect, but ruthless men gain only wealth.* Her bum went numb on the hard seat, but the reading captured her thoughts. What should her behaviour be towards others? What sort of heart did she have? *A kind answer turns away wrath.* How *should* she respond?

Six months later her father died. She continued reading.

Wouldn't he be proud now?

The press corps didn't want to disrupt the polite handshakes following the 1982 British Amateur Championship final, but, if *their* stories were to take centre stage in the Sunday papers, copy needed to be filed before the football results were in and it was already 3.50 p.m. and they were in the middle of the sixteenth hole. This being golf, however, the rush to circle the winner was dignified.

The usual cliché questions surfaced first, about the game and how she came from behind. *Daily Telegraph* reporter Marie Clark then slipped in her question. This one, however, came as a shock to the young champion: 'Wouldn't your father have been proud of you now?' Clarke asked, as much as a statement or assumption as a question. The journalist's story had, of course, already been written, about the *21-year-old* who *only started golf four years ago*, and had taken *a year off school, beaten every member of the British team* and that *her father had died a few months earlier.* Clarke simply needed a *yes* from the player to show she actually interviewed the girl.

The reply was as much a shock to the journalists as the question had been to the player: 'No.'

Faces looked up from notebooks, pens stopped, earnest expressions and eyes pinned attention on the relative unknown. The words were out, however, before the young player realised she was disagreeing with the world's top journalists. The words were out before she had thought through the ramifications of annoying this group of men and women. The pause in the furious scribbling provoked a further response, but, in those few moments, she could not find words to bridge the divide, so she once again stepped on thin ice. 'No,' she said firmly shaking her head and waiting for words, 'my father was proud of *me*, not what I did today, not hitting a ball round the golf course.'

How might these insights illuminate the lives, stories and enculturation of athletes more generally? In answer to our first question – *Are we born with a story?* – we would say, yes in part, we are. A child is born into an already unfolding story, a script with ways to talk about life, particular family with links and values that extend backward as well as forward to what he or she might become. Paradoxically, however, the answer to our question is also *no*. A child is not born *telling* a discovery, relational or performance narrative. Rather, the values, expectations and stories of the family he or she is birthed into provide a narrative heritage that encourages one story over another. From these historical legacies the foundations of a life story are birthed.

For the individual storyteller (as Georgi's, Kandy's, Leanne's and Kitrina's stories illustrate), what happens next depends on many additional factors. Given that our identities are never solely our own, our parents and caregivers provide the initial resources to make sense of events that happen in our lives. When Mary falls over (an event) and bruises her knee (evidence of an event) she may be given a 'there-there, little girls shouldn't run so fast' (comfort and gender-limiting) story or a 'no blood no tears' (tough-love) story. How her story develops is then down to what other building blocks become available at a later stage, what types of story clusters accumulate over time to scaffold other identity-defining moments.

Critically, 'People's access to narrative resources depends on their social location: what stories are told where they live and work, which stories do they take seriously or not' (Frank, 2010: 13). When it comes to building identity and opening up or closing down life possibilities, social location matters and cultural context has very real effects. The following extract, shared with us by an Olympic canoeist, provides an illustration that helps clarify the importance of social location:

I even enjoyed sports I wasn't very good at to be honest with you.... Years ago I did a TV interview when I made the Junior's World's team and I've got a video and it's got me, a little 13-year-old, and they say, 'Why do you like canoeing?' and I say: 'Cause it's hard.' ... I was quite a physical child, there was lots of outdoor activity. My father climbed and it was a non-competitive environment, much more outdoor sort of hill walking, running and climbing, swimming in rock pools, that kind of thing. And so when I went to school obviously I would join in all the running around that was to be done [laughs] but because my father was a mountaineer I grew up, essentially, mountaineering from when I was only 3 ... he didn't stop doing that. But my family, they didn't do any competitive sport or games or anything like that – that was, kind of, what was at school. I think you are limited in a way, by your horizons, by your experiences. So I had a kind of outdoor experience with my family and I had school sport. Well there was a multi-sport club, one of the people who ran it was kind of like a rough-and-tumble-type guy who paddled around the North Pole and Alaska and I thought that was brilliant. So, like, if you fell in, you had to get your boat and you'd have to swim down the river in minus-five-degrees and it seemed really exciting to me as a young person. I know it sounds silly but it was very scary and rough and exciting. And so that environment was very different to my school sport and I'm always very wary of the terms 'natural' and 'talented' because I'd been running up mountain scree since I was 3 and sliding down glaciers when I was 4. So I think that life experience has a lot to do with how you're perceived. When I was 14 I got selected in the under-18 category in the World Junior's and I did quite well. I actually got a medal and I don't know if it was a lucky day, or I was talented, whatever you want to say, but I'd had no pressure on me. All the other 17- , 18-year-olds had tons of pressure on them. So obviously then, you know, I'm 14, third in the World under-18, I think I'm pretty good at this. So, that sort of channels you towards training for it. Because I wouldn't have said that I was seriously trying. I wasn't trying to win. I was doing what I was doing, but I did it very well. And everyone thinks you're talented then.

This account, when combined with Kitrina's stories above, helps respond to our second question – to identify *the processes behind the adoption of one story over another*. Both Kitrina and the canoeist above are *predisposed* towards a certain kind of story by their particular narrative heritage. The stories they are predisposed towards are *not* the performance narrative type, but the relational and discovery types. In the case of the canoeist, the narrative resources made available through activities such as 'sliding down glaciers' at age four and 'running up mountain scree' at age three are not available to most children. Unsurprisingly, this athlete is able to self-identify as being a 'physical child' which provides a resource where she is 'able to cope' with conditions for which other children may feel unprepared. Unlike Georgi's links to a father who valued winning, she states 'I wasn't trying to win' after situating her story within an already unfolding family narrative of non-competitive mountaineering and outdoor activities. Despite 'everyone' within sport culture viewing her as simply 'talented', she did not story her ability as 'in the genes' or arising as a result of planned intervention, but rather as developed organically over time. In her words: 'I was doing what I was doing, but I did it very well.'

Ryan and Luke

We now turn to the stories of two male early-career athletes who have experienced national success at junior level. Ryan's success has come through rowing while Luke's has been through track and field. By recounting key moments from their contrasting stories we consider the other questions posed in the introduction. We explore how narrative heritage – access to particular narrative scripts at a young age – affects whether an individual conforms to or resists the dominant narrative in sport culture. We also consider the personal effects of sustained exposure to the performance narrative.

Ryan: 'It's more the winning that I've liked'

A number of studies have shown that young people commonly describe multiple reasons for playing sport, perhaps beginning to focus on winning only once they progress or get older (e.g. Côté and Hay, 2002). In the following extract Ryan sets the scene for his involvement in sport:

RYAN: I did swimming, tennis and rugby with not much success.... Then when I was 16 ... there was a governing body world class start programme and I got tested for that. I was put forward basically because of my size more than anything else and then I got on the programme and that was basically where I started from.

KITRINA: And do you remember, did you like it?

RYAN: It was more the fact that – it's more the winning that I've liked. I've gone through sports and tried to find one where I could be better than other people and just found that this was the one that I could hack. I could get better than other people at quite a high level. So it wasn't that I was particularly passionate about the activity – it was a vehicle that I could beat other people and, yeah, just get better than other people.... I think it's just, succeeding, like, winning, knowing that you are better than everyone else. How I got into the sport, and the programme I'm on, it's purely about achieving success. As soon as I got into the sport I knew that was why I was doing it. It's purely – that's where I am and that's where I want to get.

This account of Ryan's early involvement in rowing is striking in the way Ryan stories his involvement exclusively around the performance outcome of *winning* and *beating others*. There is no sign in Ryan's stories – even at the start of his career – of other reasons for participation such as (for example) enjoyment, passion for the activity, discovery, learning or sharing with others. Instead, his stories portray involvement with rowing – and any other sport – as 'purely' about 'winning'. On this basis, Ryan's story closely follows the performance narrative.

Neimeyer and colleagues (2006: 130) write: 'self-narratives represent importations of the themes, roles, and discourses available in a given culture, for better or worse.' Ryan's story may usefully be understood as an 'importation' of the culturally dominant performance narrative. Ryan's account exhibits similarities to the performance plot, which signal the cultural origins of his personal story. This is particularly so given that Ryan's initiation into rowing occurred under the auspices of a talent identification initiative through which he was identified (on the basis of physical characteristics) as a potential elite rower. In saying, 'that was basically where I started from', Ryan suggests that there is nothing worth noting in his sport history before he was identified as talented. That he considered this the start of his story is a mark in itself. The basis for Ryan's initial involvement in sport was geared around his potential to *win* and the cultural context of his participation centred on performance outcomes. These cultural conditions permeate Ryan's stories.

Luke: 'I just did it because I enjoyed it'

In the following excerpt, Luke shares a very different story of his early involvement in sport:

> The first thing I remember athletics-wise was – 'cos my dad ran – I remember being really small and watching him run. And mum used to make us little vests, sort of the same colours as his. There weren't many kids who'd go down, and I used to go down and watch the athletics, and I kind of got lost in that.... I only got involved in the [athletics] club really when we moved up here, like [at] 12, it wasn't when I was younger. I liked playing football ... if you were good at it then you kind of got accepted at school ... because I'm dyslexic – academically absolutely atrocious – I used to try to hide that as best as possible. All my school reports they were always, like, I would try to help anyone out to try to stop having to do my work! So you'd get out on the playground and, when you were younger, play football. And you wanted to be good at it because you felt accepted playing football. That's the only reason I liked playing football. I can't think of any other reason ... When we were in Year 7 they had a cross-country league throughout the winter – I'd never done anything like that before – and I remember standing on the start line and everyone was: 'Oh Luke will go off, Luke will win,' and their kind of attitude was like you're gonna, you know, there was almost an expectation. Which for the first time was a bit strange 'cos I never really had an expectation – I just did it because I enjoyed it and because I felt good at it.

Evident within this account – at two moments – are echoes of the performance narrative. First, Luke describes being 'good' at football, which suggests an awareness of performance outcomes being potentially valuable. Second, he describes a general attitude among others at his first race that 'Luke will go off, Luke will win'. These references to winning/being good signal the presence of a performance story. In contrast to Ryan, however, both of these examples refer to *others'* interest in performance outcomes, rather than Luke himself internalising this cultural story-line. In the first example, *others* value Luke being good at football and therefore 'accept' him on this basis; in the second, *others* make the judgement that 'Luke will win' and, thereby, signal *their* belief that winning is meaningful. Luke's own story, however, seems somewhat at odds with the performance narrative. When Luke senses an 'expectation' of success, he has tapped into the subtle ways the assumptions of those who subscribe to a dominant narrative are circulated – in this case the assumption that those who are 'talented' will inevitably go on to compete and win. Both of these moments illustrate how the culturally dominant perform-ance narrative (exemplified in the words and actions of others) can influence the experiences of an individual within sport culture.

Luke's story also differs from Ryan's in that diverse narrative threads are present throughout, beginning with his earliest stories. While Ryan's story does not veer from the performance script, Luke draws on a relational narrative when he describes attending athletic events with his family as a young child. He again draws on a relational narrative in his account of his reasons for playing football at school: as a route to 'acceptance' by his peers. For Luke, it is not his ability at football that is storied as meaningful, but the fact that his ability leads to him establishing positive relationships with others (e.g. being respected, taken seriously, accepted by his peers). Thus, Luke's stories of his initiation into sport demonstrate an early resistance to the performance narrative in a way that Ryan's stories do not.

Sustaining narrative heritage

Luke: 'It's the best feeling ever'

As Luke recounts his subsequent experiences in sport, further narrative threads become evident. In the following account, Luke sheds light on his reasons for continuing to run at the elite level:

> It's a place that's, it is strange, because despite the fact that when you're fin-ished, when you're completely knackered and maybe, sometimes, if you're tired or lethargic beforehand and you might not want to run beforehand, but when you're there it doesn't matter … it's the best feeling ever. Because you're feeling tall and you're running well you don't feel anyone else can get you – you're completely on your own. But at the same time, you just feel like – you're almost justifying your existence…. It's what you do well, you feel good doing it, that's what you can do well.

This excerpt demonstrates links to a variety of cultural narrative resources, including a discovery narrative, an action narrative (Carless and Douglas, 2008) and the experience of flow (Sparkes and Partington, 2003). Further narrative strands are also evident in this excerpt, in which Luke describes playing football in the school team:

> The PE teacher noticed I was reasonably good and put me on the wing … and because you'd been selected, or scored a goal, or played well, everyone seemed to give you respect. I remember they'd say: 'Oh come and play for our team!' But because it was on a Sunday Mum and Dad wouldn't let me play. So I couldn't take that next step.

At this point in Luke's story, a further narrative thread is introduced which is important in Luke's later experiences. Although Luke was 'good' at football (i.e. he met the terms of the performance narrative for progression), he was unable to progress because his parents 'wouldn't let [him] play' on a Sunday owing to the family's beliefs. This moment portrays a tension between two narratives: the culturally dominant performance narrative (in which sport is the priority) and a counter-narrative of shared belief or faith (in which going to church on Sundays is the priority). On this occasion, the actions of his parents (not letting him play) meant that the counter-narrative 'trumped' the performance narrative.

These moments are significant because they are instances when Luke was shown that the terms of the dominant performance narrative are not the *only* way to experience and story life in sport. Instead of a singular narrative script, these moments illustrate how diverse and multi-layered story threads permeate Luke's life story, revealing an array of cultural influences, obligations and expectations. As a result of repeated moments like these over time, we suggest that Luke became resistant to storying his life and developing his identity solely around the contours of the performance narrative. In sharing these stories, Luke reveals that since his earliest memories there have been more threads to his life story – and hence his identity – than being a sportsperson.

Ryan: 'I want to get ahead'

Ryan's developing story, in contrast, shows little deviation from the performance narrative. His story remains monological with every story seemingly told from the self-position of athlete. At no time, as Ryan progressed his story, was the central theme of performance seriously challenged – for example, through stories about enjoying the activity, travel, play, fun or friendship. Instead, these other dimensions are either never mentioned or are subsumed within his quest to win. As opposed to broadening out his life story, Ryan's later stories serve merely to strengthen and entrench a number of values typical of the performance narrative. For example, Ryan describes how his desire to win is 'the only thing' that enables him to endure the pain associated with training and competition:

> In a sport like rowing the actual process of rowing is really painful – you get 10 strokes into the race and already you can feel your legs burning up and you've got to, the only thing that keeps me in the race and pushing myself is the fact that I want to get ahead of the other people.

Narrating pain in this way links one's personal embodied experiences with wider cultural expectations of what it means to 'be' an athlete, and, as White and colleagues (1995) note, serves to depersonalise the experience of pain and objectify the body. Chapman (1997) suggests that regimented expectations – such as enduring pain while training – are a way in which some athletes create a *disciplined body* (Frank, 1995) through rationalising the acceptance of injury and physical harm in the pursuit of improved performance. A disciplined body tolerates pain through dissociation, and this is demonstrated in the extract above when Ryan disassociates from the pain of maximal exertion by focusing on dominating the opposition.

Lieblich and colleagues (1998: 8–9) observe that 'People are meaning-generating organisms; they construct their identities and self-narratives from building blocks available in their common culture, above and beyond their individual experience.' Ryan's life story may be seen as dominated by the 'building blocks' of the performance narrative. Ryan has either never been exposed to alternative narrative types, or has ignored or discredited these as being incompatible with his quest to win. As a result, Ryan's stories incorporate culturally dominant performance values, at the expense of other possible stories. This is potentially problematic because dominant narratives ' "colonize" an individual's sense of self, constricting identity options to those that are problem saturated' (Neimeyer *et al.*, 2006: 132). By storying his life in line with the dominant but monological performance narrative, Ryan risks an exclusive athletic identity which threatens long-term well-being (Sparkes, 1998). Not least is the danger of a single-minded striving for success and achievement to the extent that the person becomes 'detached from the humanizing web of emotional connections and social commitments' (Jackson, 1990: 209).

Challenges to one's story

At times, stories are challenged by embodied experience (see Carless, 2010). When this happens, in McLeod's (1997: 93) terms, the storyteller needs to reconsider 'the fit between his or her individual experience and the storylines that are available' within his or her culture. One of two responses is possible: the individual either modifies their behaviour to better fit the dominant narrative, or modifies their story so it better fits their experience. In the first response, the individual's actions 'fall into line' with the culture in which they are immersed, while in the second, the individual's actions transgress that culture. Ryan's and Luke's stories illustrate both of these processes unfolding. Ryan's story portrays a detachment from emotional and social connections when he modified his behaviour to conform to the performance script. Adhering to this story helped Ryan eradicate the tensions and doubts he experienced about his actions and, over time, cemented an athletic identity. Luke's established dialogical story was at odds with the monological performance narrative that dominated the culture in which he was becoming immersed. This led to a period of doubt, reflection, and eventually rejection of the performance narrative.

Ryan: 'In the boat'

One tension occurred when Ryan described pursuing his education while trying to enhance his rowing performance. In the following extract Ryan reveals how he expects his school to value his sport performance ahead of his education:

If you do the rowing right you don't have the time or the energy to finish off homework and then you get stressed about that and then the stress will affect your performance. It's bound to. So I put rowing first. They [school] give me the time off to go to camp but if you get homework set you get people saying 'ah I haven't done it' and making up excuses whereas I've got a *valid* excuse and I'm trying to get somewhere *outside*. Whereas, you've got people who didn't do it because they went out last night and got back late and they [school] don't seem to get it. It's the same response to me who's saying 'Sir, I've had really tough training the last couple of days' and them saying 'Sir, I went out last night'. They still expect the homework in – there is no allowances from that point of view.

Here, Ryan stories the 'stress' of finishing his homework (should he complete it) as adversely affecting his rowing. In keeping with the performance narrative, Ryan puts rowing first: he *does not* complete his homework. In contrast, the school's response follows a different narrative plot: rowing has to make room for homework. From Ryan's perspective, the problem is the culture and values of the school and the teachers who 'don't get it'. His decisions are solely made from the perspective of the performance narrative – from how it affects his position in the boat.

The friendships Ryan initiated at county level become a second casualty of the performance story. Ryan first tells of a mutual interdependence between crew members as they work together towards a shared goal. But, as sometimes happens, Ryan is selected to progress to a higher level which then, for him, prohibits friendships with his *former* crew while remaining completely focused on beating them with his *new* crew. The story he has advanced so far does not allow him to be 'friend' and 'winner' because the effort needed to win is generated by disliking the opposition ('I want to get ahead of the other people'). At this moment, two narratives – performance and relational – clash. Trying to unpick this issue Kitrina asked: 'Would you say that you hate the opposition?'

RYAN: You build yourself up to doing it. It's more the fact that you'd hate them to beat you. I'm probably worse than other people. When I got into, kind of, the group at national level you get to know people – before you're selected to the squad – you still train with. You get to county and you'd seen them before. Before a race a lot of them would be talking to each other and that's the sort of thing I'd have to, if I talked to them I'd forget that *[pause]*.
KITRINA: *You didn't like them?*
RYAN: Yeah. Which is *[pause]*. Yeah.

In this excerpt Ryan communicates a concern that maintaining a connection to his former crew (by talking to them before the race), would compromise his 'hate' of them beating him and, therefore, his determination to win. The *way* he recounted this part of his story (i.e. pauses and hesitations) suggested to us a degree of discomfort as he reflected on these feelings and actions. Faced in the moment, however, with the decision of whether or not to interact with his former crew, he elected to follow the script of his story by disassociating from them. This behaviour 'fits' the performance story he advanced and 'makes sense' in terms of the plot of this story. It is accepted by tellers of performance tales that relationships are, if necessary, sacrificed in pursuit of success (as Georgi's story revealed in Chapter 4). Yet in the terms of a relational narrative, the same actions make no sense at all because they result in the breakdown of relationships. From a relational perspective, Ryan's behaviour could be interpreted as selfish, insincere and/or uncaring. Ryan's story remains within the contours of the performance narrative, thereby relegating relational concerns and sidestepping any need for ethical or moral reflection on his actions. His story justifies them as necessary in the pursuit of performance.

A further tension occurred when Ryan described his experience of national training camps in which his girlfriend also took part. Although Ryan believed spending time with his girlfriend did *not* affect his performance, he suggested that spending 'too much time' with his girlfriend was *perceived by others* as a threat to performance. He offered this account of how coaches responded to him spending time with his girlfriend:

> They make a massive issue of the fact that if you've got half an hour free time in the evening or in the middle of the day, they go out of their way to say you can't see that person. So it just creates tension because you have bad feelings towards the coach because you can't think or see a logical reason why. I mean you can say if you're spending your whole time with them that your crew mates won't like that 'cos you're not focusing on the job in hand. But I know my crew were perfectly happy with me seeing her. So I don't – they just seem to go out of their way to make it difficult.

This example illustrates behaviour control that has been identified in elite sport culture (Denison, 2007) where training camps present a unique opportunity for coaches to put the behaviour of athletes under a 24-hour microscope, policing even how they use their leisure time. While those outside sport may dismiss coaches' influence on such matters, Shogun (1999) suggests that what a coach says carries great weight for many elite athletes. While voicing his frustration, Ryan takes the coach's words seriously and decides to modify his actions to demonstrate his commitment. By doing so, he again sacrifices relational values in favour of sustaining a performance story.

Ryan makes sense of his response (spending less time with his girlfriend) by highlighting his responsibility to his crew:

> You have to limit it, 'cos I can see if I spent all my free time with her then that would annoy my crew, 'cos for them, they would look at it that my focus wasn't on performing. And when I've trained all year and they've trained all year to get to one point they'd want to know – I'd want to know – that everyone else in my crew was completely mentally, sort of, in the boat.

In this account, Ryan does further 'narrative work' to reframe his embodied experience (that spending time with one's girlfriend does not affect his performance) within the terms of a shared performance narrative. In the light of a totalitarian performance narrative, spending 'all [his] free time' with his girlfriend implies that Ryan is not mentally 'in the boat', and any action that suggests he is not 'in the boat' weakens his commitment to the crew and is seen as a threat to performance. Consequently, Ryan adjusts his behaviour (i.e. he reduces the amount of time he spends with his girlfriend) to fit a story.

Luke: 'Selling myself short'

Luke's progression to the international scene was typical, and included school, local club, county and national competition. Up to this point, Luke lived with his parents, established friendships and connections within sport and outside, and regularly attended a local church. This all began to change when Luke attended a prestigious national performance centre:

> I broke the British record, went to the Worlds for the first time, and met the coach of the two best athletes in the world. He was the top dog. And when he says, 'Do you want to come and train with me?' you think, 'Right! OK, that's going to another level.' So I upped sticks and moved there. Every morning [we] trained 'til 12, go to lectures for two hours, go back to training, go home. It was just that for two years, training all the time with the best athletes in the world ... you're wandering in and it's like *Sports Personality of the Year*.

Over time, Luke began to experience tensions with the culture of the performance centre. One example is evident here, when Luke looks back on his time at the centre:

LUKE: It wasn't me. Having been someone who was brought up in church and stuff, all of a sudden Sunday mornings was training, and that was sort of non-negotiable.
KITRINA: So they wanted you to train on Sundays and you decided not to?
LUKE: No, I decided to train. I went to church in the evenings. But it was the principle – I felt that I was kind of selling myself a little bit short in that I knew really I should make more of an effort to go to church and stuff. But then I wanted to train and I wanted obviously to get better and so you've got that kind of nagging away at you.

The 'nagging away at you' that Luke describes may be understood as a result of a clash between the culture of the centre (which prioritised performance) and his personal story (which prioritises religious faith and church). McLeod (1997) suggests that individuals whose stories do not fit dominant cultural narratives are often silenced – their stories cannot be told within that culture. This was the case for Luke, as his personal values and beliefs were side-lined by the centre's 'non-negotiable' culture of training on Sunday.

Luke described temporary changes in his behaviour – and even the kind of person he considered himself to be – that occurred over two years as he tried to 'fit in':

> You kind of became consumed in your athletics. You became at the end so into it that you couldn't see your perspective on other stuff.... I dumped Naomi, I didn't want – I got to the point where I just felt that *I want to be an athlete, I'm meant to be. I just felt that athletics is what I should be involved with. I've come this far, I've invested money, I've invested time, I need to give it as good a shot as I can and I can't be doing with you, you know, moaning at me down the phone. I need to be single minded.* I wasn't giving her enough time, or I wasn't at church, or I was becoming a different person.... Because she had known me obviously before I went to Uni and I was quite, I always felt, I was quite laid back. But I don't think I was when I was at [the performance centre]. I was just really kind of channelled to wanting to just run faster.

In the italicised passage in the above, Luke tells a performance story, using phrases that characterise this narrative type. For a time, Luke modifies his behaviour in an effort to conform to this script. Evident, however, is a degree of discomfort, revealed as a tension between Luke's established life story (focusing here on connections to his girlfriend and church) and the storyline that was impressed upon him by the culture of the performance centre ('sport comes first'). For Luke, striving for success under the terms of the dominant performance narrative resulted in him becoming detached from humanising social and emotional connections. This is demonstrated in his story when he moved away from home (loosening ties with his family), trained on Sundays (loosening ties with church) and 'dumped' his girlfriend. Luke's actions at this time held different meanings for different people. For those within the performance culture (his coaches and teammates), they provide evidence that he is 'dedicated', 'focused' and 'wants to win'. For those outside (his girlfriend and parents), they indicate a dramatic shift in his priorities. For Luke, his actions leave him feeling guilty and uncomfortable.

Initially, despite the tensions his actions create, Luke tries to adopt a performance script. This is not surprising, as these behaviours are sanctioned in elite sport and storied as the only route to success. However, two experiences led Luke to question the performance story. First, despite his commitment, his performance *was not* improving:

> You'd go to [the centre] thinking I'm training with the best in the world – I can't fail to get better. And that didn't happen. And so you feel, well hang on a minute, what's going on, is this working for me? In the back of your mind you're questioning it.

According to the performance narrative, total commitment is the route to success: the compromises Luke made should result in him running quicker. However, the objective details (i.e. times) showed that this wasn't the case. The performance story wasn't working.

Second, as Luke came to know two other athletes – Tom and Erik – he reflected on how they lived their lives:

> Tom wouldn't go to a cinema because how you have to sit in a chair would affect his hamstrings. And you think, flipping heck, if that's what a world record holder does, then I'm not that! Is that what I have to be like? I've seen what a lot of the best athletes in the world are like, because as much as Tom was like that, Erik wasn't, and he also won an Olympic medal. Having spent time with him I realised Erik wasn't like that and he still performed. And I realised Erik had a kid, his wife and they bought a house, he was settled, this place was home. Whereas everyone else was there because the coach was there, they'd come from other places.

In this excerpt Luke sees that it is not the case that the *only* way to be successful in elite sport is to follow a performance script. While Tom did, Erik – who was also successful – did not. Around this time Luke realised that if there were alternatives for other athletes, perhaps *he* did not *have* to be this way (a way that was causing him personal tension and guilt) to be successful. As a result, the promise of the performance narrative was weakened, and Luke began to consider alternatives.

He found those alternatives by returning to the life story he had previously developed, characterised by a strong relational thread:

> I remember being back in [the centre] pretty much deciding that really I'd given everything to my athletics in probably the most single-minded way I could do. I felt that I had upset a few people. Naomi, most definitely, Naomi. I hadn't spent time with her. I'd kind of broken up with her and I didn't really speak to my mum and dad when I was there. I didn't really see much of my family. As much as I had friends at training and stuff, I didn't really have any other friends outside of training, I didn't know anyone from church, it was all pretty much everything was based around training – completely. And I just felt that really that's crazy, what happens when I'm not an athlete? I've got to start to look at where I'm going in the long term and then weave athletics into it and I think that's the way it's got to be for me. Because I love athletics, and I love running, and I want to achieve … but I think the only way for me to do that is for me to get certain areas of my life sorted, in the sense that now I've moved [back home], got married, kind of established friends, got involved in the church quite a lot, and got friends within university, in training and church and stuff. I feel like I've really gone back to basics but in a way I've got back to me…. I've kind of eased back a little bit on the intensity of the training I was doing but I'm not as injured and I'm running just as well.

The availability of an alternative story (which encompasses moral dimensions of life) provides the resources needed for critical reflection on one's own actions from a moral and ethical perspective. Luke's stories demonstrate this journey unfolding. Initially, Luke modified his behaviour to follow the contours of the dominant performance narrative. As he later put it: 'I've tried it – I turned into a person I didn't like.' This dislike of his 'new self', we suggest, relates to the tensions that arose when the new behaviours that were required of him by the performance script no longer aligned with his personal story. Eventually – supported by the presence of alternative narratives alongside his awareness of cracks in the performance narrative – Luke abandons the performance story to return to the values of his previous dialogical life story.

Despite being of a similar age and having both achieved national success, Luke's and Ryan's stories and actions are dramatically different. We take the view that the biggest single factor behind this difference is their narrative heritage – i.e. the reservoir of stories available to them during their early years. At a time when the pressures on young athletes to adopt performance values seems to be increasing, we may well see more and more young people following the trajectory described in Ryan's story. This is a major concern given the dangers of the performance narrative which we outline in the chapters that follow. Luke 'escaped' these dangers. But doing so required significant courage to act *against* the culture in which he was immersed.

Note

1 This chapter contains material adapted and developed from Carless and Douglas (2013b).

8 Living, playing or resisting the part of 'athlete'[1]

> I think we are all actors and actresses and I think you have to be. It's just like a big stage. You've got to go on there and you've got to perform.
>
> (Golfer on Ladies European Tour)

In Chapter 4 we presented and explored a particular type of story – a performance narrative – that is dominant within elite sport culture. In this chapter we ask you to think of the performance narrative as a *script* that operates within sport culture to define the part of 'athlete'. Just as the script of a play serves to define the words and actions of the actors, so the performance narrative can serve to define (more loosely perhaps) the words and actions of high-level sportspeople. In short, the performance script articulates what is supposedly necessary to *be* an elite athlete. Of course, sportspeople are not required, in the same way that actors are, to follow the script. In sport the script has not even been written down, let alone circulated amongst those involved to be learnt verbatim. In sport, we assume, there is no director hiring and firing on the basis of whether or not the individual follows the script. *Or is there? Are selectors', coaches' and managers' decisions always and exclusively based on objective performance?*

Whatever the answer to these questions, we invite you, for the purposes of expanding shared understanding and stimulating reflection, to hold the metaphor of a script in mind as you read on. Using this metaphor, our purpose in this chapter is to ask: *how do athletes exist within the culture/s of high-level sport? How do they navigate and negotiate the way of being articulated in performance stories?* This is a way of being that is – supposedly – necessary in order to stand any chance of success at a high level in sport. As the title of the chapter suggests, we have found three distinct ways: by *living* the part of athlete, *playing* the part of athlete or *resisting* the part of athlete, as defined by the performance narrative.

Living the part of athlete

Individuals who we describe as *living the part of athlete* story their life and act in ways that conform to the plot of the performance narrative. Georgi and Ryan are two individuals who we would see as having come to *live* the part of athlete. Both Georgi and Ryan articulate sport as their *raison d'être* and identify achieving performance outcomes as of primary importance to them. Ryan's story, in particular, demonstrates how performance stories are routinely circulated within elite sport culture (through being told and retold by powerful others such as coaches), encouraging or coercing athletes to narrate their life in ways that follow its particular plot.

There is more to it, though, than 'just talk'. Through the process of interpellation, stories call on a person 'to acknowledge and act on a particular identity' (Frank, 2010: 49). In other words, a story calls for actions and behaviours that fit its plot. A particular story calls for a particular way of being. On this basis, those who tell performance stories are called to act in performance-oriented ways if they are to be able to sustain their story. Thus, individuals who *live* the part of athlete must do more than just 'talk the performance talk'. Rather, over time they must, if they are to sustain their story, *act* and *behave* in ways that align with the performance script. By doing so, they are likely to exclude or deny aspects of their lives that fall outside or threaten the performance narrative's primary focus on performance outcomes.

In a simple way this process is evident in Georgi's story when she describes stopping sitting by the pool with a drink in her hand one evening to go to the practice ground. In a more profound way it is also evident when she describes her attitude to partners: that her golf is, and always will be, more important than their relationship. Ryan, too, recounts times when he has sacrificed or relegated actual relationships (with ex-teammates and with his girlfriend) in favour of sport. Acting in these ways has been necessary if he is to legitimately sustain his 'performance comes first' story. Over time, these kinds of stories and actions, when repeated, can serve to foreclose identity, isolate individuals from others and (as we show in Chapter 9) pose a threat to long-term well-being and mental health.

The story shared by Suzanne (a 29-year-old member of the British hockey team) provides a good illustration of the process by which some individuals live the part of athlete. In the following excerpt, Suzanne looks back over her sport career:

SUZANNE: I have to say that relationships have suffered because of my hockey. So if I hadn't been playing hockey then I still think maybe I would have still been with a certain person. So I chose hockey really ultimately. Yeah. But things like family illnesses, 'cos with hockey you do so much travelling and you know you could be on the other side of the world, and if something happened I'm sure within the drop of a hat I'd be home. But then when I was younger, sometimes you can be so blinded by the fact that it's so good to be an elite sportsperson that you'd sacrifice absolutely anything for it. I've seen things where people have done certain things and I think: will you regret that in, like, a couple of years' time?

KITRINA: Can you give us an instance of that?

SUZANNE: Yeah, I probably can. A teammate's sister had a miscarriage and she was away on a training camp and her sister really wanted her to go home. And the coach kind of suggested she shouldn't go home so she didn't. And, you know, as her teammate I – [pause]. It's your sister – you can't ever forget that. If someone needs you at the time then – [pause]. To them it's just her sister. It's: she's away playing hockey. And hockey's just, you know, pathetic. And in the grand scale of things it is just a game. And I think a lot of people just lose sight of that. I think you do just have to keep one eye on reality because when you are surrounded by people who want the same goal you can be blinded by it. And coaches can be blamed for that, totally for that. They can totally blind you and in some instances they can, you know, emotionally bribe you about things.

Much like Georgi and Ryan, Suzanne's life story largely conformed to the performance narrative. This is illustrated above when Suzanne says, 'You can be so blinded by the fact that it's so good to be an elite sportsperson that you'd sacrifice absolutely anything for it.' Here, her story connects to the values of a performance script where *being* an elite athlete is storied as desirable and achievable only through sacrifice. The magnitude of sacrifice Suzanne describes ('absolutely anything') is in line with the tendency for performance stories to be totalitarian, prioritising sport performance ahead of other values, story plots and ways of being. It connects, too, to the intoxicating power of the hero narrative for many and suggests a possible aggrandised or glorified self.

In the excerpt above, a distinct sense of tension is evident, present from the first sentence ('relationships have suffered because of my hockey'). We suggest that particular characteristics of the performance narrative discussed in Chapter 4 (e.g. that it is a monological and linear story which privileges the individual and their personal agency) underlie this tension. By contemplating no longer being with a previous partner and whether or not to be with family members at times of illness and miscarriage, Suzanne evokes a counter-story – a *relational* narrative – which prioritises interconnectedness, relationships and living or being *with and for* another. These characteristics (discussed in Chapter 6) are, at a fundamental level, at odds with the individual agency that underlies the performance script. They directly challenge the monological and linear nature of the performance narrative. Therefore these two aspects of Suzanne's story exist in some degree of tension.

According to Frank (2010: 14), 'Stories *act* in human consciousness, with individuals sometimes being aware of what story is acting and sometimes not.' Suzanne's story clearly portrays how the culture of elite sport acts upon not only athletes' thoughts and stories, but also on their behaviours. In this example, Suzanne experiences expressions of the performance narrative *by others* as shaping her own actions, as well as those of teammates ('the coach kind of suggested she shouldn't go home so she didn't'). When Suzanne says, 'You do just have to keep one eye on reality because when you are surrounded by people who want the same goal you can be blinded by it', she reveals how sport culture operates through relationships between people via the circulation and reproduction of a dominant storyline. Suzanne's account suggests that immersion and participation in a culture where performance stories were told and retold over time 'blinded' her to alternative stories.

It may be that the subculture of team sports is particularly powerful in terms of 'encouraging' (or coercing) individuals to conform to a particular way of being and type of story. While athletes in individual sports potentially have significant time out of the view of other players, management and selectors (as Kitrina did in professional golf), team sports often provide a more closely monitored environment. Both of us have personally witnessed and experienced the kinds of process we describe here unfolding in team sport.

I (Kitrina) remember staying at the Palazio Hotel in Portugal for a particular tournament and going off, after play, to explore the area and begin to learn the language. In contrast, a professional football team also staying at the hotel seemed to live the kind of life recounted in the *Golf course, hotel, airport* story in Chapter 2. They appeared to exist solely to train, play, eat and rest. They went from the airport to the hotel to the football pitch. Other than for training or for a match, they never seemed to leave the hotel! But what alternative did any individual within the squad have? They had all likely been immersed in the subculture of professional football for several years – a culture that had taught them, through stories and modelled behaviours, that *this* is what professional footballers *do*, that *this* is what it is to *be* a pro soccer player. In contrast, I had been exposed to a very different set of stories – such as discovery stories (see Chapter 5) – which value and even prioritise experiencing and exploring a full and multidimensional life beyond sport. I had access to a reservoir of stories that enabled me to avoid living the part of athlete.

From the other side of the coin, I (David) have experienced some of the effects of team sport culture while playing hockey. One weekend we were staying in a hotel for two away matches – one on the Saturday morning and other on Sunday afternoon. I had the dubious honour of being selected as reserve goalkeeper for both! On the Saturday afternoon, having returned to the hotel after the match, I played a game of squash with the first-choice goalkeeper. I had sat on the bench that morning while the other goalkeeper had little to do, as we had won easily. We both wanted some exercise. The team coach, though, was not pleased, saying our actions were somewhat irresponsible. As this was amateur sport and *both* goalkeepers were involved in the 'misdemeanour' there was little the coach could do in response. Had the first-choice goalkeeper played squash with a different player, I wonder if I would have been selected to play the Sunday match? Had it been professional sport, I wonder what repercussions might have ensued? With the benefit of hindsight, I can see that while our actions had no adverse effect on performance the next day, they did clash with the performance script: we hadn't prioritised winning tomorrow's match. Looking back, I suppose this was a story that I did not fully embrace at the time, but I don't believe I would act differently if faced with the same situation today.

Within Suzanne's story, however, there *is* a sense of personal change over time. Like several of the older and more experienced athletes we have interviewed, Suzanne came to question the performance script as she moved through her sport career. Evident in her reflections ('when I was younger...') and the questions she asks ('will you regret that in a couple of years time?'), is a sense of temporal progression that sees her *weighing* or even *judging* her own and others' prioritisation of sport ahead of family and personal relationships. 'The challenge,' Freeman (2010: 12) writes, 'is to identify the ways in which these cultural narratives have permeated one's being and, in the process, to break away from them and sap them of their coercive power.' Suzanne's account reveals how she came to recognise the ways in which the performance narrative had permeated her own life and reject some of the moral and ethical assumptions that underlie it. For Freeman (2010: 5), the narrative reflection, possible through looking back, through hindsight, 'plays an integral role in shaping and deepening moral life'. Similar to some other sportspeople whom we have interviewed (see Chapters 6, 7 and 10), Suzanne seemed to achieve – through reflection over time – a new self-understanding of a moral and ethical kind that led her away from a performance story and towards the values of a relational narrative.

Playing the part of athlete

Other sportspeople consciously and deliberately *play the part of athlete* under certain conditions, in much the same way as an actor plays the part of a particular character when on stage or in front of the camera. Rather than *living* the part of sportsperson as scripted by the performance narrative, these individuals *present* or *perform* themselves in ways that align with the performance script when they perceive it necessary to do so. They do so by consciously modifying their story (what they say) and behaviours (what they do) by telling and enacting performance stories in public. At these times, they align their stories and actions with the expectations of powerful others (such as selectors, managers and coaches) and are thereby able to survive, or even thrive, within the culture of elite and professional sport. In private, however, they articulate a different life story and enact another set of behaviours that draw upon alternative narrative types. Thus, these individuals *covertly* maintain a multidimensional life story but silence aspects of their story when they perceive that powerful others expect or demand a performance story. At the same time, they monitor their behaviour (allowing certain actions to be seen while others are hidden) to ensure it aligns with the performance-oriented expectations of influential others.

A sense of playing the part of athlete is evident in moments of both Kandy's and Luke's stories. Although both individuals sustain relational and discovery threads in the life stories they shared during our interviews, they recount moments when they have consciously and deliberately told or enacted the performance script. Kandy, for example, described how because 'the media only wanted the good news' she would silence stories about the difficulties she was facing being away from her young daughter. The press wanted performance stories, she felt, so that is what she gave them. There is a strong sense in Luke's story of him 'trying on' the part of athlete, rather than embracing and internalising the performance script. For a time, for example, Luke stopped attending church on Sunday mornings (which, it was felt, interfered with training) yet continued to attend church in the evening. As far as the coach was concerned, Luke had stopped attending church. Thus, Luke appeared to others to be putting sport before his faith and thereby demonstrating 'commitment' to the performance script. Berni too (in Chapter 9) describes playing the part when she deliberately presented a very different (confident, optimistic, improving) self to potential sponsors.

Tony (a 24-year-old professional rugby union player) is one individual whose life story demonstrates clearly how, at times, he plays the part of athlete. This excerpt, shared while talking about his attempts to regain a place in the first team following an injury, provides an illustration:

TONY: I went to see him [the coach] and said, 'Look, I thought I've been playing well for the second team, what's happened the last couple of months?' And he said, 'Well, you haven't been to see me. Your attitude stinks.' Basically my fitness coach had snaked me and said I hadn't done any extras and what killed me was I had to go and see him for him to tell me this. If I had known that that was the way I was being perceived then I would have done something about it. I wouldn't have done anything drastic because I felt like I was working hard anyway but I would have probably done something so that they know I've been working hard, sort of thing. For an example, they do a core group – like core stability through here every morning at 8 o'clock. There's special people need to do it, so once I got this bollocking for being last, being perceived as being lazy, the next day I went to this core group – and to be quite honest with you I don't think it makes any difference – and I went and did it for a week.

KITRINA: So the sole reason you're doing it is to be perceived as more serious?

TONY: Yeah. So I go in there, get my folder, I'm in there at 8 o'clock every morning with one other bloke, something like that, and then I got a tick for saying I'm in there and then I'm perceived for doing work. It's not really made that much difference to my body, but to the way they perceive me it's massive. By the end of the two weeks: 'Oh, his attitude has really changed.' Know what I mean? And it was bollocks and we knew it was bollocks! Every Wednesday we sit around after eating talking about perception and how it's happened to every one of us, how we've all gone in and seen our fitness coach and he's said something to me like: 'You haven't done this.' And then you'd have to prove it to him, you have to go up and say: 'I've been working really hard on this, I need another programme 'cos I've just been working really hard on this one. I'm on the end of my phase two, can you give me another programme for phase three 'cos I feel like I'm putting on loads of muscle?' And he'd be, like: 'That's really good, really impressed with you.' Then the next meeting … he'll say to the coach: 'Tony is just outstanding at the moment, I really think you should give him a go. His body is unbelievable.' He hasn't even seen my body! He hasn't done any calliper testing! He just knows from what I've said to him.

This account offers valuable insights into psychosocial dynamics within elite sport culture – particularly the ways in which athletes both *shape* and are *shaped by* the expectations, perceptions and behaviours of (powerful) others. When Tony describes how 'my fitness coach had snaked me and said I hadn't done any extras', he alludes to a widely shared assumption or belief within sport culture (here, on the part of coaches) that hard physical work, dedication and doing more than asked is required to perform at the highest level. This orientation is consistent with the contours of the performance narrative where dedication is considered essential, a particular attitude is expected and sport is storied as work. In Tony's account, two members of the coaching staff are portrayed as subscribing to the values of this narrative type, expecting – or demanding – signs of dedication (i.e. a particular attitude) and hard work (i.e. commitment to additional physical training) as a prerequisite to being a professional athlete.

This excerpt also reveals that as a professional athlete Tony considers it is, first, *necessary* and, second, *that he is able* to control, manage or influence the decisions of powerful others. As he put it: 'If I had known that that was the way I was being perceived then I would have done something about it.' Here, Tony works in a planned, active, self-conscious and targeted manner to manipulate the perceptions of powerful others whose decisions exert a very real influence on his career development and earning potential. These decisions, in Tony's account, are subjective judgements made on the basis of Tony's behaviour and talk. In other words, the coach's observations of what Tony does and the stories he tells (publicly) provide the basis for the decision that Tony is not ready to return to the first team.

To effect change in the coaches' perceptions, it is less that Tony sees a need to change what he actually *does* (in a concrete, embodied way), but rather that he sees a need to publicise, market or promote those aspects of himself that are communicated as desirable by the coaching staff. In his account: 'I wouldn't have done anything drastic because I felt like I was working hard anyway but I would have probably done something so that they know I've been working hard.' Thus, Tony consciously and deliberately changes the kinds of stories he tells the coaching staff and adjusts aspects of his behaviour (such as attending the morning 'core training' session) to appear in a way that is consistent with their expectations. Tony makes these changes even though they result in neither subjective improvement in performance nor objective reduction in body fat. The direction of change or realignment is, we suggest, towards the script of the performance narrative: Tony realigns his *public* stories and behaviour to fit more closely with the kind of performance story that is expected – or demanded – by the coaching staff.

Tony's actions may be understood, in Goffman's (1959) terms, as a particular *presentation* of self designed to manage or influence the responses of others. In the preceding excerpt, we see this process in action as Tony presents himself in the role commonly expected of professional athletes. This is *not* an identity or self that Tony stories outside of sport culture, but rather an aspect of self that is presented or performed when required. He behaves much like an actor does when playing a particular character. The role that he plays fits the script of the performance narrative. Thus, Tony plays the part of athlete (as defined by the terms of the performance narrative) while immersed in professional sport culture, where his career and earnings depend on decisions made by powerful others who subscribe to the performance narrative.

Yet this is not a part that Tony takes as his authentic self; it is not a story he routinely tells elsewhere. Rather, Tony is consciously aware that he is giving a performance. Within different cultural settings – where there is no need to tell this story or fulfil this identity – Tony presents a broader, multidimensional, dialogical self. During the interview, for example, Tony variously shared stories of his family, his partner, his passion for cooking and desire to train as a chef, and his love of theatre and dance. These diverse stories demonstrate that Tony has established a repertoire of self-positions from which he narrates his life. It is not the case that Tony's life is storied from the singular, monological position of 'athlete'. Rather, Tony's stories demonstrate a dialogical self that is constructed through an array of stories told from multiple self-positions (Lysaker and Lysaker, 2006).

Through this process, Tony is able to both survive (or thrive) in professional sport culture while covertly resisting cultural pressures towards a singular athletic identity. Without at times playing the part of athlete, it seems likely that Tony's sport career would be hindered through his continued exclusion from the first team. On the other hand, by adopting or internalising the performance narrative as his own story and authentic self, he risks sacrificing valuable and important aspects of his identity. This is important given the threats that adherence to the performance narrative poses for identity development and well-being.

When Tony says, 'It's not really made that much difference to my body, but to the way they perceive me it's massive', he suggests that particular performances or presentations of self really do work (and may even be necessary) for success in elite sport. They work not because they affect objective performance, but because coaches and selectors (and others too) typically *expect* them. Matching the kind of self an athlete performs and the stories he or she tells to the preferences of coaches and selectors can be an effective way to modify their perceptions and decisions. Doing so can significantly affect career development and earning potential. Tony's story suggests that these processes are not uncommon: he recounts how, in behind-the-scenes or backstage conversations, teammates shared similar experiences, leading to agreement that 'it's happened to every one of us'.

For those individuals who do not live the part of athlete, a relevant question at this point might be: is it possible to get on within elite sport culture and not, at times, play the part of athlete? We think the answer is likely to be no. This is not because performance stories are necessary for high-level performance (as Chapters 5 and 6 show), but that performance stories are expected or required by 'gatekeepers' in elite and professional sport. By this we mean those who have power and influence over sportspeople's careers – coaches, selectors, managers, performance directors, sponsors and media professionals. Our research to date has led us to the view that few successful sportspeople have been able to navigate elite sport culture without – from time to time – playing the part of athlete.

On this basis, should sport psychologists who wish to help and support aspiring high-level athletes begin teaching their clients how to play the part of athlete, in the name of career progression? Tony's ability to do so demonstrably improved his professional prospects. Our position is that there would be much potential value in aspiring athletes developing a more *informed understanding* of the mechanics of elite sport culture that we have described in this book. Being aware of the myth of the performance narrative – that it is *not* the only route to success and that it is a story which ends badly for the teller – would be a good start. An understanding of the distinctions between *living* the part and *playing* the part of athlete, as we have described in this chapter, would also be helpful. It seems to us that developing and sustaining awareness of the difference between these two ways of being would help an individual avoid internalising a potentially limiting and dangerous exclusive performance script. While we see playing the part as preferable to living the part, we are cautious advocating it as an entirely benign strategy. This is because it poses some risks to identity development as, over time, we risk *becoming* the parts we play.

In Judith Butler's terms, Tony's words and actions may be seen as the *performance* of a particular identity that is valued and rewarded within a specific cultural setting (in Tony's case, professional sport). Butler (1990: 25) argues that 'identity is performatively constituted by the very "expressions" that are said to be its result'. Our understanding of this point is that we create our selves by performing particular roles, behaviours and actions. By continually performing a certain self, do we eventually take on the characteristics of that self? Butler's point, as we understand it, is that while we may *think* we are performing a certain self through our words and actions, we are actually *creating* that self, both in terms of others' understanding of us and our understanding of ourselves.

Transferring this insight back to Tony's example, we might consider the following questions: is there a point where performing so many 'required' actions leaves no time or space for the behaviours that support a multidimensional life story (for Tony: cooking, theatre, ballet, time with family, time with partner)? How long would Tony have to go to core training before it begins to change his story in this way? How many further actions would Tony need to be called upon to perform (to show he is 'serious') before the self he is 'playing' takes over from the self he is 'living'? To be sustainable, stories must be *believable* in that they are connected (in some way) to the material conditions of the teller's life (Gergen and Gergen, 2006). Telling a certain story calls for certain actions that fit its plot (Frank, 2010). Telling and enacting performance-oriented tales and actions is therefore risky on three counts. First, recounting more and more performance tales erodes the actions and behaviours that stem from alternative story types. They cannot be sustained because they do not fit the stories the teller is currently advancing. Second, there is a danger that by imposing more and more actions (that follow the performance plot), other actions and behaviours are eroded. They cannot be sustained simply through lack of time. As a result, the alternative life stories that are derived from those actions may perish. Third, if we are continually presenting an illusory self, how can others ever really get to know us? It may well be that adverse relational consequences may follow for those who continually play the part of athlete.

Resisting the part of athlete

In contrast to individuals like Suzanne whose stories align with the performance narrative, we have established that the stories and actions of some athletes – like Tony when he is outside sport culture – do not follow the performance plot. While individuals like Tony *covertly* sustain alternative stories and actions, another group of highly successful sportspeople *overtly* maintain a range of stories and actions that contravene the performance script. These individuals avoid living, 'buying into' or internalising the performance narrative. Instead, they *resist the part of athlete* by sustaining a life story that deviates from the performance narrative by drawing on alternative narrative types. We describe their resistance as *overt* because they *publicly* recount stories and demonstrate actions that align with their multidimensional story. These individuals, it seems, are able to resist pressures to story or enact elements of the performance script.

Kandy (in Chapter 5) provides one example of an athlete who is able, at times, to resist the part of athlete. While her story portrays moments where she plays the part of athlete, there are many other moments when she explicitly rejects this role. For example, she describes times when she is a mother, a wife and herself as entirely separate from, and different to, the world of professional golf. Kandy rejects the performance script's prioritisation of winning and being the best, to narrate instead *her* prioritisation of joy, exploration, relationships and freedom through golf. By the end of the story he shared with us, Luke (in Chapter 7) had arrived at a place where he explicitly and overtly rejected the terms of the performance narrative. He left the centre of excellence to move back home, marry his girlfriend, attend church again and embark on a teacher-training course. Luke said these changes had no effect on his objective results, his times. Luke, however, felt a need to exit a significant cauldron of elite sport culture (the performance centre) in order to embody and sustain his resistance.

The following excerpts shared by Alex (a 29-year-old British Paralympic swimmer) provide a further illustration of the ways in which some individuals are able to resist the part of athlete:

> Where I live is a prime example. I live there because I want to be happy. And I have to travel eight miles to get to my training venue, which isn't far

anywhere else in the country, but I have to do it through London traffic so sometimes it can be a 45-minute journey and I knew that when I moved to London. But I thought I would much rather be in London and be surrounded by all of my friends and able to almost check in and out of a swimming training session. I can just leave it behind. I knew that when I moved to London, that just my sort of living costs would go through the roof but I thought it would be worth it in terms of just being happier. 'Cos I was training in Manchester before and it was all swim, swim, swim. I'd moved to Manchester and, as you can tell, I'm not from the north, and I moved there and I didn't ... know anyone who lived in Manchester.

Education was very important to me.... I didn't want to be beholden to swimming because sometimes the people you get mixed up with in sport at a management level are just the worst people on earth. They're bad managers, poor communicators.... I'm talking about performance managers, team managers, performance directors. Sport is littered with them. One of the things that has been great when I've been on the team is I've just thought if I want to I can just quit this now and I can go out and I can get a job earning the same amount of money and my life, where I live, isn't in danger and all that sort of thing. There are, you know, a lot of people on the sports teams now, on the swimming team now, and I think in a lot of sports now, where they haven't got an education, any sort of further or higher education, and you do kind of look at them and think, what are you going to do if you don't swim? Literally, what are you going to do?

Within Alex's story is a sense of deviance – even mischievousness – as this multiple Paralympic medal-winning athlete is able to disregard the terms of the expected performance script, yet still reach the highest level in sport. His story challenges the argument that achieving excellence prohibits exploration of alternative roles and behaviours (e.g. Warriner and Lavallee, 2008) and requires the sacrifice of relationships (e.g. Holt and Dunn, 2004). It also contravenes a core premise of the performance narrative that the *only* way to be successful in elite sport is to place sport performance at the centre of one's life story in four ways: Alex (1) puts happiness before performance; (2) places maintenance of friendships alongside or ahead of training; (3) believes there is more to life than just 'swim, swim, swim'; and (4) refuses to be 'beholden to swimming'.

According to McLeod (1997: 94): 'Even when a teller is recounting a unique set of individual, personal events, he or she can only do so by drawing upon story structures and genres drawn from the narrative resources of a culture.' In other words, as we suggested in Chapter 2, personal stories draw on culturally available narrative scripts. Evident within Alex's story are (at least) two alternative narrative types or scripts. The scripts of these dialogical narratives call for connection, interdependence, exploration, diversity and multiplicity over and above individuation, personal gain, singularity and linearity. These alternatives are, we believe, important because they provide *a point of resistance* to the dominant narrative.

The first of these is the relational narrative, as described in Chapter 5. In this type of story relationships with others are storied as equally important as – or more important than – training or performance outcomes. Gilligan (1993) describes a host of positive developmental consequences that arise through successfully sustaining a relational orientation. Alex's story explicitly reveals relational strands when he talks about leaving Manchester where he didn't 'know anyone' to return to London to 'be surrounded by all of my friends'. He doesn't merely 'talk the talk', but also *enacts* relational values by relocating. He prioritises, in both words and actions, being able to see his friends alongside or ahead of sport performance.

The second alternative story type evident in Alex's accounts is the discovery narrative (discussed in Chapter 5). In discovery stories, self-worth is not related to sporting achievement, and the need to explore and discover a full life takes precedence over the need to perform in sport, regardless of the expectations of others. For example, Alex expressly chose to continue his education, as doing so, he felt, would provide him with freedom and independence from swimming. It offered a means that he was able to continue exploring and discovering life without being, in his words, 'beholden to swimming'. Gaining qualifications provided a sense of freedom that would allow him, should he wish, to 'just leave [swimming] behind'. It provided a level of reassurance and independence which meant, as he put it, that 'I can just quit [swimming] now and I can go out and I can get a job earning the same amount of money and my life, where I live, isn't in danger'.

The two excerpts from Alex's story illustrate how, rather than being linear and monological like the performance narrative, his story is instead *dialogical* or *polyphonic*. According to Lysaker and Lysaker (2006: 59), within dialogical models of the self, 'complementary and opposing aspects of the self, or self-positions, are thought to bring significance to one another through their interaction or dialogue, leading to the experience in the moment of a sense of personal depth'. In a similar way, Douglas Ezzy (2000: 613) describes polyphonic narratives as characterised by 'overlaid, interwoven and often contradictory stories and values'. Alex's story is notable in that, like Kandy's story, it is told from multiple self-positions, in contrast to the singular self-position from which performance stories are articulated. In contrast to tellers of linear or monological stories, Ezzy (2000: 613) suggests, 'polyphonic narrators embrace many of the contradictions and tensions in their accounts rather than suppressing them'.

Research suggests that the distinction between a monological (linear) story and a dialogical (polyphonic) story has implications for both psychosocial well-being and long-term personal development (e.g. Ezzy, 2000; Hermans, 2006; Lysaker and Lysaker, 2006). Not least of these is the assumption underlying linear narratives that individuals can control their lives, minimising the significance of other people and of environmental constraints. 'In contrast,' Ezzy (2000: 616) writes,

> polyphonic narratives recognise the limited control humans have over their environment and that outcomes are contingent on these environmental and

social factors. In polyphonic narratives people are both active agents and passive recipients, pushed around by forces beyond their control.

A sense of this two-way or reciprocal process unfolding is present in Alex's story when, although recognising the limits to the control he has over his sport career (e.g. through the influence of managers and directors), he creates and sustains future options for himself through conscious, concrete actions. Critically, these actions (e.g. choosing to live where he can maintain relationships, continuing his education) provide the embodied material or resources for authentic relational and discovery stories. Again, these actions are important because, as Gergen and Gergen (2006) note, building a life story is never simply a matter of inventing a story. Rather, they suggest, the individual's story needs to be *believable* (i.e. connected to current life conditions) and *actionable* (i.e. may be put into practice). In this sense, we are never entirely free to invent our life story; instead, our personal story is shaped and constrained in particular ways by our embodied experience (see Carless, 2010). At the same time, through the process of *interpellation* (Frank, 2010), stories call upon a person to behave or act in ways that are appropriate to its plot. The two – embodied experience and story – therefore exist in a reciprocal relationship, with each affecting the other.

On this basis, and in light of career transition research among elite sportspeople (e.g. Carless and Douglas, 2009; Douglas and Carless, 2009a; Sparkes, 1998; McKenna and Thomas, 2007), Alex's story may be regarded as a positive one from the perspective of long-term development and psychosocial well-being. A particular feature of his story is a refusal to adopt an exclusive athletic identity in favour of sustaining a broad-based, multidimensional identity. While at times this places Alex's story in tension with elite sport culture, he reasons that this friction is worthwhile for the benefits it brings.

In earlier chapters we discussed how the dominant performance script insists that, to be successful at the elite or professional level, athletes must be single-minded, resist other facets of life and relegate relationships. For those who follow the performance script, so total is the focus on sport performance that the person and the job become inseparable. This is clearly not the case for athletes like Alex who achieve excellence while overtly resisting the monological performance narrative. These individuals story their lives instead around the contours of a dialogical relational and/or discovery narrative. While relational and discovery stories are at odds with the dominant narrative, the experience of sportspeople like Alex underscores our suggestion that they do not compromise performance excellence yet promise positive consequences for identity and well-being.

Resisting a culturally dominant narrative is, however, never easy and rarely without costs. One cost is the risk of being excluded or ostracised from a culture on the basis of perceived difference from 'norms' or expectations. For elite and professional athletes, this kind of exclusion has the potential to lead to loss of earnings and/or career development through, for example, de-selection or loss of sponsorship. On this basis, sustained resistance may be close to impossible within the contemporary culture of high-level sport. It may only be individuals like Alex who – as a well-established athlete competing in an objectively measurable sport – have the realistic possibility of sustained and public resistance.

According to Nelson (2001: 150), counterstories provide 'the necessary means of resistance' when faced with an oppressive dominant or master narrative. 'Through their function of narrative repair,' she writes, 'counterstories thus open up the possibility that the person could attain, regain, or extend her freedom of moral agency'. Nelson goes on to distinguish three levels of resistance to a dominant narrative: refusal, repudiation and contestation.

> To *refuse* a master narrative is to deny that it applies to oneself and to tend one's own counterstory, perhaps without serious effort or any hope that others will take it up. To *repudiate* a master narrative is to use the self-understanding arising from a counterstory to oppose others' applying the narrative to oneself, but the opposition is piecemeal. To *contest* a master narrative is to oppose it with a counterstory both publicly and systematically.
>
> (Nelson, 2001: 169)

Reflecting on the stories of the sportspeople we have interviewed in the light of this theory, we can see different levels of resistance taking place within the culture of high-level sport. Luke's story provides an example of a young athlete who has *refused* the dominant performance script. Prior to sharing his story with us, his resistance appeared to be predominantly a personal process: he tended his own counter-story (moments from which we presented in Chapter 7) but did not seriously use his story to challenge the picture or understanding others in sport held of him. In contrast, Kandy and Alex demonstrate a further level of resistance, akin to Nelson's repudiation of a dominant narrative. Not only did these individuals refuse to identify themselves under the terms of the performance narrative, but they actively challenged (at times) *others* who tried to impose performance values upon them.

To contest a dominant narrative 'both publicly and systematically' seems to us to be beyond the abilities of any one individual. Nelson (2001) provides the black power movement and the gay and lesbian activists as examples of times when oppressive master narratives have been successfully contested. Both of these examples required entire communities to join together to publicly and systematically challenge and overturn racist and heterosexist cultural narratives. Contestation was not possible for anyone alone. A community of stories was necessary. We believe that the time is right for a similar (though admittedly more modest) contestation of the ways in which sportspeople are represented and constructed by the performance narrative. We hope the collection of stories we offer in this book will galvanise this task.

Note

1 This chapter contains material adapted and developed from Carless and Douglas (2013a).

9 The consequences of stories at retirement[1]

> It's just a viewpoint from someone who's just finished, as opposed to when you are
> in the middle of it. You think: 'Oh sod it!' You think you're bullet-proof, you're
> invincible. And now I've found myself not as bullet-proof as I thought I was.
>
> (International cricketer)

It is widely recognised that understanding retirement necessitates seeing withdrawal
from sport as a transitional process as opposed to a one-off event (e.g. McKenna and
Thomas, 2007). Retirement experience can only be understood in light of earlier
events in the athlete's life and the personal meaning of sport. In this chapter, therefore, we build on earlier chapters to explore the consequences of stories at retirement. In Chapter 7 we showed how the process of enculturation provides young
sportspeople with a particular toolkit of narrative resources to scaffold identity development and to shape how they make sense of events. We also explored how being
embedded in different environments affects the repertoire of stories that are available. In Chapter 8 we examined how individuals negotiate the culture of high-level
sport by either living, resisting or playing the part of 'athlete' as scripted by the performance narrative. In this chapter we consider the consequences of these processes
for sportspeople's experiences over time, with a particular focus on retirement.

We do so by exploring the life stories of two multiple tournament-winning
professional golfers, recounted during our longitudinal research, spanning pre-
and post-retirement. The first, Christiana, we consider to have predominantly
lived the part of athlete, narrating her life in ways that align with the performance narrative. We begin the chapter by telling Christiana's life story in her own
words, gathered through interviews with Kitrina over a six-year period. The
second, Kandy, we see as mostly resisting the part of athlete and storying her life
in line with the discovery narrative. We shared Kandy's story in Chapter 5.

The kinds of questions we want to address in this chapter are: how do professional athletes experience retirement? What factors shape whether or not withdrawal from high-level sport is experienced as traumatic? What are the
consequences at retirement of storying one's life around the performance
narrative? What might be the consequences for those who resist this narrative
type? Can withdrawal from professional sport ever be experienced positively?

Christiana's story

I went to boarding-school, so most of my memories of sport start there. We played tennis, rounders, lacrosse and hockey – typical team sports mostly. I just played simply because I loved playing in a team – the camaraderie, the banter. And I was good at it. I just like playing sport. That's the trouble, I don't mind what it is, I love competing.

You'd see me going out to play hockey at school with my friends – if I could get anyone to join in, which was always difficult. We used to go out on the tennis court with a hockey ball and make up drills, and we had loads of fun running around trying to practise little bits of technique ready for the next week and the match. It's funny, looking back, I taught myself so much. I love learning like that. If I could learn other things on a sport pitch I'd probably remember it better. There was one teacher, Mr Bramley, who used to do that – he'd take us out to the hockey pitch to teach us about angles. Maths for people like me who didn't like sitting down in a classroom!

Perhaps, because I hadn't really done anything academically at school, I'm not saying that it was 100 per cent of my motivation to be a pro, but it was a part of my motivation to succeed at something or to be good at golf, because I wasn't good at anything else. I didn't do very well in exams and nearly all the teachers at school said I was useless. School is so result orientated – if you don't produce the results then you're viewed as a failure. That's been an ongoing problem I've had since I was at school – lacking belief in myself because I was told I was useless. Except for sport that is.

I started golf in my teens and, as I said, I just loved sport – any sport. You introduce me to any sport and I'll have a go. I was very competitive. So I took lessons for six months and then entered a few tournaments. I was rubbish to start with, when I first started playing, but it didn't bother me then really. Then I got into the club side and then got into the county golf setup and then it starts, you start to think about being a pro then, it's at the back of your mind. Once I got in the Curtis Cup team, that was when I thought: it's about time, I should be earning my living from golf. I wanted to turn pro. I had no doubts. I wanted to win and I wanted to earn a living out of it. So it wasn't a huge decision. It took me about half a day – not even that long, a couple of hours. I wanted the next challenge.

Golf consumed me. It was everything to me. I just went out and played and tried to compete. Compete against anybody, everybody. I didn't think about who I was competing against. It's just: I've got to play the golf course and I've got to try and shoot the lowest I can. And of course you have your sights on the Solheim Cup and I wanted to win the big events – the Open – and I wanted to go and test myself in America because that's where the best players in the world were playing. I wanted to see if I could compete against them or not. And it was great – I could!

I suppose the fact that I was good at something was important to me, boosts your confidence. But with sport you tend to be on an imaginary roller-coaster. When I play well, you're less tense and just ride on a wave of doing well. Other times I can't seem to cope with not doing well. I find it very difficult to laugh on the golf course – I'm a miserable, miserable cow on the golf course. Miserable if I didn't play how I wanted to, really in horrible bad moods, all day. You know how I played by my face. I've always been a bit like that, but what I'm saying is in recent years I'd be able to stop that but I am finding it difficult at the moment. I tend to get annoyed, irritated. I'm all right as long as people don't bug me and start talking about the game or saying 'you should have done this' or 'you should have done that'. I've gone, 'for goodness sake shut up and leave me alone!' But most of the time I can handle that. I mean, sometimes it does affect me inside, you just feel – it drains you. You are not doing as well as you think, you have bad breaks. But, you know, I've come back fighting. But then I do get tired fighting sometimes.

Once it becomes a job it becomes more of a grind because it's all based on performance. If you get to top level or you become good, you start thinking about the result rather than just the playing. When you're a winner it's something you get used to and if you're not winning it is kind of frustrating. You think, or I have thought, *'perhaps it is the end, it's the end of my career'.* And those thoughts are coming into my head quite a lot. I am struggling. I don't particularly enjoy the travel any more. Places like this, OK, yes, it's just superb. And I enjoy some of the golf courses. And I've got a lot of good friends out here. But the sacrifices are tough, the costs are high, more so now that I am getting older than when I was younger. You give up home life, being with my family.

I would have loved to have children. I don't know, but I think it's probably too late now to be honest. That's history. I would like to have done but I don't think I could cope with it now. And you know that is something, as a woman – I don't know whether it's something you yearn for, or if that's innate, or being a woman? And it's the same with getting married. Sometimes I think, *'Yeah! I would love to'.* And then other times I think, *'No! I'm not made out to be married.'* I would probably say that if I hadn't been successful at golf then I may well have been successful at something else. But the fact that I haven't been married or I haven't had any relationships or stuff – that is something that I will always wonder about, whether I failed at, you know? So my emotions go up and down but are not particularly constant. And there's pressure and tension just trying to do well. You know that sort of mental pressure.

Recently I've been thinking, *'perhaps I don't belong here'.* I never really experienced that before. Before I always thought, *'I'm gonna show 'em!'* Not that it really mattered whether I did or not – but that was how I felt inside. I wanted to get on with it and enjoy the moment. Now I feel frightened – not frightened, but tense.

I Love Competing, Not Faffing About

Unless I can win, don't want to be here
As long as I'm competitive, I'll stay out here
I *just* want to win ... *just* a couple more

But, you think, I'm getting on
Older, frightening to be honest
What am I going to do?
Not sure

You don't want it to end:
Fun, being successful, winning, the attention
Coming down the last, the crowd cheering
Here I am!

Last week, came second
Disappointed
Wanted to win
But it was fun being up there again

I want to go out on a high
So hang on, stay out there
It is what you are used to!
It's my comfort zone

I haven't been up there at any point recently but in Atlanta I did a good first round and was up there and then my game fell apart. So I'm a bit confused about it really. I've always liked it up there – can't wait to get out there and compete. Whereas now I'm thinking, '*I can't wait until this is over*'. Ridiculous. I don't know why really. Maybe I'm frightened to fail? It could be that. I'm frightened to fail and make a mess of it – which I never used to worry about.

I get upset with the crowd now and I can't be rational about anything. I can't even enjoy it when people are clapping for me. It was always a goal of mine to win a major and then I found myself in a position to do it. I just wanted to finish it off. The last day was unreal. The thing was, the crowd wanted Yvonne to win and they were cheering for her. But I pretended it was for me. I would run up on to the green when she was walking on and when the crowd applauded her I was right next to her going 'thank you' as if they are all clapping for me. None of it was for me! Now they *are* clapping for me and I just want them to go away. It's ridiculous.

Thing is, like I said before, my emotions were up and down. Some days I *think* I want to be in contention and then if I do reasonably well I think, '*I don't want to be here*'. I've always coped before, but now I don't feel like I can. That's the emotion I am going through. It's like I'm gone – I can't cope.

S T R E S S

Not thinking, no perspective
Nothing in the right order
Emotions up and down
One day runs into the next

Like you said, yesterday:
'Chris, move on'
But I am not able

I am tired out for some reason
Not able to do what I know
Up and down, round and about
That's me at the moment

I think most sportspeople would say: 'I'm gonna pack it in 'cos I'm going through a tough time.' Because sport isn't an exact science. The last couple of years I've had that feeling, sort of, slowly coming, creeping up – rather than one 'puff!'

I Forgot to Mention:

Osteoarthritis, physio van
Every week, joints swelling up
Couldn't turn left, nerve referral
Aches and pains, stiff and sore
Terribly tight, knees and neck
Losing fitness, putting on weight
Risking injury just going to the gym
Tablets, injections ... look out liver!
I'm a ticking clock

I think with society – I'm not just talking about family, I'm talking about comments that I've had from other people – people expect things of you. My Mum got into that a little bit, possibly. I don't think she meant it in a bad way. She couldn't quite understand why I wasn't shooting good scores, she said: 'You used to shoot good scores what's happened to you?' You're not that bothered about it yourself, but suddenly, you *do* become bothered about it because it's been put in your mind. Not necessarily directly, it's indirectly. It's the same with other people, your fans. It's the first thing they say. It's not 'How are you?' They want to know 'What did you shoot today?' And you get into that syndrome because of other people too. It's not necessarily something you think yourself but that influence is forced upon you. And you start thinking about yourself and then you get upset with yourself and think, *'well hang on, what's going on here?'* I think I'm afraid of upsetting people. I'm always worried that I've upset people or hurt people. It makes me feel terrible, guilty. Thinking: *'Why did you do that? That was horrible.'*

I can see that much more clearly now than when I was in the situation. But *then* you start getting tied up with what *they* ask about – when you didn't really want to. In fact, when you're trying *not* to. Influences from fans can be very difficult. It happens much more in the media 'cos you're taken to the press tent regardless of whether you win or not – when you're not even in contention. Luckily I've got a great rapport with the people who report on women's golf but I'm guarded about controversial issues. I don't feel threatened by them, so I told them I was depressed, but they've just not necessarily reported it. It's not newsworthy. I told them but they haven't written about it. They're worried about who is winning the tournament – not whether Christiana Anderson is going to retire.

I think it was relief when I did retire. Because I did find it difficult at the end there – with my short game and stuff, the mental battles, sleepless nights. It was a huge relief. But it's been harder. I've had huge support from my family but what to do next has been very difficult. 'Cos when you're in sport you get that sort of buzz, the adrenalin rush, the nervousness and the crowds and adulation. I used to love performing in front of crowds and all that. Some of the tournaments where I've won there, there have been lots and lots of people coming up to me afterwards.

Last week, when I went to an event, I thought, '*Crikey! I do miss that.*' But I had a long chat with Tess on the phone and I've talked to you, had lots of chats. There was a programme on television about two footballers and they were talking about how they missed the buzz of going into a stadium with thousands of people there and they said you'd never replace that. Other people were saying to me that you'd find something else that gives you that buzz. And I said, 'Well, I don't know if I can.' Someone else says to me, 'You need to find something that gives you a buzz.' But it wouldn't be the same – digging my potatoes up and eating 'em, you can't connect the two. It's like chalk and cheese. I went to an event recently to see a couple of players and I was waiting at the eighteenth, you know, you stand there and you see them coming up the eighteenth and that's when it hit me again. It brought back those same feelings. Euphoria! I used to love walking up the eighteenth and waving at the crowd, being on a stage, performing I suppose. Towards the end I didn't. I got stage fright.

But what I'm saying is that when I saw somebody walking up the eighteenth and it wasn't me, those memories came back to me again. But it only lasted about five minutes and then I went inside and had a coffee with Tess. I said to her, 'I've got those feelings again.' She said, she was brilliant 'cos she said, 'Chris, you know, I've talked to a lot of people and they said they didn't get a sense of equilibrium for some time. Some people do and some don't. In the end we're all different.' I know some of the footballers who've retired, they get much more support from the PFA in terms of getting them into some other work. But I'm thinking, '*Crikey! What am I going to do?*' Suddenly you lose your confidence and you think, '*Well, I'm no good at anything.*'

Hindsight is a wonderful thing. Perhaps I should have done a bit more. But I was under the impression, because of certain things which had been said to me, they said to me, 'When you retire you'll be all right because of what you've done in golf you'll be able to get into something easily.' And I'm thinking, '*I don't know about that.*' I did feel depressed. In fact it consumed me. There were two things. One, missing the buzzing excitement of walking up the last, the crowds and all that business. Then there was: *what am I going to do next?* That sort of hit me all at once. I was depressed and then you start to question whether you made the right choice. I felt, *well why am I here? What am I going to do? How am I going to earn a living?* The money wasn't the concern – I didn't want to do *nothing*.

When it happened I thought, '*I haven't got anything.*' I'm not qualified or anything. So people don't want to touch me. That's what I've found. They talk about a seat on a bus; the trouble is, we haven't got a seat for you. We think you're valuable, but we don't know what at. So, I don't get anywhere. And that's what hit me. I'm valuable, but what are my skills? They need to be channelled in a direction to get some qualifications so I can move forward. Everyone I talked to said I was very valuable – but unfortunately we haven't got a seat on the bus for you.

The troubling psychological space in which Christiana found herself following retirement is suggested by the last paragraph of her story above and crystallised in the phrase 'we haven't got a seat on the bus for you'. Despite similarly successful careers in golf (in terms of, for example, professional tournament wins, national and European representation) Kandy found herself in a very different place following retirement. 'For me,' she said some 18 months after retiring, 'all the seats are mine and I go with the bus wherever I want.' Kandy told Kitrina:

I thought, when I retired, I am pretty sure 200 per cent I am not going to miss golf, competition. But maybe, I thought, after the excitement is gone maybe life is going to be boring because when you have that kind of life you never stop, you're never at home. So I thought maybe being home, you know, the quiet life, normal life, I wasn't sure after the excitement is gone. But no, no, no, no! The excitement is still there, every day, you know. I wake up and I am so happy to have the life I have. I think anything I do, it doesn't matter what, I enjoy it, every day I say, this is a beautiful day, I am glad to have this day and I enjoy everything I do – golf or no golf.... That is behind me, it's closed. I never want to go back and play! Never!

These remarkably different stories beg the question: *what led each of these women to experience retirement in such profoundly different ways?* To answer this question it is necessary to consider the kinds of stories that each woman developed and sustained across her life in sport.

Building a personal story

Lieblich and colleagues (1998: 7) suggest that one's life story '*is* one's identity, a story created, told, revised, and retold throughout life'. In a similar vein, Spence (1982: 458) argues that 'the core of our identity is really a narrative thread that gives meaning to life provided – and this is the big if – that it is never broken'. Christiana's and Kandy's life stories differ notably, as do the identities they developed over time. This observation is key to making sense of their contrasting retirement experiences – which may be understood in simple terms through Spence's metaphor of a 'narrative thread'.

The narrative thread that Kandy created through her discovery life story contains many strands that she wove intricately together. The thread of Kandy's narrative was strong by virtue of being multidimensional and dialogical – it was able to survive intact across her sport career and into retirement. In contrast, Christiana's life story may be characterised as relying on a single strand: sport performance. The thread of her performance story, while strong when sport was going well, became vulnerable whenever her performance was threatened. In what follows we explore this premise in more detail.

Christiana: 'Golf was everything to me'

Christiana's stories of her childhood portray a love of sport and a competitive nature (e.g. 'I started golf in my teens and as I said, I just loved sport – any sport. You introduce me to any sport and I'll have a go. I was very competitive'). Stories of her childhood suggest that sport was the *only* activity in which she achieved success and, thus, the *only* avenue through which she was able to develop a positive sense of self. In noting how 'everyone is result orientated' and not producing is 'failure', Christiana indicates the type of culture in which she was immersed at school and expresses a perception that there is no altern- ative *but* to be 'result oriented' if one is to avoid 'failure'. As time went on, Christiana storied her progress through the amateur game and into the profes- sional ranks as 'natural' and a result of her 'hunger' for further competition and success. Her stories of smooth progression in sport contrasted with the dif- ficulties she described in other areas of life where she recalls being told she was 'useless'.

These characteristics mirror several hallmarks of the performance narrative that we discussed in Chapter 4. We see similarities – in terms of plot – between Christiana's, Georgi's and Ryan's life stories. Like Georgi and Ryan, following this narrative plot left Christiana little space for meaningful talk of alternative roles, interests or activities beyond those that related directly to improving performance. As a consequence, it seems her identity came to be almost exclusively constituted in and through performance-related talk. Further, the identity Christiana constructed through these stories wasn't just *any* golfer but a very specific kind of golfer: a player at the top of the profes- sional game. The sense of self she developed was tenuous and dependent upon continued success on the professional tour. Golf was, as Christiana later put it, 'everything to me'.

Kandy: 'I never felt better because I won a tournament'

The types of stories Kandy told of her life – and consequently the self and iden- tity she created – differ markedly from Christiana. Kandy talks of excitement, exploration, playfulness, discovering travel and food, as opposed to competition and winning trophies. This is illustrated in the following exchange where Kandy explicitly resists the performance narrative definition of success (i.e. winning tournaments) to create a personally meaningful criterion of success.

KITRINA: How important was it for you to be successful at golf? How would you describe it?

KANDY: Successful for me is if you have a goal and you want to reach it, and if you reach it, you are successful. Not because you win a lot of money or because you win two or 22 tournaments. It is because if in your mind you want to realise a red square, if you have blue triangle, well, it is not really the same. But if, because of your work or because of your interest or because of your sacrifice or because of a lot of different things, you reach the red square, you are successful.

KITRINA: Was it important for you to reach the red square?

KANDY: Yes. Because I was brought up and educated to have a goal and to reach a goal. That's my mother's type of dedication and she always said you are born to play golf, you are born sporty, you are born to be a good player, and you *have* to do it.

KITRINA: Did you believe that?

KANDY: No. I thought, well no, at that time I thought I don't care. I don't mind. For me it was not the goal. The goal was to play good golf, to escape, and to go out and to discover other worlds. That was my red square.

Here, Kandy articulates a way of being that differs dramatically from the performance narrative where tournament wins are storied as the overriding priority. In doing so, she contravenes the expectations of others (e.g. her mother) who buy into the performance story, creating an alternative story (*her* 'red square') through which to evaluate her life.

This is not to say that Kandy did not work hard at golf. But, critically, her stories locate performance within the broader context of her life rather than being, as is the case with Christiana, the priority of life. Two examples should clarify this distinction. First, Kandy stories her motivation for golf as based upon the belief that being successful would improve the conditions of her life. As she put it, 'if I was working in golf and was good I could discover more, and to discover was interesting for me. So ... I had to work at golf.' Thus, golf was a *conduit* for other things, rather than the central *purpose* of her life. Second, as a consequence, Kandy's sense of self and identity were not storied as being dependent upon her golf performance. As she put it: 'The day I played badly, or the tournaments I played badly, it was not like, I am not good enough or I am bad. No! ... I never felt better because I won a tournament.'

Instead of revolving around performance, Kandy's stories evoke and prioritise a multidimensional life – in terms of interests, roles, an identity, a sense of self – *outside* golf. One example is her decision to give up her golf scholarship in the USA so she could move to Europe to marry. Another example was her decision to have a baby. In both instances Kandy's story deviates from the performance plot. Significantly, the discovery stories that underpinned Kandy's life *in* golf – being *life* stories rather than *performance* stories – held the potential to be projected into her future life after golf bringing the possibility of narrative continuity rather than disjuncture.

Living in sport culture

The stories both women developed had consequences for their day-to-day lives before they reached retirement. These consequences may be understood through the lens of narrative theory, in particular the need to create 'a satisfactory-enough alignment between individual experience and "the story of which I find myself a part"' (McLeod, 1997: 27). Narrative theorists suggest that the stakes in this task are high as success is associated with personal development and adaptation while failure can lead to stagnation and mental health problems (Crossley, 2000; McAdams, 1993). According to McLeod (2006), individuals are either positioned *by* a dominant narrative or, alternatively, they must proactively create personal stories that enable a different, more personally satisfactory position to be maintained. We use these points now to reflect on Christiana's and Kandy's stories of their lives within the culture of professional sport.

Christiana: 'You used to shoot good scores, what's happened to you?'

For much of her career Christiana is able to achieve a satisfactory-enough alignment between her life experiences and the dominant narrative in which she is embedded through telling performance stories. She is, however, only able to maintain this alignment *provided* she continues to win *and* dedicate her life to golf. When both of these conditions are met, Christiana's stories – alongside her sense of self – are relatively coherent and culturally endorsed, resulting in narrative 'fit' and relative psychological well-being. Problems occur, however, when there is a change in either her lived experience of performance (i.e. results) *or* the culture in which she is immersed (i.e. life outside golf). At these times, her changing circumstances begin to fall out of alignment with her personal performance story and tensions become evident.

The consequences of these tensions are illustrated, for example, when Christiana describes herself as a 'miserable, miserable cow on the golf course. Miserable if I didn't play how I wanted to, really in horrible bad moods, all day.' Her emotions are like 'an imaginary roller-coaster. When I play well, you're less tense and just ride on a wave of doing well. Other times I can't seem to cope with not doing well.' Revealed here are some of the emotional and psychological costs Christiana experienced during periods of poor form. Christiana's emotional ups and downs may be understood as a consequence of a lack of alignment between her performance story (which demands tournament wins) and her objective experience of poor form and disappointing results. Previously, when Christiana described success at the amateur and professional level she told of positive effects on the self in terms of self-esteem and confidence. At these times, her experiences aligned closely with the ideals of the performance narrative and, we suggest, she experienced harmony. When she fails to perform, however, her experience *does not* align with the performance story. The result is tension and emotional suffering.

It is significant that the emotions Christiana experienced during such periods are not only a result of her own stories. Christiana reveals that emotional difficulties resulted from being immersed in a culture where the expectations of *others* influenced her. At these times, Christiana describes being adversely affected when her experience (her golf performance) fails to align with (live up to) others' performance stories. Christiana shows that while she is at times able to reconcile this difference in herself, she exists within and is constrained by a culture where continued adherence to the performance narrative by family and fans perpetuates tensions.

The extent of Christiana's commitment to the performance narrative is underscored when she considers her life after tournament golf. Four years before retiring she stated: 'I think I can still be competitive, got a couple of goals still left that I want to achieve. I think as long as I feel, as long as I am competitive I would like to stay out here.' Two years later:

> I just love competing. Last week I came second, it was obviously disappointing in that I wanted to win, but it was fun, I enjoyed being up there again, it was just fun to be able to compete. I still like competing and I want to go out of it on a high.

These excerpts illustrate how Christiana told, and continued to tell, performance stories throughout her career. Despite failing to meet the terms of the performance narrative (i.e. not winning), she did *not* modify her personal story through adopting an alternative narrative template. In sticking to a performance story, Christiana had little in the way of a future orientation outside this narrative type. She seems to have experienced what Freeman (2003) terms *identity foreclosure* through self-narrowing, self-erosion, and a loss of multidimensionality and potential future selves.

A sense of identity foreclosure is illustrated in this excerpt:

CHRISTIANA: I think the fact that I haven't been married or I haven't had any relationships or stuff like that, you know, that is something that I will always wonder about, whether I failed at.

KITRINA: Would you like to have a family, children?

CHRISTIANA: Oh, I would have done but obviously I have had to sacrifice that. It's history. I am not sure I could cope with it now, you know, that is something, as a woman, you yearn for that. I don't know whether that's innate or being a woman *[pause]*.

KITRINA: What about getting married?

CHRISTIANA: The same. Sometimes I think, yeah, I would love to, and then other times I think, no, I am not, I'm not made out to be married, you know. So my emotions go up and down, not particularly constant.

In responding to a present-tense question of whether she would like to have a family, Christiana replies in the past tense. Here, Christiana seems to have *finalised* her own life: she believes it is too late for her to have children and she is 'not made out to be married'. Importantly, by saying that having a family is something she has 'obviously' had to 'sacrifice', Christiana sustains the view that *being a mother* and *being an elite athlete* are fundamentally incompatible. For her, in common with many female athletes (McGannon *et al.*, 2012), having a family *and* performing at the highest level in sport seem mutually exclusive choices. Christiana articulates the emotional costs of the conflict between what is expected of her as an athlete and what she feels is 'innate' as a woman. Within the sport culture, few (if any) question her sacrifice, yet in contemplating life outside professional sport she is unable to articulate a satisfactory alternative story.

Kandy: 'I am the owner of my life'

In contrast, Kandy's discovery stories *did not* align with the dominant performance narrative and tensions were apparent in golf contexts. This is evident, for example, when Kandy portrays a lack of alignment between her story and the expectations of other people and the press. In her words: 'People were expecting, the press, people, but in my mind golf was not a priority. "You have to play well because they expect and have an image." No! Golf was important because it was money and education for my daughter.' Rather than acquiesce to others' performance stories, Kandy is determined to stick with her own story: she explicitly says 'No!' to the pressure to conform to performance values. This is evident at moments throughout Kandy's story, such as her decision not to return to the USA for a golf scholarship.

At these moments, it seems that others in sport could not accept Kandy's transgression of the dominant narrative (which stories performance over relationships). Like Christiana's stories, Kandy's stories also suggest that others *expected* her to act in ways that align with the performance narrative. However, the plot of Kandy's story is characterised by her continued resistance to these attempts. We suggest that Kandy is able to resist and re-story her mother's reaction (which stories Kandy's plans as 'a disaster' and 'not what I was supposed to do') by drawing on her established life story of exploration and discovery.

The general absence of alternatives to performance stories in sport culture is further illustrated when Kandy describes a lack of interest within golf of her life outside sport: 'No one ever asked about my daughter or how I was coping. The media only wanted good news. My problems did not interest them at all.' As a result, Kandy did not feel able to voice her 'red square' in public arenas. She kept these aspects of her self to herself. But by privately sustaining these silenced stories, Kandy was able to maintain her discovery life story in the face of its rejection by others. By saying 'golf was important because it was money and education for my daughter', Kandy positioned herself as a *mother* before a *golfer*. We suggest that Kandy thereby achieved a high degree of narrative alignment – *not* with the dominant performance narrative but with a culturally endorsed narrative of motherhood which focuses on caring and providing for one's child.

By storying her life along the lines of a discovery narrative Kandy was able to achieve a high degree of narrative authenticity, continuity and coherence. Although not without emotional difficulties, Kandy's stories fit with the way she lives her life, remain consistent across her career and allow her to make sense of sometimes difficult experiences in golf. Thus, although Kandy experiences narrative tensions and a degree of emotional trauma *within* golf (because her story does not align with cultural expectations within sport), *outside* golf she experiences a high degree of narrative alignment and relative psychological well-being.

Consequences of life stories at retirement

The risk of narrative disruption (and, consequently, identity trouble) increases at times of significant change. Neimeyer and colleagues (2006: 131) suggest that: 'Dramatic life events, and especially those of a traumatic kind, have the potential to introduce experiences that are not only radically incoherent with the plot of a person's prior life narrative, but that invalidate its core emotional themes and goals as well.' While this did not seem to happen for Kandy when she retired, it did seem to happen for Christiana, who experienced significant emotional and psychological trauma following withdrawal from tournament golf.

Christiana: 'We haven't got a seat on the bus for you'

Soon after officially retiring, Christiana began to experience psychological difficulties. She identified two contributing factors: 'missing the buzzing excitement of walking up the last' and the question 'what am I going to do next?' In her words: 'I was depressed and then you start to question whether you made the right choice. I felt, *well why am I here? What am I going to do? How am I going to earn a living?*' Here it is apparent that Christiana felt the loss of the (glorified) athletic identity that characterises her earlier stories. Because golf had, from her teenage years, been *the* thing upon which her identity and confidence depended, it is hardly surprising that its loss led her to question her worth and lose confidence in more general life contexts. As a consequence of the changes she was experiencing, Christiana became depressed.

In the months following withdrawal, Christiana described fluctuating between episodes of depression and periods of more positive psychological health. In addition to revealing a glorified athletic identity, Christiana's stories of retirement as loss were reinforced by the media and other sportspeople whose words reinscribed the dominant performance narrative. Alternative narrative types did not seem to be available – or acceptable – to Christiana to provide the resources with which to construct a 'new' self. For example, Christiana recounted how: 'Someone else says to me, "you need to find something that gives you a buzz." But it wouldn't be the same – digging my potatoes up and eating 'em, you can't connect the two. It's like chalk and cheese.' In stories like this, the glorified athletic identity she developed through her life in sport is portrayed as irreplaceable. In Christiana's stories, *anything* else is portrayed as a poor second.

Over the coming months, the gap between her previously established glorified self and what she was experiencing post-retirement continued to widen. Christiana described a continuing deterioration in her mental health as a string of possible work opportunities failed. After repeated disappointments she remarked: 'People don't want to touch me. That's what I've found. They talk about a seat on a bus; the trouble is, we haven't got a seat for you.' These troubling circumstances, we suggest, served to reinforce Christiana's commitment to the only story which has ever 'worked' for her. She asks herself, 'if I have made the right choice' retiring, and wonders whether she should return to golf. In so doing, Christiana increasingly focuses her present and future on the past – a strategy that, according to Crossley (2000), is a dangerous one. In Crossley's (2000: 151) terms, 'such an occupation with the past to the detriment of the future rapidly deteriorates into a loss of sense of meaning in life and subsequent mental and physical decay'.

Kandy: 'All the seats are mine and I go with the bus wherever I want'

Four years before retiring, Kandy had started to consider what she might do following her withdrawal from professional golf. Her story, as told in Chapter 5, ends with the following words:

> A lot of players think: '*What shall I do later on?*' I don't have that problem. When I finish and I retire I will play golf for my pleasure but I won't work in golf. I want to learn to play the guitar. I want to learn Russian. I want to learn to restore antiques because I love wood, the smell, colour, I love it. I love gardening. I'll have a big garden. I want a dog. I want to go and bicycle with my dog and I want to do many things and I want to travel. And my boyfriend is the same. We want to travel and discover the countries we don't know because we don't know the food, we don't know.... It's like: *Oh my goodness! I want to have time to do all these things.*

Entirely absent from this prospective view of retirement is any talk about loss. Instead, Kandy sounds positive – *excited* even – about her future after golf. This story is wholly consistent with the terms of a discovery narrative and is reminiscent of Kandy's stories of her childhood involvement in sport. Since winning, competition and glory did not underpin her sense of self at any stage of her life, there is no reason why she should fear their impending loss. Instead, Kandy resists the performance narrative by drawing upon the alternative stories (and identity) she has created throughout her life which looked to a broad range of factors (for example, travel, relationships, her home and garden) to bring interest, excitement and meaning to her life. Eighteen months after retirement Kandy had no doubts about whether retirement had been right for her.

It is evident that Kandy's discovery stories, which tell of her earliest involvement in sport through to post-retirement, display a high degree of consistency and coherence. She *never* tells performance stories in which winning, success and competition are prioritised over and above other activities, roles and goals. Instead, Kandy progresses a story which remains focused on experiencing life in the fullest sense, of discovering new experiences, of making the most of *now*. Kandy's experiences exemplify Spence's (1982: 458) point that 'the core of our identity is really a narrative thread that gives meaning to life.' Critically, sustaining this narrative thread necessitated *resisting* and *rejecting* the dominant performance narrative.

During her final interview with Kandy, Kitrina spoke anonymously about Christiana's feeling that, for her, there were 'no seats on the bus'. Kandy's response was: 'For me, all the seats are mine and I go with the bus wherever I want.' We suggest that while Kandy was able to sustain a discovery-oriented narrative thread which gave meaning to her life throughout her golf career and after her retirement, Christiana's almost exclusively performance-oriented narrative thread was lost when she retired from professional golf. It is this point – above all else – that makes sense of their profoundly different retirement experiences.

Reflections on Christiana's and Kandy's stories

We see Christiana's stories as powerfully shaped and constrained by the dominant and monological performance narrative. Here, the role of 'golfer' is storied not only *above* all other possible identities, roles and selves, but at times to their *exclusion*. Kandy's dialogical discovery narrative resists, contravenes and challenges this dominant narrative, inevitably resulting in tensions, personal difficulties and emotional costs. In this light it should not be surprising that many sportspeople, Christiana included, seem unable to avoid storying their life around the contours of the performance narrative. Individual athletes cannot be held solely responsible for this – more or less the entire fabric and culture of elite sport (from parents, coaches and fans to the media and other athletes) is permeated by performance stories. This culture steers athletes towards the kinds of experiences and identity recounted in Christiana's stories. Kandy's stories show that an alternative exists.

We hope that placing Christiana and Kandy's stories side by side shows how the stories individuals tell of their lives make a difference later in life. In short, stories matter. Although in performance terms *both* Christiana and Kandy were highly successful golfers, the stories they told, the identities they developed and the retirement they experienced differ dramatically. The very existence of their stories shows that alternative routes to and through elite sport are possible: it is simply *not* the case that there is only one way to achieve success and that withdrawal will inevitably be experienced as loss.

The life histories of these two women also reveal that it is not the case that at any time in life we can simply switch to a 'new story' when the one we have been telling becomes problematic. Instead, life stories developed over time become engrained and entrenched. Kandy was able to story retirement as an exciting opportunity (e.g. 'I love gardening. I'll have a big garden') because this was a story (and self) that she had created and reinforced over a period of many years. In contrast, within the monological performance story that Christiana established, there was little room for excitement or opportunity through any activity other than winning a golf tournament. Thus, Christiana could not suddenly enjoy gardening ('digging potatoes up') – not because it is impossible to enjoy gardening, but rather because this requires a self too removed from the one she had created.

Note

1 This chapter contains material adapted and developed from Carless and Douglas (2009).

10   Asylum and the conditions for story change[1]

> *I'm gonna walk down the mountain*
> *With my head in the sky*
> *I'm gonna walk down the mountain*
> *If I stay here I will die*
> (Martyn Joseph, 2003)

What happens when an individual, metaphorically speaking, has reached the top of the mountain but is no longer able to perform? The performance narrative maps one route *up* the mountain that seems adequate so long as the individual is winning or performing well. However, the journey the performance narrative offers *down* the mountain doesn't appear to be so appealing. Post-retirement, Christiana (for example) experienced trauma, mental health difficulties, identity foreclosure and narrative wreckage. She found herself with no way to go forward – the things she valued were lost and could never be replaced.

The map offered by the discovery narrative, in contrast, seems to suggest a way to walk down the mountain with your head held high. Kandy, for example, was excited about all the 'little things' in life, such as gardening and walking her dog. The fact that gardeners all over the world also gain so much from gardening and dog walkers value the time spent with their dogs shows it is possible to derive meaning from these activities. Kandy could and did. Yet Christiana could not. Is it possible, we might ask, for someone whose life story and identity has been shaped from a young age by a narrative script where 'winning is everything' to recognise that there can be more to life? That other activities and roles can be meaningful? Can someone, for example, who says 'digging potatoes' can never compare to standing on the winner's rostrum come to value gardening?

In this chapter we consider these kinds of questions. We ask: is it possible for an individual who has adhered to a performance life story to re-story their life in line with an alternative narrative type? If it is possible, what are the conditions necessary to support this change? To explore these questions we draw on the life stories of two women who aligned with the performance narrative. Both women adhered to this way of narrating their experiences even when it became problematic to their well-being to do so. What is unusual with Berni and Debbie, however, is that both women went on to adopt a new story. We believe that exploring their life stories may offer hope to those who feel stuck with a narrative map that no longer works. Perhaps these stories can provide resources to help performance storytellers negotiate their journey down the mountain more safely.

We tell Berni and Debbie's stories in three sections: (1) *living the part of athlete*, which relates to their involvement in elite and professional sport; (2) *narrative wreckage*, which focuses on the factors preceding and accompanying withdrawal from sport, and (3) *asylum*, which explores how, following withdrawal from professional sport, each woman achieved identity construction and personal development through the adoption of an alternative narrative type.

Living the part of athlete

For a period of time, both Berni and Debbie lived the part of athlete: their life stories aligned with the contours of the performance narrative. During this time, which stretched from their initial involvement in golf through turning professional, several shared characteristics were evident in both women's life stories.

First, both described positive feelings from their earliest involvement with golf, which they associated with being 'good at golf'. Debbie, for example, was able to remember her father's reaction to her first-ever golf shot as a small child: 'I think you're very good at this!' Significantly, as their golf careers began to develop, these positive feelings became more exclusively associated with achievement in terms of scores and results. Within these accounts, both women used metaphors and evocative descriptions to communicate the powerful ways in which winning affected them. Phrases like 'floating on air', 'just so happy', 'ecstatic', 'on a high', 'a lot of satisfaction', 'excitement', 'heightens all your awareness' and 'you're so confident as well, you *know* you are good' communicate a feel for their experience of successful performances. In each woman's story of her journey from beginner to elite level, positive feelings through golf became increasingly intertwined with winning prestigious matches, competitions and tournaments.

A second characteristic of both women's stories, also integral to the performance narrative type, was the ascendancy of a *glorified self* (Adler and Adler, 1989). The beginnings of this process were evident in their descriptions of their earliest golf memories which linked being 'skilful' with gaining recognition and social esteem among family and friends. In Debbie's words,

> It makes you feel good that people want to watch you because you're good, gives you a buzz, you can show off how good you are, you know, 'Look at me!' People clapping, cheering, it puts tension in the air, I like that, I get off on that, it pulls you along, it lifts you, it, like, makes it all worthwhile.

Similar to Georgi's and Christiana's stories, as each player began to win more prestigious events, the recognition and esteem they received spread to a wider social circle which included coaches, parents, selectors, colleagues, and ultimately sponsors, fans and the media.

A third hallmark of a performance narrative evident within Berni's and Debbie's stories was a tendency to assume a totalitarian belief that winning is, and must be, the primary focus for all professionals. Debbie, for example, stated, 'I just can't understand people who don't want to get to the top', while Berni described how:

> I never believed people who say that they don't dream about winning tournaments. For a long time I've dreamt of winning the British Open, dreamt of playing in the last pairing with Annika Sorenstam, you know, [I've] seen so many putts drop.

In providing a personal account of their own beliefs, Berni's and Debbie's stories illustrate again how a dominant narrative can silence alternative stories. Despite Berni alluding to some players not dreaming about winning, their beliefs are dismissed because *not* dreaming about winning is incomprehensible within the culture of sport. In taking this approach, alternative and future options are denied as players restrict themselves – and others – to believe that winning is the primary goal. From this perspective it is difficult to imagine playing golf for comradeship, to support others' progression, to travel or for the enjoyment of the game, because the overriding focus must be winning.

A fourth characteristic of both women's stories concerns the way in which their identity came to be constructed almost exclusively through – and in the context of – golf performance. This was evident in both women's decisions to prioritise golf above other developmental and social activities. Like Ryan in Chapter 7, Debbie described how golf took priority over her education:

> Mum said, 'What's this Debbie's not going to college? She *is*!' And then mum and dad had a bit of an argument and dad said, 'Look, she's really good at golf, if we stop her, if we make her do both, each will suffer. She won't pass her A levels, she won't be as successful at her golf, so we've got to let her choose and we've got to stand by her.' So I chose golf.

These types of choices, over time, point to each woman coming to value the athletic role over other roles and identities. Berni, for example, described being a professional golfer as being 'a big part of me' and, when asked if it was the biggest part, replied, 'Ah, probably yes, but reluctantly.' In light of these kinds of remarks, we suggest that both women had developed an exclusive athletic identity. In terms of identity construction, Sparkes (1997: 101) observes: 'the problem of identity is the problem of arriving at a life story that makes sense (provides unity and purpose) within a sociohistorical matrix that embodies a much larger story.' From this perspective, we suggest, both women were able to create a coherent identity through exclusively telling performance stories which aligned with their life experiences and the dominant performance narrative in sport.

However, Berni's use of the phrase 'but reluctantly' in the preceding excerpt hints that telling exclusively performance-type stories is not without its costs. When Berni was asked to talk further about this reluctance she reflected on some of these costs:

> It is quite frightening in the last couple of years. Through playing golf and being away I've missed the wedding of my favourite cousin, the birth of my nephew, the funeral of a very close friend and, however much I say that friends and family are more important, I've never had to prove it and am quite grateful I haven't.

This excerpt captures a degree of tension between the self that is constructed within the performance narrative and the self that the narrator desires to become. Berni's remarks resonate with those of Suzanne in Chapter 8. Adler and Adler (1989) suggest that it can be impossible for athletes to resist putting sport before other life domains because the lure of glory and celebrity is so powerful. In the excerpt above, Berni illustrates this point but also highlights a degree of conflict between her need to be a 'dedicated athlete' and her need to value family-oriented roles. Thus, in keeping with Adler and Adler's research, these examples illustrate how a glorified self gains ascendancy at the expense of other dimensions of self and relationships, but that this process is not without tensions.

Narrative wreckage

Reliance on a single dominant narrative can be problematic when a person's experiences no longer fit the narrative type. At these times, there is a risk of *narrative wreckage* (Frank, 1995), when a person's experiences no longer fit the contours of available or dominant narrative types. As a consequence, McLeod (1997) suggests, sense of self, identity, mental health and personal development are threatened as the narrative fails to provide a workable template for her life.

Evident within both Berni's and Debbie's life stories was a stage when their expected career trajectory was disrupted through being unable to fulfil the requirements of the performance narrative. While the reasons behind this change differed between the two women, the result – from the perspective of narrative theory – was the same: the performance narrative ceased to provide a workable template for life, identity and sense of self, and, as a consequence, both women experienced narrative wreckage. At this time, neither Berni nor Debbie was able, within the constraints of the dominant performance narrative, to construct a coherent story through which to make sense of their current life circumstances. In Sparkes' (1997) terms, neither woman could find meaning and unity in her life story and, as a result, both women experienced significant personal trauma and suffering.

Berni: Failure, shame and humiliation

Signs of narrative tension in Berni's life story slowly grew throughout her professional career. Although she had been a successful international amateur, success in the professional game eluded her. After turning professional Berni consistently missed cuts, failed to keep her player's card at tour school and failed to earn much money. As a result, she described experiencing stress and anxiety about her golf career which she believed had led to 'unexplained' physical health problems and depression. However, despite her lack of tournament success Berni's story did not change. In short, the story she constructed promoted a view that winning would solve her problems. In keeping with the performance narrative, her stories during this phase, as they had been earlier in her career, were about working harder and harder in an effort to improve. Eventually, however, the gulf between the stories she was telling herself (and others) and her experiences became too great:

> At the end of the day I can say, 'if I improve my game, fitness and organisation then that's all moving me forward' but what actually shows up, the tangible evidence, is the results. So, you know, I can stand in the car park talking to a member telling them I am happy with my game as long as I like, but if I've just missed four cuts in a row I am not going to be convincing either probably to them or to myself.

In this excerpt, Berni communicates a growing unease and dissatisfaction with the disjuncture between her story – of working towards future success – and the 'tangible evidence' which suggested she was not improving.

One strategy for continuing to play in tournaments was writing to tournament sponsors to gain entry to events. Although doing so made it possible for her to play more tournaments, it also had drawbacks in that she had to repeatedly create a story for the sponsor that was more optimistic than she actually felt. Describing how writing these 'begging' letters made her feel, Berni said:

> It is humiliating. You feel that you can't be totally honest. You don't want to write to a sponsor and say let me play a tournament because I played badly at tour school last year and I really need your help, which is the truth, but instead you write and say, 'It didn't quite work out for me but I know that I am a good player and if you could just give me this opportunity then everything will be all right.' You have to sound a lot more positive than you feel.

Although her experience is 'begging', 'humiliation' and 'failure', her story type, once again, remained constant. The problem, therefore, became the disparity between how she felt, which was not positive, and how her story was presented to others as optimistic, and therefore, at best, economical with the truth, or, at worst, dishonest. What she believed was the truth – that she was a failure in performance terms – is not a story she could tell because her dream was to win. Further, as Berni was embedded within sport culture, she was influenced by the expectations of those in that culture: *failure isn't an option*. She held a totalitarian view: a golfer who fails to perform should not be on tour.

Unable to voice what she considered to be an untellable truth, Berni continued to offer the more acceptable story of 'I know I am a good player' and 'it didn't quite work out' while hoping that her performance would improve. Her perception that she was being dishonest caused a moral dilemma but, such is the importance of winning, her story shows that 'the end justifies the means':

BERNI: As long as I stay in golf I have an opportunity of doing well and thereby justifying everything I've done. Whereas if I leave, it, uh *[pause]* not quite it's been for nothing but, you know, the investments have been so big. [The] previous 15 years have to have been for something, have to have a point.

KITRINA: If you still haven't succeeded how will that make you feel?

BERNI: Um, pretty worthless. Yeah. It means that I don't really think that I make a contribution to the people around me and to, not exactly to the world, but I am trying to think of a smaller, you know, if I wasn't here I don't think it would really matter – OK – a feeling that my life or what I do has *[pause]*, at the end of the day if I wasn't here or if I hadn't even been here it wouldn't really matter or, you know, have made any difference.

Several researchers have suggested that there is a strong link between a golfer's rank, tournament record and their self-worth, social esteem (Crosset, 1995; Ravizza, 2002). When Berni achieved success as an amateur she felt good about herself and others responded positively towards her. In contrast, for a player who endorsed the values of the performance narrative, failing to win on the professional tour, over a sustained period, had the opposite effect, bringing humiliation, shame and loss of self-worth to the extent that a future devoid of success would mean that she would see herself as 'pretty worthless'. Here, the gravity of her situation was spelled out clearly when Berni said that without winning in golf her life would have no point. In her words, 'if I hadn't been here it wouldn't matter'.

Debbie: Depression and self-harm

Although the biographical particulars were different, Debbie came to a similar position regarding her worth as an individual after becoming pregnant and deciding to have the baby. Here, her story is one where she had to make a choice: 'When I got pregnant, I thought, well, it's career or babies and I decided to have the baby.' Lenskyj (1986) suggested that dominant cultural and societal values concerning what it is to be a woman are in tension with the role of being an athlete. Western cultural expectations hold that 'good mothers are selfless and sacrifice their own wants and needs for those of their children' (Collett, 2005:

340) to the point that, 'to be a remotely decent mother, a woman has to devote her entire physical, emotional, and intellectual being 24/7, to her children' (Douglas and Michaels, 2004: 4). Thus, the social expectation of what it is to be a mother – to be 'available' and to prioritise the needs of the child – is, we suggest, incompatible with the demands of the performance narrative which demands an exclusive focus on one's self and achievements in sport. A result of this perceived incompatibility is that many female athletes, like Debbie and Christiana, believe it is impossible to combine a career in professional sport with having children. From this position, being a 'good mother' would require Debbie to abandon the performance narrative, thereby, as she saw it, sacrificing her career in professional golf.

It was after the birth of her son that the implications of this perceived incompatibility became evident in Debbie's life. Reflecting two years later, she told, with remarkable honesty, how:

> I didn't want my baby. I resented him because my golf career was over. I'd care for him, I wouldn't want to hurt him or anything, but I blamed him for my golf – I felt I was out of the environment I knew and I felt lost. I tried to hide it. I couldn't cope. I wouldn't talk.... I didn't think I could make any contribution to life.

Thus, as opposed to embracing motherhood and it providing a complementary dimension to her identity, Debbie found herself unwilling to relinquish her golf career and, caught up within the constraints of the performance narrative, mourned the loss of her career and blamed her son for this loss.

This moral dilemma, and the emotional turmoil it caused, was compounded by Debbie's unease with voicing her feelings. In her words: 'The last thing I could say is I don't want my baby.' In short, cultural expectations concerning motherhood served to render Debbie's story untellable. Eventually, Debbie decided to break her silence by sharing her feelings in the hope of gaining the support and assistance of close friends:

> Finally, I said to two close friends that I couldn't cope, that I was struggling. Their reaction was totally unexpected: they said I was selfish, I'm not a good mother *[pause]*. I walked out. They found me in the next village, I don't know how I got there, I just walked out. I couldn't cope, I was very tearful and they took me to see the doctor. He said it was postnatal depression and just bunged tablets at me.

The 'totally unexpected' reaction of Debbie's friends was, we suggest, entirely consistent with cultural attitudes towards motherhood, yet entirely inconsistent with the sport culture in which Debbie had been immersed since childhood. Thus, Debbie found herself in a situation where whichever course of action she chose (being a 'good mother' or a 'good professional golfer'), her life story would inevitably clash with the values of one of two powerful narratives. Given these constraints, and the tensions her situation created, it is perhaps not surprising that Debbie became seriously unwell. As she put it, 'I just couldn't live life. I couldn't get off the sofa. I was manic, shaking, hearing voices, terrible.' Seven months after her son was born, seeking escape from her turmoil, Debbie attempted suicide. Following this incident, she was admitted to a psychiatric hospital.

Asylum

Until this point in their life stories, Berni and Debbie constructed an identity and sense of self that was almost entirely dependent on success in professional golf. Shortly before withdrawing from professional golf, Berni felt 'if I hadn't been here it wouldn't really matter', while Debbie believed 'I couldn't make any contribution to life'. These kinds of remarks suggest that neither player perceived an alternative route to self-worth outside golf. McLeod (1997) suggests that even when we story unique personal events, we still draw on narrative structures from our culture. We suggest that, although Berni and Debbie indeed recounted unique personal experiences, the construction of these experiences was powerfully shaped and constrained by the storyline of the performance narrative in which they had been immersed since childhood. The performance narrative was the primary – or perhaps only – resource available. But both women had now reached the point of narrative wreckage, where the performance narrative no longer worked in the context of their life experiences. To reinstate mental health and well-being – to be able to get on with life – it became necessary for each woman to rebuild her identity through creating an alternative story which more closely fit her current life experiences.

Both women achieved this by developing new life stories that drew upon a different narrative type. Following a period of asylum, the narrative type that came to underlie both women's stories is a relational narrative. As we noted in Chapter 6, relational narratives have 'an emphasis on interpersonal dimensions rather than the separate self' (Lieblich *et al.*, 1998: 87), focusing on care and connections. Inherent within this type of story is a sense of 'offering self to others' needs' (Josselson, 1996: 8) through an empathic and attentive other-orientation instead of a self-orientation. Importantly, the process of coming to tell relational stories required the abandonment of the performance narrative which was only possible once each woman had removed herself completely from the culture of elite sport.

Berni: Cancer and caring

Berni's unforeseen withdrawal from the professional tour was triggered midway through the season when her mother was unexpectedly diagnosed with cancer and an operation was immediately scheduled. Reflecting later on this event, Berni described being 'stunned' and feeling 'disbelief' when she heard about the severity of her mother's illness. Carolyn Ellis (2001) describes a metamorphosis that may occur in an individual when a loved one is in need. Berni described this epiphany in her life as:

> a time when I didn't want to be away from home. And I remember I'd been playing in Sweden the week before her op and I came home the day before the operation and a week later I realised that my clubs were still in the flight bag, I hadn't even got them out. I began to prioritise.

Here Berni communicates a feeling of the metamorphosis that occurred in her life when she didn't even think about golf during the week of her mother's operation. In the context of her life in elite golf to date, where golf had been her first and perhaps only consideration, this action, or lack of it, allowed her to create a story by which she showed that these pivotal and dramatic events surprised even Berni herself. While putting her golf performance before family had previously caused her considerable moral tension, this action provided her with an opportunity to create a new type of story unconnected with golf performance.

In the weeks that followed her mother's operation, Berni cared for her mother as well as for her father. During her mother's recuperation Berni also cared for her niece and her nephew. As her mother's condition improved, Berni took on work locally and was quickly promoted. Approximately 18 months later she enrolled in a coaching degree course and accepted a job teaching at a local golf club. Four years later Berni was able to reflect on these events:

> Mum's illness was a catalyst, definitely. Those years in the pub were time out from golf. You realise there is so much more to golf than playing tournament golf. Doing this [teaching] would have felt like second best [while playing the tour]. I wasn't ready, I needed time away to realise how lucky I am. Now I *want* to do it. I didn't want to do it, everything revolved around my score, you know, if I shot 68 everything was great and if I shot 75, ugh! Whereas now, it's really exciting when people you help start to improve and I'm enjoying coaching. Every Tuesday I've been straight into the ladies' locker room to look at the results and see who's done well every week. I know someone will be round to tell me they shot 67 and someone else to say they need a lesson. I'm happier and more content. I enjoyed pro golf but I wasn't content because it didn't live up to my expectations – everything depended on winning.

For Sparkes (1997: 101–102): 'As individuals construct past events and actions in personal narratives they engage in a dynamic process of claiming identities and constructing lives.' The events and actions recounted above provided Berni with an opportunity to reconstruct an alternative story about her identity and sense of self. First, she identified her mother's illness as a necessary catalyst of change. She then went on to highlight the importance of 'time out from golf' and how she 'needed time away' from the game. We suggest that this time provided her with a kind of asylum in an environment where winning wasn't important. Asylum therefore provided her with both new kinds of experiences to story *and* access to alternative valued narrative templates that were not available within elite sport culture. By caring for her mother, and subsequently working as a golf coach, Berni was able to bring together a story that more closely aligned with her experience. Her story ceased to resemble a performance narrative, to favour instead the storyline of a relational narrative with an orientation towards others. Berni's stories suggest that this shift in orientation led to her finding happiness and contentment, not in what she achieves in performance terms, but by caring for and helping others with their needs and aspirations.

Debbie: Hospitalisation and breaking silence

Although the particulars of Debbie's story differed from Berni's, the same underlying theme of needing time away from the culture and values of elite sport was evident. For Debbie, removal from the world of elite sport was extreme and total as she spent approximately one year in a psychiatric hospital. Like Berni, Debbie's stories of this time encapsulate a change of narrative type away from the values of a performance narrative towards the relational narrative type. Thus, Debbie's story shifted away from a focus on the self, and her own problems and difficulties, towards a consideration and desire to help others. This process is illustrated in the following excerpt in which Debbie described her slow recovery:

> It took me two years, you know. We can do it, with the help of family, although I suppose not everyone has that, people who care, counsellors. My mental health counsellor, Alice Morton, was fantastic. I would see her once a week. It took Alice a year before I would tell her what was on my mind. Now I just want to tell others about what happened to me, I'm not ashamed, I don't mind if people know what's happened to me. I said to my husband, I would like to get my story out. We were trying to think of who to write to. I think it might help other people. We think we're the only ones, you feel so alone and you can't talk.

When an individual's story fails to align with dominant cultural narratives, it may be deemed untellable and therefore silenced. As McLeod (1997: 100) points out:

> taking into account the fact that storytelling is a performance, an event that requires an audience, very often the existence of a personal 'problem' can best be described as a response to *silencing*, the unwillingness of others to hear that story that in some sense 'needs' to be told.

The experience of being silenced is, we suggest, central to understanding Debbie's experience of narrative wreckage and subsequent mental health problems. Debbie's story of putting golf before her baby, while being sanctioned by the terms of the performance narrative, was simply too dangerous to tell within the context of cultural expectations of motherhood. When she did find the courage to tell this story to close friends, their rejection served to reinforce the unacceptable nature of her story and to perpetuate her silence. In the excerpt above, Debbie illustrated how difficult it was to break this silence – how, even with the benefit of a 'fantastic' counsellor, it took 'a year before I would tell her what was on my mind'.

A second important element in Debbie's story is the demise of her glorified athletic self to be replaced by a relational focus characterised by an overriding consideration for others. Similarly, her story came to focus on people who care about her as a person rather than individuals who are in awe of her sport talent. Considering the stigma associated with mental illness and attempted suicide, the courage behind Debbie's willingness and desire to speak out to provide help to others who may, like her, 'feel so alone', and those who 'can't talk', should not be underestimated. In many ways, her current relational orientation is a complete contrast to the performance-oriented self-focus that was promoted in the earlier parts of her life story. Debbie's moral stance – of bearing witness to a life-changing experience for the benefit of others – has much in common with Frank's (1995) descriptions of cancer survivors who struggle to tell, and find an audience for, their personal illness stories in an effort to help those in similar situations.

This period of asylum opened up space for the women, in Michael White and David Epston's (1990: 75) terms, 'to re-author or constitute themselves, each other and their relationships according to alternative stories or knowledges'. The alternative type of story by which both women created meaning and coherence in their lives may be characterised as a relational narrative. Through telling her life story around the contours of a relational narrative, and enacting these values in her daily life, each woman was able to reinstate a coherent identity which provided a sense of meaning and worth to life after golf. While this may be healthful for these women and their families, we believe there are broader implications for other athletes who struggle to 'fit' with the expectations of the performance narrative in professional or top-class sport, but who are equally unable to re-story their lives.

Conditions for story change

Berni's and Debbie's stories reveal how difficult it is for an individual to change the way in which they narrate their life, to scaffold their personal story around an alternative narrative template. For athletes like Christiana, this fundamental change appears impossible. If Berni or Debbie could have 'just' changed their story, it seems to us that they would have done so sooner. Re-storying one's life is never easy because one's story has been engrained over many years. Yet Berni's and Debbie's experiences show that it *is* possible, even within the context of high-level sport. Significantly, however, their experiences show that one's personal story cannot change in isolation – other social, cultural, psychological and material conditions must also change.

We see these changes together providing *asylum* for the individual – a place of refuge from the culture of elite and professional sport. In essence, asylum offers protection or insulation from the values and script of the dominant performance narrative. Within this 'safe space' personal transformation becomes possible as alternative life stories have a chance to be developed. One athlete whom we interviewed used the word 'greenhouse' to describe the nurturing environment that was placed around him during a critical time in his life. In his words, this allowed him 'to re-grow' while being protected from a culture he experienced as hostile. The metaphor of asylum – as place of refuge – is also present in the accounts of some other participants when they described their recovery following sport-related psychological trauma.

It seems to us that a number of conditions are necessary if an individual is to have any chance of revising their life story. On the basis of the experiences of the participants in our research and existing narrative theory, we have identified four interrelated conditions that support story change. One of these alone is unlikely to offer a sufficient level of asylum. It appears to us that some combination of these four conditions is necessary for those who have lived within the culture of high-level sport. This was certainly the case for Berni and Debbie. In what follows, we consider the four conditions that support the kind of narrative transformation – comprising a movement *away* from the performance narrative – evident in Berni's and Debbie's stories.

Access to counter-stories

Throughout the book we have heard about athletes who seemed to have limited resources to story their lives differently. The stories of Georgi, Ryan, Christiana, Berni and Debbie all demonstrate this: they storied their lives in line with the dominant performance narrative, a story that has much in common with the master narrative of elite sport that we discussed in Chapter 1. Creating, sharing and developing only one type of story seemed to foreclose other identity possibilities and life horizons. We have suggested that this narrowing of personal stories is due (in part at least) to an absence of alternative narrative templates – or *counter-stories* – that contest the dominant performance narrative. According to Nelson (2001: 8), counter-stories:

> are stories that define people morally, and are developed for the express purpose of resisting and undermining an oppressive master narrative. They ordinarily proceed by filling in the details that the master narrative has ignored or downplayed. Through augmentation and correction, the master narrative is morally reoriented, thus allowing the counterstory teller to dissent from the interpretation and conclusion it invites.... They are, then, narrative acts of insubordination.

Within the context of elite sport, discovery and relational stories may be considered counter-stories that contest the dominant performance narrative. Throughout the book we have heard discovery and relational counter-stories from Kandy, Leanne, Luke, Tony, Alex and Kitrina. Counter-stories are also evident in the later experiences of Berni, Debbie and Suzanne. Their stories fill in details which the dominant narrative ignores or downplays. They are, in Nelson's terms, 'narrative acts of insubordination' which morally reorient the performance narrative, allowing the teller to 'dissent from the interpretation and conclusion it invites'. The counter-stories we have presented throughout the book show, for example, how it is possible to sustain worth without performance success, maintain an identity and self beyond sport, and experience career transition without suffering and trauma.

It seems to us that rather than the terms of the performance narrative *loosening* over time to welcome greater diversity and difference, the opposite is the case. Player pathways, talent development schemes, rules, regulations and expectations of elite and aspiring sportspeople appear to be becoming more tightly defined and enforced. *You must do this, in this order, at this time, if you want to be successful.* Within sport policy and practice, the range of routes to success in high-level sport is being narrowed and reduced. One result is an increasingly constricted and prescriptive culture that adheres more and more exclusively to the performance narrative. This is worrying, given the adverse effects of this way of storying one's life. We believe that the need for counter-stories to be made available to sportspeople (in educational and consulting settings, for example) is becoming more urgent.

A damaging aspect of master or dominant narratives is their tendency to operate beyond the individual's awareness, thus obscuring their influence (Phoenix and Smith, 2011). It is therefore important to identify and recognise damaging *story fragments*. One small example of a damaging story fragment is captured in the phrase 'education is something to *fall back on*'. Parents, coaches and teachers often use this phrase to persuade young people that education is worth continuing alongside their sport careers. However, presenting education in this way diminishes the potential for education to be valued as a worthy investment. It also obscures the way in which learning can be liberating and transformational during as well as following a sport career. As Alex's story reveals, education can be empowering *during* the athletic career (which may be why it threatens the hierarchical systems within which many athletes' careers are held). If the story offered about education is that it is only beneficial 'when things go wrong', then it isn't surprising that athletes like Debbie decide to leave school, and Ryan decides to train rather than do his homework. We are not suggesting that education be enforced but, rather, that we make available within sport culture counter-stories that articulate learning as independently valuable. Failing to capture what is transformational, liberating and empowering about education – by describing it as 'something to fall back on' – does a disservice to young sportspeople.

Others who value counter-stories

Other people play a major role in either coercing an individual to conform to the performance narrative or supporting them to contest its script. Throughout the book we have heard stories of athletes being pressured *towards* the performance narrative. We have also heard how other athletes were helped to resist this script by those around them. All athletes will to some extent be influenced by the stories of those around them. Others' stories become particularly problematic when they cement, finalise or hold an individual in an identity that prohibits development or change. The types of stories that are particularly oppressive are those which normalise or naturalise aspects of the performance narrative, for example, by making it seem that sport participation is a 'natural' condition of birth (such as 'you were born to run'). Normalising actions (for example, taking over other roles and responsibilities to allow the athlete to 'concentrate on their training') hide how they impede identity development. Another potentially oppressive story looks only backwards to who or what the athlete *has been* or *has achieved.* For Lindemann (2009: 420), 'When we interact with someone solely on the basis of these stories, we impede the person's ability to change.' Because sports enthusiasts enjoy talking about and analysing sport performance (and because it can be validating reminiscing about shots, goals and trophies), the stories told or shared about particular athletes tend to focus on their past. Over time, only talking about and remembering that past takes its toll on the possibility of the sportsperson expanding their identity and establishing new areas of expertise and enjoyment.

The following example provides an illustration. A decade after I (Kitrina) ceased to play professional sport I was out walking along the cliff path near my home and passed a woman walking in the opposite direction. Moments later the woman shouted out: 'You're the golfer!' The language this stranger used ('you're *the…*') and the particular role and identity she chose to single out ('*golfer*') is an illustration of how an identity can be cemented by the stories of others. After asking, 'What are you doing now?' and upon learning I no longer played golf, the woman further cemented and elevated the golfer identity by saying: 'What a waste of all that talent!' Even this brief exchange is not as innocuous as it may seem – although we imagine the woman was unaware of the damaging message in her story. What this woman was effectively saying is that because a sportsperson excels at sport that is all they should devote their life to – for ever! This story ('what a waste of talent') places athletic skills above other skills and relationships within the individual's life, and is entirely in line with the performance narrative. It suggests that unless an individual devotes their 'talents' to sport then that individual has failed in their moral responsibility. Story fragments like these are oppressive because they subjugate an individual's moral agency and naturalise their athletic identity. In Nelson's (2001: 163) terms, they make it 'seem inevitable that certain groups of people must occupy certain places in society'. My response to the woman was: 'What about all the talent that was being wasted while I was playing golf?' These few words draw on a counter-story to resist the foreclosed identity which this woman's words imply.

In addition to having *access* to counter-stories, sportspeople need other people who *invite, support and value* them. For Debbie, the person she credits with making it possible to create a new story was her mental health nurse – who coaxed, nurtured and encouraged other accounts of Debbie's life. For Berni, it was the people in her local pub, who interacted with her on the basis of who she *might become*, as opposed to what she *had been*. The mental health nurse, pub customers and staff, who were unknown to these women while they were on tour, had a sufficiently open vision of these women to allow narrative trans-formation. But this isn't always the case. Christiana, for example, recounted how other people continually led her back towards performance stories. Given that sport is so highly valued by many people it seems likely that there will always be those who prefer to keep the identity of their heroes fixed in the past. When an athlete is exposed to people like this, they are likely to feel as though they are swimming against the tide – always being in danger of being swept downstream. One of the potential hazards of excelling in sport is that identity development and maintenance require ongoing narrative resistance as a lifelong necessity. Being surrounded by others who *do not* endorse or value the performance nar-rative is, we believe, critical to long-term well-being. Berni and Debbie could only achieve this by exiting sport culture.

Other events to narrate

Stories are predicated upon actual concrete events and identities are created as we weave together stories about these events. It is impossible to develop or sustain a life story that does not connect in some way to the material conditions of one's life. If an individual's valued experiences are all to do with sport performance (e.g. training regimes, diet, scores, statistics, events, wins), what else do they have to story? A further requirement for story change, then, is alternative events and experiences to narrate. Because we are social beings and stories exist in and through relationships, it is also important that the storyteller has someone to share her or his stories with – someone who will listen, witness and value the story.

For Kandy there were numerous events to story while she played professional sport and she often shared stories of these events with friends outside sport. Berni, in contrast, primarily told performance stories (about competitions and training) during her golf career. By the time she was working in the pub, she had accumulated stories based on other events – such as caring for her mother, cancer survival, nursing, treatment, child-minding and so on. Her 'new' stories drew upon very different events and experiences than her earlier stories. We therefore see a further condition for story change as engaging in activities that are outside of an individual's 'sport' frame of reference. Typically, these are not the events or activities valued by coaches, the performance team, fans or team-mates. Like the woman on the cliff path, these people are more likely to ask 'When are you coming back?' or 'How come you no longer play?' For people like Debbie and Christiana – who wrestle with doubts over whether they should have retired – this is an ongoing threat to their well-being. At the time of writing, we are unsure whether Debbie will be able to resist the constant persuasion of others (family, friends, media) to lure her back to the performance narrative and the person she once was. If she is to do so, we suggest she will require a range of other (not sport performance-related) events and experiences to narrate.

Time

Alongside the three conditions we have described above, story change also requires time. The passing of time provides the *temporal distance* needed to initiate and grow a new story and identity. For Freeman (2010: 208), temporal distance promises not only a panoramic view of life but also a narrative context 'within which one can situate the various episodes of one's life in relation to one another and to the emerging whole'. Time makes it possible to re-story events from a different horizon and then to lay down roots which allow this new story to grow. The new narrative script, while remaining true to events, also makes it possible for the individual to account for change to themselves as well as to others. Freeman suggests that events that seemed one way in the past may come to be seen differently from the present.

Time out from the demands of sport (where life is framed by the next season, Olympic cycle, tournament, league championships and so on) provides an individual with the opportunity to consider and reflect upon their life and the type of identity they value. 'Somehow,' Freeman 2010: 209) writes, 'we need to achieve that sort of self-distancing, often only achieved in the face of death, that can orient us vigilantly to what is of true value in our lives.' Both Berni and Debbie experienced an extended period of time outside sport before they were able to re-story their lives. That they both also experienced 'the face of death' may not be insignificant in that it provided a strong impetus to reconsider their previous values and beliefs. During this time, with the support of a counter-story, other people and different life events, both women were able to develop a new life story. Arthur Bochner (2001: 140) writes that by adopting a new self-narrative it becomes possible for an individual to 'turn mere existence ... into a meaningful social and moral life that is self-validating'. This seems to describe well the process Berni and Debbie have been through, which involved abandoning the performance narrative to story their lives instead around a relational narrative. Given the problems the performance narrative can create, we suggest that this change is a necessity for athletes who have storied their lives around the performance script. Without asylum – through access to counter-stories, other people who support the transformation process, events to story and time – this profound change appears unlikely or impossible. Yet without this transformation occurring, the long-term well-being of performance storytellers appears bleak.

Note

1 This chapter contains material adapted and developed from Douglas and Carless (2009a).

11 Reflections

Humans live their lives getting themselves into stories. We need help reflecting on what these stories are, and what the choices among them are.

(Arthur Frank , 2010: 124)

Throughout this book, and indeed across all our research, we have been mindful of the difficulty – the delicacy – in moving from one individual's story of their unique and particular experience, to more general claims that apply to others within similar contexts. In writing the book we have experienced ongoing tensions in making this step. It has been and remains an uneasy process that contains a degree of doubt and uncertainty. Time and again we have asked ourselves: *Should* we make general claims? *What* claims should we make? *How* should they be voiced? *When* should they be offered?

The primary goal we have set ourselves is to understand and faithfully represent the experiences of those individuals who take part in our research. We have worked with each case, one by one, to ensure that we have understood the individuals' stories, and the experiences they describe, as well as we are able. Often, this task has required us to return to the individual to discuss our emerging understanding.

Over time, we have come to see some more general processes underlying the experiences these unique individuals describe. Broadly speaking, we see these commonalities as cultural issues that impinge (in one way or another) on the lives of the individuals who exist within that culture. In other words, sport culture acts in non-unique ways on the unique athletes who exist within it. It is here that we have employed forms of analysis and interpretation that allow us to move towards a more generalised theory regarding the experiences of high-level athletes.

We have, though, moved towards general claims with caution. A key reason behind our decision to include more general theoretical claims is our awareness of others who are only too willing to make sweeping generalisations regarding the lives of elite sportspeople, usually on the basis of much less intensive, thorough and in-depth study. Given that we *have* engaged in intensive, in-depth, longitudinal study, we feel morally obliged to write in a way that challenges and contests certain individuals' and organisations' views about elite athletes.

It is important to us that we do this in a way that avoids finalising the lives of those athletes whom we have interviewed – and, indeed, the lives of other elite athletes who did not take part in our research. We have tried to remain open to diversity and difference to avoid foreclosing the life possibilities of high-level sportspeople. To do this, we have included an array of *voices* throughout the book that speak of diverse and sometimes contradictory, ambiguous or paradoxical experiences. Incorporating multiple voices by privileging personal stories allows different experiences to be heard, valued and given space, possibly for the first time.

The term 'voice' also refers to the tonal vibrations produced when we talk, hum or sing. When different notes are produced simultaneously in the same melody, we refer to it as a harmony. This metaphor aligns with our ultimate aspiration for this book: to share a voice which is both melodic and harmonious yet retains difference. It is an aspiration to initiate and sustain dialogue by placing diverse voices – through different personal stories, analyses and theory – side by side within a harmonious whole.

To this end, we conclude the book by reflecting on some of the questions we have been asked by others about our research. We have often asked ourselves similar questions. By reflecting on a selection of these questions, we hope to anticipate some of the questions you may have, having read the book. Of course, we cannot address every possible question, so we invite you – within your own circles – to engage with the dialogue we have set in motion.

Is the performance narrative really so extreme and dominant? Are we overstating the case?

There are two issues that have informed our thinking on this issue. First, in Chapter 4 we focused on a 'classic' form of the performance narrative to present as clearly as possible its key characteristics. Doing so allowed us to distil a range of hallmarks that are not necessarily evident in *every* performance story. We have, however, heard other individuals tell performance stories that are comparable in strength to Georgi's. These stories trouble us. It is true that some individuals tell more 'moderate' versions of the performance story, perhaps drawing at times upon other narrative threads. However, we consider that even these stories can be dangerous because of the tendency of the performance narrative to be totalitarian and monological. Within performance stories, performance *must always* come first: this type of story demands exclusivity and does not tolerate other stories taking precedence. It is this singularity – which prioritises the self-position of athlete above all other roles – that signals potential trouble.

Second, feedback from other people has suggested that we are not overstating the case. Others, too, have real concerns about the athletes they work with who seem to have no alternative than adhere to the values and terms of the performance narrative. Following a conference presentation, David met an individual who used to work at a football academy for young aspiring professionals. He said that he began to reflect on his role and the values of the academy after having his own child. As a result of this reflection, he said, he quit his job, having decided that he would not want *his* son to experience the extreme performance-oriented practices of the academy. Students, too, have offered us powerful feedback. On hearing Georgi's story, for example, one Master's student reflected upon his previous role as a PE teacher in a secondary school. He said that the terms of the performance narrative were exactly what they tried to teach their sport students – he believed that they were needed to do well in sport. Hearing and discussing Georgi's, Kandy's and Leanne's stories led him to question the practices in which he had previously engaged.

Do these narrative types apply across all sports?

Our research originated in golf and it is here that we have conducted our most intensive longitudinal work. However, we have subsequently conducted research into other diverse sports, including rugby union, judo, track and field, rowing, hockey, netball, canoeing, swimming and cricket. Others, too, have extended the work into other sports (e.g. Papathomas and Lavallee, in press). On the basis of the research conducted to date, our findings and interpretations seem to hold across sports. It is always possible to criticise research or researchers on the basis of what *hasn't* been done. No matter how many studies we conducted, this criticism would probably be levelled by someone, somewhere! In the absence of research that challenges or discredits our interpretations, we put our trust in the studies that *have* been conducted – rather than the possible findings of those that have not. These findings suggest that across sport culture a dominant performance narrative exists which places athlete well-being in jeopardy. Performance stories script not only the nature of the activity, but also what the individual must *be* or *become* to engage successfully in that activity. We suggest that the story that *life is competitive*, that we *must* therefore compete and strive to be the best, is very evident in contemporary Western culture. A sport-based model seems to have crept into many aspects of life, such as dance and cookery television programmes that are run as competitions. Increasingly, it seems to even underlie the management and administration of organisations such as schools and universities.

How much of all this is to do with what athletes say, and how much concerns what they actually do?

This is a difficult question to answer. How can we know what athletes *actually* do? It is clearly impossible to observe an athlete 24 hours a day across their entire life! Even then, would we really know? We cannot really access and understand what people do, other than by asking them to *tell us* what they do. This means that it is difficult or impossible to determine for sure whether something results from what a person *says* or what they *do*. In practice, stories and actions affect each other in a reciprocal manner. There may be no tight correlation, but they are not independent. Using narrative theory as a lens to understand the stories of the participants in our research, we can see that what athletes say both shapes the self *and* creates the 'reality' that is experienced by the storyteller and, potentially, their audience.

Illustrations of this complexity may be drawn from the highly publicised actions of Lance Armstrong and Tiger Woods. Both of these individuals may have been seen (for a time) as offering a utopian vision of what sportspeople could be. They were, for a time, 'ambassadors' for sport. But there was another truth that they were living by. In our terms, both of these individuals were *playing the part* when the public generally assumed they were *living the part*. When it was revealed that they were actually playing the part, responses were typically disbelief and anger. The truth was too much to bear. People were shocked – not only at their behaviour but also at their deceit. In our view it is impossible to tell from a public portrayal – such as a blog, media interview or television appearance – whether an individual athlete is living or playing the part. In modern-day sport, there is simply too much riding on their public persona for us to be able to take these accounts at face value. That is why the interview approach we have used in this book is necessary: to provide the protection of anonymity within the context of an accepting, trusting researcher–participant relationship.

The following extract, taken from a recent interview with a practitioner who provides psychology support, is a further example of how athletes are called on to play a certain role:

PRACTITIONER: I would say there are a high number of athletes I work with who are not being authentic to their 'true self' in the sport environment, it is very much a façade or role. You can catch them on brief moments when you feel they are being more authentic and you see difference.

KITRINA: Can you give me an example?

PRACTITIONER: I would say we have some athletes going to a major Games recently, who I have been having a conversation with and then someone who is part of [name of organisation removed] came up and asked them a question. I think they asked if they were excited about going to this major Games, and the athlete said: 'Oh Yes! I've been waiting for this since I was such an age.' And it was almost, this media response, although it wasn't for the media, it was almost a given story they felt they should tell.... And the response was so different to what they had just told me about what they were thinking before going to this event.

KITRINA: What had they said to you?

PRACTITIONER: Well, they said – they expressed some nerves, not knowing what it was going to be like. 'I'm not looking forward to this and don't really know.' Whereas to this other person [the athlete] had turned round and gone 'Great!' and 'I can't wait!' and 'I'm handling everything well.' It was just a very different response. And another athlete going to the same event – and this is someone I've known for a long time – and we had lots of media in that day and [this athlete] said 'Oh I don't like the media, it's just not me, and I'm going to have to put this show on this afternoon.' ... So it's interesting to see that 'part' isn't just played to the media, it's played to the coach and its played to performance director.

In sum, we see the influence of stories – both those an individual athlete tells and those circulated by others in the culture – as having a larger and more powerful sphere of influence than is typically recognised.

Can an individual athlete be more than one narrative type or can a person move through different narrative types over time?

Given the right conditions, it may be possible for an individual to develop two contrasting life stories and identities. We don't rule this out. Narrative theory shows us that there are always more possibilities than we can imagine. At the same time, the life stories we have recounted here suggest it to be unlikely for an individual to incorporate – in the same moment – the performance narrative with any other narrative type. A performance-discovery combination is unlikely because the performance narrative is the antithesis of the discovery narrative. If winning is everything, necessitating discipline, sacrifice, hard work and the prioritisation of sport ahead of all other areas of life, it would be very difficult for that same person, in the same moment, to accommodate defeat in a way that avoids feelings of shame and disgrace.

A performance-relational combination is similarly unlikely. When sport is prioritised ahead of relationships and the individual depends on adulation, competition, beating others and hates to be beaten, how can that person simultaneously prioritise relationships, put the needs of the other first? Expectations and behaviours are woven into the fabric of the plot line.

The potential for an individual to move through different narrative types at different phases of life seems to be a more realistic possibility. In Chapter 10 we outlined the conditions for story change, exploring how an alternative story can be seeded, developed and grown over time. In our research to date a small number of athletes have shown signs of making such a journey during their sport careers. A triple Paralympic gold medallist whom we interviewed provides one example. After hearing about the three narrative types, he described to us how, at his first Paralympics, he felt his life story aligned with the performance narrative. The same athlete, who also won gold at his second Paralympics, suggested that what motivated him towards his second gold medal four years later was his parents (like Leanne who wanted to win for her dad). This athlete wanted to win for his parents as a way to acknowledge their investments in his sport career. Thus, he believed he aligned with the relational narrative. By the time this athlete reached his third Paralympics, he felt he was oriented towards the discovery narrative: a desire to enjoy and focus on the journey and life possibilities that were offered as opposed to focusing on the performance outcome. He won gold at this event too.

Tracking and documenting these changes through the stories which athletes share was possible during our research among women tour players because we stayed in contact with participants for up to a decade. This provided opportunities to listen to their stories at different phases of life and life circumstances. Doing so taught us how difficult it is for any individual to adopt an alternative narrative template for their life and how the process is predicated on accessing alternative narrative resources and embodied experiences – and these being valued by others in the individual's culture. Therefore, while we seek to leave open the potential for narrating life in multiple ways, and the possibility of changing narrative types, we are also aware of how inescapable the influence of the performance narrative has become given its cultural prevalence and dominance.

Should practitioners be trying to change athletes' stories? Should we steer athletes away from the performance narrative?

In previous chapters we showed how sport culture leads young people towards a particular script and, potentially, to live according to its values. *Living* the performance narrative means that the athlete is likely to always feel pressure to cut off other story options and life possibilities that fail to align with the performance plot (dedication, training, focus and so on). If a young person begins their sport journey having already established a discovery or relational life story, changing this orientation may be damaging and potentially threaten well-being or/and continuation in sport. We see this most often with young women for whom friendship circles are more important than sport performance. Too often girls are called – in the context of school sport, for example – to make choices between what is culturally sanctioned and valued (performing in sport at increasingly higher levels) and their friends. We have seen how elite sport culture can challenge, undermine and sometimes trivialise the core values held by discovery or relationally oriented young people (as Kandy's, Leanne's and Luke's stories showed). We therefore consider it imperative that practitioners support these individuals to *sustain* their pre-existing relational or discovery story.

Given the potential dangers of performance stories, it may, on the face of it, seem a good idea for practitioners to actively seek to change individuals' stories *away* from the performance narrative. We would urge caution. *Enforcing* any narrative script may be damaging to the individual. We see the process of supporting individuals to 'change stories' (because it relates to action, behaviour, experiences, meaning and identity) to be a challenging and long-term intervention. It is very much a therapeutic initiative, aligning with the processes of narrative therapy, which take place in a supportive and professional context through numerous sessions (over months, if not years). We do, however, advocate that practitioners consider ways in which they might, through their day-to-day practice, work to offer the kinds of conditions (outlined in Chapter 10) that support story change and include a variety of story options.

For some practitioners these ideas are already being applied, as the following extract, from one practitioner whom we interviewed, suggests:

> I like that concept of the stories that we can encourage *them* to tell, and that *other people* can tell about *them*, to reinforce that fact that they are not *just* purely determined by performance results and actually, 'I've got a lot more going on'. Those are quite easy terms to apply, because you see it a lot – where it's all just sport performance – and of course, across a career you're not going to be able to sustain great performances.

Ensuring alternative stories are available, sustaining opportunities for actions and behaviours that align with these alternative stories, and actively valuing and supporting diverse stories are three powerful ways in which practitioners can help challenge the dominance of a monological or totalitarian story. All this can be beneficial on many levels as a way of extending horizons and developing a better understanding of the athletes with whom we work. A place to start is for us all (coaches, psychologists, researchers, performance directors, athletes, parents, etc.) to open ourselves up to the realisation that there are different ways to exist and achieve success in sport.

It may be that a more entrenched psychological/cultural schism ultimately underlies this issue. This question, and our response to it above, focuses on the individual athlete as a 'bounded self'. This conceptualisation is commonplace in contemporary psychology. In reality, much of the problem lies not within the individual but within sport culture, as research in cultural psychology has evidenced (see e.g. Schinke and McGannon, 2014). An alternative and potentially far-reaching solution is to work together to challenge and change what is accepted within elite sport culture. Rather than seeing sportspeople as walking problems needing to be fixed (whether they are too performance-oriented or not performance-oriented enough), we could usefully shift the attribution of blame from the individual athlete to ourselves as a collective. It's not just down to *them* – it is also down to *us*.

In Chapter 3 we shared a story about golf union officials demanding to know the name of a golfer who cheated by 'throwing' a match in the World Team Championships. The response of that governing body was to apportion blame to the individual. These officials believed that the individual had to be singled out and punished. In contrast, when the same research was presented in the Netherlands, officials responded by calling an emergency meeting to reflect upon potential factors within the culture of Dutch golf that might provoke a young performer to self-harm and 'throw' an event as a means of release. Rather than seeking to change the individual (through punishment), they sought to change golf culture to ensure that similar experiences would not result for Dutch golfers.

How might elite sport be better? What may be done to improve things?

The words of one practitioner (during a recent interview) provide an aspiration in line with the one we have espoused in this book. Reflecting on how athletes may perceive a need to play a particular role (which may not be one they feel is authentic), this practitioner commented:

> I think that is the challenge – creating an environment where individuals feel comfortable to be authentic without the constraints of 'you have to go this way'. I think that's one of the agendas of people who are involved, like myself, where we want them to explore who they are, we want them to feel comfortable being who they are, being authentic, and how many people can be authentic across their career? It's usually when they become established, they go, 'this is me', whereas how can we encourage them [athletes] to be authentic from day one? And that's where education and not just education and not just supporting the individual, but the system, the coaches, the pro-gramme managers, this is something I talk about a lot. I want you to be an individual, I want you to be comfortable being an individual, and that will influence the performance agenda, which you can't neglect. But I firmly believe if you look after the person you are going to get the performance.

For us, making diverse stories available to sportspeople is an essential aspect of this task. Another practitioner (who wrote to us) suggested that he found the nar-rative and storytelling approach useful in his applied practice because it is *accessible*: 'I can read it and I can get it and I can see how it applies to the athletes I work with.' He went on to say:

> The life story stuff fascinates me inasmuch as we often neglect that, we look at the here-and-now and we don't understand the full process of where an individual has come from and how that influences what they are going to do now, and how that influences what they are going to do in the future. So that has certainly influenced my thinking.

The 'life story stuff' mentioned above has been a time-consuming research strategy requiring a long-term investment from ourselves as well as from parti-cipants. This type of research isn't always possible and the significant costs aren't obvious. It isn't a method that is particularly suited to doctoral research or investigations where a quick turnaround is required. Feedback of this kind helps us justify the investment and, we hope, encourages others to recognise and value the benefit of life stories and how they may be used in applied practice.

At the same time, there is a perhaps even more important point being made above: that by focusing too closely on the 'here-and-now' a performance team may neglect or even become blind to how an athlete's cultural heritage (as described in Chapter 7) influences their present identity and future interests. That is, without taking a wider lens it will be difficult to understand and make sense of how past events, roles and identities play a part in directing the present and future actions, behaviours, motivations and expectations of sportspeople. This is perhaps particularly relevant when we consider marginalised, ethnic and minority populations in sport (see Martens *et al.*, 2000; Ryba and Wright, 2005; Schinke *et al.*, 2006, 2010). Paul Nesti (2004, 2010) has also called attention to a similar lack of awareness in sport regarding how an individual's spirituality or faith influences the way in which an individual understands their sport career, responsibilities, morality, life choices and relationships (as Luke's story showed).

An issue frequently raised by parents regards what appear to be unnecessarily narrow (and perhaps even unbalanced) player pathways instigated by sport governing bodies. Although, on the face of it at least, player pathways have been created as a *guide* (a story about how to achieve sporting excellence), many have come to mirror the performance narrative where one particular route is *enforced.* Many parents feel pressure to accept this route, even when they have concerns about it. Many experience pressure from sport culture regarding talent development. This results in parents being blamed for being 'trouble-makers' if they question 'the system' or as ruining the chances of a young, talented sportsperson should they opt out. 'Going-it-alone', as one parent described it recently, removes financial support and potentially jeopardises future national team selection. Given the different routes to excellence described here, it seems that there is convincing evidence for a need to widen and expand player pathways.

A further aspect of improving provision within sport culture relates to asylum as discussed in Chapter 10. The concept put forward was that a route to a new story and well-being can be achieved within a protected environment outside of sport culture. We wonder to what extent it may be possible to provide 'asylum' *within* sport culture. It seems, theoretically at least, that it is possible to provide counter-stories within sport – as they already exist (as Kandy and Leanne showed). There are also sportspeople who value other dimensions to life, as well as other non-sport experiences, and have provided ways to narrative these differences (see Douglas, 2009, 2012, 2014; Nesti, 2010). It may therefore be possible to protect the individual in order that he or she may re-grow without them needing to leave sport. Some stories which athletes have shared with us have led us to believe that there is potential for coaches, performance directors and parents to provide a protective 'greenhouse' around a fragile and/or vulnerable individual.

What seems important is to encourage and develop stories that value diversity and continuing development. These stories can legitimise other interests and activities (e.g. music, literature, life, health). Such a move, it seems, has the potential to contribute to the type of self-knowledge, self-awareness and self-reflections Nesti (2004) and Miller and Kerr (2002) advocate. However, we do not see this as the domain of the sport psychologist, or lifestyle practitioner exclusively. One participant enjoyed telling us about his interest in literature, theatre and ballet. He didn't need or want a practitioner to 'pre-scribe' these for him. However, he was unable to talk freely about these inter-ests within his particular sport subculture because of the teasing he anticipated would come from his teammates. What *we* need to move towards is building a culture in which interests beyond sport performance would be welcomed rather than belittled.

Stories and artful pedagogy

We believe that there is untapped potential to use storytelling and narrative approaches across sport and education as a way for practitioners (as well as athletes and students) to become more self-aware, self-reflective and self-critical. It also seems that stories can challenge sport systems that have become life and health limiting. As Frank (2010: 59) puts it: 'Vital, breathing stories can break through the filters and grids. Stories can make themselves heard whether or not they fit a narrative habitus.' While coaches, sportspeople, fans and the media have, it seems, always told stories, these stories haven't always been critically reflective, emancipatory, inclusive, empowering or speedy to challenge homo-phobia, sexism, racism or able-bodyism in sport.

We have found that the use of arts-informed approaches (of which story-telling is part) enhances the way in which we understand and present our 'data'. At the same time, these approaches make our work more accessible to audiences outside academia and sport, whether it be research in professional sport (Douglas, 2014b: www.youtube.com/watch?v=M3YQaeNekwU) or the physical activity experiences of women (Douglas, 2014c: www.youtube.com/watch?v=IuUFDMLGfiE) and these we see as playing a part in challenging ster-eotypical portrayals of sportspeople as well as the dominant narrative. As such, we have come to take the view that storytelling of this kind requires an artful mind, and we hope our work contributes to valuing and developing artful minds and critical learning within sport settings.

We have both learned a great deal through writing the life stories of athletes here and through the process of writing stories about our own lives and research practice. One dimension to expanding self-understanding – for each of us – has been through becoming more aware of our own cultural heritage and storytelling repertoire. Our final thoughts therefore are about the part these story fragments play in the origins of the performance, relational and discovery narratives.

Perhaps the performance narrative has its roots in the hero who faced danger and death in Hades to return with the prize that saved his people. This seems a noble reason for telling this tale. Perhaps the relational narrative has its roots in the stories about the *Good Samaritan* who attended to the needs of a brutally beaten traveller left for dead on the highway and ignored by passers-by. The traveller's injuries were tended by a Samaritan who took him to a nearby refuge and paid for his care. Perhaps the discovery narrative has its roots in tales of Arabian Knights, spawned by exotic images of ancient travellers and merchants as they journeyed along the Chinese silk trail. We cannot know for certain the origins of any narrative type, but we recognise that each has value. Each, in unique ways, contributes to making sport a more balanced culture. Are we not better off with a culture that reflects and embraces the breadth of human experience, interests and interaction – rather than being oriented towards one type of story alone? It seems we are at risk of losing something very special from our lives, our relationships, our communities and our culture when the performance narrative becomes the only story worth telling.

References

Adler, P.A. and Adler, P. (1989). The gloried self: The aggrandizement and the constriction of self. *Social Psychology Quarterly 52(4)*, 299–310.

—— (1991). *Backboards and blackboards: College athletes and role engulfment.* New York: Columbia University Press.

Althusser, L. (1971). Ideology and ideological state apparatuses. In *Lenin and Philosophy, and Other Essays* (trans. Ben Brewster). London: New Left Books.

Andersen, M. (2009). Performance enhancement as a bad start and a dead end: A parenthetical comment on Mellalieu and Lane. *The Sport and Exercise Scientist 20*, 12–14.

Anderson, E. (2005). *In the game.* Albany, NY: SUNY Press.

—— (2009). *Inclusive masculinity.* London: Routledge.

Atkinson, R. (2007). The life story interview as a bridge in narrative inquiry. In D.J. Clandinin (ed.) *Handbook of narrative inquiry* (pp. 224–245). Thousand Oaks, CA: Sage.

Bamberg, M. (2004). Considering counter-narratives. In M. Bamberg and M. Andrews (eds) *Considering counter narratives: Narrating, resisting, making sense* (pp. 351–371). Amsterdam: John Benjamins.

Barone, T. and Eisner, E. (2012). *Arts based research.* Thousand Oaks, CA: Sage.

BBC Horizon Special (2006). Winning Gold in 2012: Horizon investigates the scientific approach to sporting success.

BBC News: Sport programming (10 November 2012). The Boat Race. www.bbc.co.uk/programmes/b01fp0x4 (accessed 14 December 2013).

Bloor, D. (1977). *Knowledge and social imagery.* London: Routledge & Kegan Paul.

Bochner, A. (2001). Narratives virtues. *Qualitative Inquiry 7(2)*, 131–157.

Boyle, R. and Haynes, R. (2000). *Power play: Sport, the media and popular culture.* Harlow: Pearson Education.

Brackenridge, C.H. (2001). *Spoilsports: Understanding and preventing sexual exploitation in sport.* London: Routledge.

Brewer, B., Van Raalte, J. and Linder, D. (1993). Athletic identity: Hercules' muscle or Achilles heel? *International Journal of Sport Psychology 24*, 237–254.

Brohm, J.-M. (1978). *Sport: A prison of measured time* (trans. I. Fraser). London: Inks Links.

Bruner, J.S. (1986). *Actual minds, possible worlds.* Cambridge, MA: Harvard University Press.

Butler, J. (1990). *Gender trouble.* New York: Routledge.

Butryn, T.M. and Masucci, M.A. (2009). Sweating through the Matrix: A qualitative analysis of sport and exercise experiences in 'technological' and 'natural' settings. *Journal of Sport and Social Issues 33(3)*, 285–307.

Campbell, J. (2008). *The hero with a thousand faces: Collected works of Joseph Campbell* (3rd edn). Novato, CA: New World Library.

Carless, D. (2010). Who the hell was *that*? Stories, bodies and actions in the world. *Qualitative Research in Psychology 7(4)*, 332–344.

—— (2012). Negotiating sexuality and masculinity in school sport: An autoethnography. *Sport, Education and Society 17(5)*, 607–625.

—— (2013). Cultural constraints: Experiencing same-sex attraction in sport and dance. In N. Short, L. Turner and A. Grant (eds) *Contemporary British autoethnography: A handbook for postgraduate qualitative researchers* (pp. 49–61). Rotterdam: Sense Publishers.

Carless, D. and Douglas, K. (2008). Narrative, identity and mental health: How men with serious mental illness re-story their lives through sport and exercise. *Psychology of Sport and Exercise 9(5)*, 576–594.

—— (2009). 'We haven't got a seat on the bus for you' or 'All the seats are mine': Narratives and career transition in professional golf. *Qualitative Research in Sport and Exercise 1(1)*, 51–66.

—— (2010). *Sport and physical activity for mental health*. Oxford: Wiley-Blackwell.

—— (2011). Stories as personal coaching philosophy. *International Journal of Sports Science and Coaching 6(1)*, 1–12.

—— (2012). Stories of success: Cultural narratives and personal stories of elite and professional athletes. *Reflective Practice 13(3)*, 387–398.

—— (2013a). Living, resisting, and playing the part of athlete: Narrative tensions in elite sport. *Psychology of Sport and Exercise 14(5)*, 701–708.

—— (2013b). 'In the boat' but 'selling myself short': Stories, narratives, and identity development in elite sport. *The Sport Psychologist 27(1)*, 27–39.

Chapman, G. (1997). Making weight: Lightweight rowing, technologies of power, and technologies of the self. *Sociology of Sport Journal 14*, 205–223.

Chase, S.E. (2005). Narrative inquiry: Multiple lenses, approaches, voices. In N. Denzin and Y. Lincoln (eds) *The Sage handbook of qualitative research* (3rd edn) (pp. 651–679). Thousand Oaks, CA: Sage.

Clandinin, D.J. (2007). *Handbook of narrative inquiry*. Thousand Oaks, CA: Sage.

Coakley, J. and Donnelly, P. (2009). *Sports in society: Issues and controversies* (2nd edn). Toronto, ON: McGraw-Hill Ryerson.

Collett, J.L. (2005). What kind of mother am I? Impression management and the social construction of motherhood. *Symbolic Interaction 28(3)*, 327–347.

Conner, J.M. and Mazanov, J. (2009). Would you dope? A general population test of the Goldman dilemma. *British Journal of Sports Medicine 43*, 871–872.

Connor, J., Woolf, J. and Mazanov, J. (2013). Would they dope? Revisiting the Goldman dilemma. *British Journal of Sports Medicine*, online first, 23 January, doi:10.1136/bjsports-2012–091826.

Cook, A. (2013). Seriously – sport is not a matter of life and death. www.telegraph.co.uk/men/thinking-man/10489571/Seriously-sport-is-not-a-matter-of-life-and-death.html (accessed 14 December 2013).

Côté, J. and Hay, J. (2002). Children's involvement in sport: A developmental perspective. In J.M. Silva and D. Stevens (eds) *Psychological foundations of sport* (pp. 484–502). Boston, MA: Allyn and Bacon.

Crosset, T.W. (1995). *Outsiders in the clubhouse: The world of women's professional golf*. New York: State University of New York Press.

Crossley, M.L. (2000). *Introducing narrative psychology: Self, trauma and the construction of meaning*. Buckingham: Open University Press.

—— (2003). Formulating narrative psychology: The limitations of contemporary social constructionism. *Narrative Inquiry 13(2)*, 287–300. http:// dx.doi.org/10.1075/ ni.13.2.03cro.

Cruickshank, A. and Collins, D. (2013). Culture change in elite sport performance teams: Outlining an important and unique construct. *Sport and Exercise Psychology Review 9 (2)*, 6-21.

Denison, J. (2007). Social theory for coaches: A Foucauldian reading of one athlete's poor performance. *International Journal of Sport Science and Coaching 2(4)*, 369–383.

Department for Culture, Media and Sport (2008). *Playing to win: A new era for sport.* London: HMSO. Crown Copyright.

Douglas, K. (2004). *What's the drive in golf: Motivation and persistence in women professional tournament golfers.* Doctoral dissertation, University of Bristol.

—— (2009). Storying my self: Negotiating a relational identity in professional sport. *Qualitative Research in Sport and Exercise 1(2)*, 176–190.

—— (2012). Signals and signs. *Qualitative Inquiry 18*, 525–532.

—— (2013). A truth waiting for a telling. In N. Short, L. Turner and A. Grant (eds) *Contemporary British autoethnography: A handbook for postgraduate qualitative researchers* (pp. 79–95) Rotterdam: Sense Publishers.

—— (2014). Challenging interpretive privilege in elite and professional sport: One [athlete's] story, revised, reshaped and reclaimed. *Qualitative Research in Sport, Exercise and Health. ifirst* DOI:10.1080/2159676X.2013.858369.

Douglas, K. and Carless, D. (2006a). Performance, discovery, and relational narratives among women professional tournament golfers. *Women in Sport and Physical Activity Journal 15(2)*, 14–27.

—— (2006b). *The performance environment: Personal, lifestyle and environmental factors that affect sporting performance.* London: UK Sport Council.

—— (2008a). Using stories in coach education. *International Journal of Sports Science and Coaching 3(1)*, 33–49.

—— (2008b). The team are off: Getting inside women's experiences in professional sport. *Aethlon: The Journal of Sport Literature 25(1)*, 241–251.

—— (2008c). Training or education? Negotiating a fuzzy line between what 'we' want and 'they' might need. *Annual Review of Golf Coaching 2008*, 1–13.

—— (2009a). Abandoning the performance narrative: Two women's stories of transition from professional golf. *Journal of Applied Sport Psychology 21*, 213–230.

—— (2009b). Exploring taboo issues in professional sport through a fictional approach. *Reflective Practice 10(3)*, 311–323.

—— (2011). A narrative perspective: Identity, well-being, and trauma in professional sport. In D. Gilbourne and M. Andersen (eds) *Critical essays in applied sport psychology* (pp. 3–22). Champaign, IL: Human Kinetics.

—— (2012a). Taboo tales in elite sport: Relationships, ethics, and witnessing. *Psychology of Women Section Review 14(2)*, 50–56.

—— (2012b). Membership, golf and a story about Anna and me: Reflections on research in elite sport. *Qualitative Methods in Psychology Bulletin 13*, 27–35.

Douglas, S.J. and Michaels, M. (2004). *The mommy myth: The idealization of motherhood and how it has undermined women.* New York: Free Press.

Drape, J. (2003). Miami's Winslow 'immediately regretted' outburst. *New York Times*, 10 November. Retrieved from www.nytimes.com.

Duncan, M.C. (2000). Reflex. *Sociology of Sport Journal 17(10)*, 60–68.

194 *References*

Eisner, E. (2008). Art and knowledge. In J. Knowles and A. Cole (eds) *Handbook of the arts in qualitative research* (pp. 3–12). Thousand Oaks, CA: Sage.

Ellis, C. (2001). With mother/with child: A true story. *Qualitative Inquiry 7 (5)*, 598–616.

Ely, M. (2007). In-forming re-presentations. In D.J. Clandinin (ed.) *Handbook of narrative inquiry* (pp. 567–598). Thousand Oaks, CA: Sage.

Etherington, K. (2004). *Becoming a reflexive researcher.* London: Jessica-Kingsley.

Ezzy, D. (2000). Illness narratives: Time, hope and HIV. *Social Science and Medicine 50*, 605–617.

Fasting, K. and Brackenridge, C.H. (2005). *The grooming process in sport: Case studies of sexual harassment and abuse.* London: Sage.

Fielding, N. (1993). Qualitative interviewing. In N. Gilbert (ed.) *Researching social life* (pp. 135–154). London: Sage.

Fisher, N. (2002). Competitive sport's imitation of war: Imaging the completeness of virtue. *Philosophy of Sport* 29, 16–37.

Fontana, A. and Frey, H. (2000). The interview: From structured questions to negotiated text. In N.K. Denzin and Y.S. Lincoln (eds) *Handbook of qualitative research* (pp. 645–672). Thousand Oaks, CA: Sage.

Forrest, D. and Simmons, R. (2003). Sport and gambling. *Oxford Revised Economic Policy 19(4)*, 598–611. doi: 10.1093/oxrep/19.4.598.

Frank, A.W. (1995). *The wounded storyteller.* Chicago, IL: University of Chicago Press.

—— (2000). The standpoint of storyteller. *Qualitative Health Research 10(3)*, 354–365.

—— (2004). *The renewal of generosity: Illness, medicine, and how to live.* Chicago, IL: University of Chicago Press.

—— (2010). *Letting stories breathe: A socio-narratology.* Chicago, IL: University of Chicago Press.

Freeman, M. (2010). *Hindsight: The promise and peril of looking backward.* New York: Oxford University Press.

Gadamer, H.G. (1975). *Truth and method.* New York: Seabury.

Gergen, M. and Gergen, K.J. (2006). Narratives in action. *Narrative Inquiry 16(1)*, 112–121.

Gilbourne, D. (2010). Edge of darkness and just in time: Two cautionary tales, two styles, one story. *Qualitative Inquiry 16(5)*, 325–331.

Gilbourne, D. and Andersen, M. (2011) *Critical essays in applied sport psychology.* Champaign, IL: Human Kinetics.

Gilbourne, D. and Richardson, D. (2006). Tales from the field: Personal reflections on the provision of psychological support in professional soccer. *Psychology of Sport and Exercise 7*, 325–337.

Gilligan, C. (1993). *In a different voice: Psychological theory and women's development.* Cambridge, MA: Harvard University Press.

Goffman, E. (1959). *The presentation of self in everyday life.* Harmondsworth: Penguin.

Goldman, B., Bush, P.J. and Klatz, R. (1984). *Death in the locker room.* London: Century.

Gordon, S. and Gucciardi, D.F. (2011). A strengths-based approach to coaching mental toughness. *Sport Psychology in Action 2(3)*, 143–155.

Gould, D., Dieffenbach, K. and Moffett, A. (2002). Psychological characteristics and their development in Olympic champions. *Journal of Applied Sport Psychology 14*, 172–204, doi:10.1080/10413200290103482.

Gould, D., Eklund, R.C. and Jackson, S.A. (1992). 1988 U.S. Olympic wrestling excellence: II. Thoughts and affect occurring during competition. *The Sport Psychologist 6*, 383–402.

Gould, D., Weiss, M. and Weinberg, R.S. (1981). Psychological characteristics of successful and nonsuccessful Big Ten wrestlers. *Journal of Sport Psychology 3*, 69–81.

Gould, D., Guinan, D., Greenleaf, C., Medbery, R. and Peterson, K. (1999). Factors affecting Olympic performance: Perceptions of athletes and coaches from more and less successful teams. *The Sport Psychologist 13*, 371–395.

Green, G.A., Uryasz, F.D., Todd, A. and Bray, C.D. (2001). NCAA study of substance use and abuse habits of college student-athletes. *Clinical Journal of Sport Medicine 11(1)*, 51–56.

Greenleaf, C.A., Gould, D. and Dieffenbach, K. (2001). Factors influencing Olympic performance: Interviews with Atlanta and Nagano U.S. Olympians. *Journal of Applied Sport Psychology 13*, 179–209.

Hallmann, K., Breuer, C. and Kühnreich, B. (2013). Happiness, pride and elite sporting success: What population segments gain most from national athletic achievements? *Sport Management Review 16(2)*, 226–235.

Hammack, P. and Cohler, B. (2009). *The story of sexual identity*. New York: Oxford University Press.

Hermans, H. (2006). The self as a theatre of voices: Disorganization and reorganization of a position repertoire. *Journal of Constructivist Psychology 19(2)*, 147–169.

Hertz, R. and Imber, J.B. (1995). *Studying elites using qualitative methods*. London: Sage.

Holman-Jones, S., Adams, T. and Ellis, C. (2013). *Handbook of autoethnography*. Walnut Creek, CA: Left Coast Press.

Holt, N. and Dunn, J. (2004). Toward a grounded theory of the psychosocial competencies and environmental conditions associated with soccer success. *Journal of Applied Sport Psychology 16*, 199–219.

Hughson, J. (2009). On sporting heroes. *Sport in Society 12(1)*, 85–101.

Hyde, L. (1983). *The gift: Imagination and the erotic life of property*. New York: Random House.

Ingham, A.G., Chase, M.A. and Butt, J. (2002). From the performance principle to the development principle: Every kid a winner? *Quest 54*, 308–331.

Jackson, D. (1990). *Unmasking masculinity*. London: Unwin Hyman.

Jansen, S. and Sabo, D. (1994). The sport/war metaphor: Hegemonic masculinity, the Persian Gulf War, and the New World order. *Sociology of sport 11*, 1–17.

Jenkins, T. (2013). War – the militarization of American professional sports: How the sports intertext influences athletic ritual and sports media. *Journal of Sport and Social Issues 37(3)*, 245–260.

John, S. (2013). A different kind of test match: Cricket, English society and the First World War. *Sport in History 33(1)*, 19–48, DOI:10.1080/17460263.2013.764922.

Jones, G., Hanton, S. and Connaughton, D. (2002). What is this thing called mental toughness? An investigation of elite sport performers. *Journal of Applied Sport Psychology 14*, 205–218.

Josselson, R. (1996). *The space between us: Exploring the dimensions of human relationships*. Thousand Oaks, CA: Sage.

Kemmis, S. and McTaggart, R. (2000). Participatory action research. In N.K. Denzin and Y.S. Lincoln (eds), *Handbook of qualitative research* (pp. 567–605). Thousand Oaks, CA: Sage.

Klapp, O.E. (1962). *Heroes, villains and fools*. Englewood Cliffs, NJ: Prentice-Hall.

Knoppers, A. and Elling, A. (2004). 'We do not engage in promotional journalism.' Discursive strategies used by sport journalists to describe the selection process. *International Review for the Sociology of Sport 39*, 57–73.

Krane, V., Choi, P., Baird, S., Aimar, C.M. and Kauer, K.J. (2004). Living the paradox: Female athletes negotiate femininity and muscularity. *Sex Roles 50(5/6)*, 315–329.

Ladies European Tour (2003). *Media guide handbook*. Ladies European tour publication.

Ladson-Billings, G. (2000). Racialized discourses and ethnic epistemologies. In N.K. Denzin and Y.S. Lincoln (eds), *Handbook of qualitative research* (pp. 257–277). Thousand Oaks, CA: Sage.

Lakoff, G. and Johnson, M. (1980). *Metaphors we live by*. Chicago, IL: University of Chicago Press.

Lenskyj, H. (1986). *Out of bounds: Women, sport and sexuality*. Toronto: The Women's Press.

Lieblich, A., Tuval-Mashiach, R. and Zilber, T. (1998). *Narrative research: Reading, analysis and interpretation*. London: Sage.

Lindemann, H. (2009). Holding one another (well, wrongly, clumsily) in a time of dementia. *Metaphilosophy 40(3–4)*, 416–424.

Lysaker, P. and Lysaker, J. (2002). Narrative structure in psychosis: Schizophrenia and disruptions in the dialogical self. *Theory and Psychology 12(2)*, 207–220.

—— (2006). A typology of narrative impoverishment in schizophrenia. *Counselling Psychology Quarterly 19(1)*, 57–68.

MacIntyre, A. (1984). *After virtue: A study in moral theory* (2nd edn). Notre Dame, IN: University of Notre Dame Press.

Madill, L. and Hopper, T. (2007). The best of the best discourse on health: Poetic insights on how professional sport socializes a family of men into hegemonic masculinity and physical inactivity. *American Journal of Men's Health 1(1)*, 44–59.

Mahoney, M.J. and Avener, M. (1977). Psychology of the elite athlete: An exploratory study. *Cognitive Therapy and Research 1*, 135–142.

Malcolm, D. and Sheard, K. (2002). Pain in the assets: The effects of commercialization and professionalization on the management of injury in English Rugby Union. *Sociology of Sport Journal 19(2)*, 149–169.

Martens, M.P., Mobley, M. and Zizzi, S.J. (2000). Multicultural training in applied sport psychology. *The Sport Psychologist 14*, 81–97.

McAdams, D. (1993). *The stories we live by*. New York: The Guilford Press.

—— (2006). The problem of narrative coherence. *Journal of Constructivist Psychology 19(2)*, 109–125.

McGannon, K., Curtin, K., Schinke, R. and Schweinbenz, A. (2012). (De)constructing Paula Radcliffe: Exploring media representations of elite athletes, pregnancy and motherhood through cultural sport psychology. *Psychology of Sport and Exercise 13*, 820–829.

McKenna, J. and Thomas, H. (2007). Enduring injustice: A case study of retirement from professional rugby union. *Sport, Education and Society 12(1)*, 19–35.

McLeod, J. (1997). *Narrative and psychotherapy*. London: Sage.

Messner, M., Hunt, D., Dunbar, M., Perry, C., Lapp, J. and Miller, P. (1999). *Boys to men: Sports media. Messages about masculinity: A national poll of children, focus groups, and content analysis of sports programs and commercials*. Oakland, CA: Children Now.

Miller, P. and Kerr, G. (2002). Conceptualizing excellence: Past, present, and future. *Journal of Applied Sport Psychology 14(3)*, 140–153.

Murphy, G., Pepitas, A. and Brewer, B. (1996). Identity foreclosure, athletic identity and career maturity in intercollegiate athletes. *The Sport Psychologist 10*, 239–246.

Neimeyer, R., Herrero, O. and Botella, L. (2006). Chaos to coherence: Psycho-therapeutic integration of traumatic loss. *Journal of Constructivist Psychology 19(2)*, 127–145.

Nelson, H. (2001). *Damaged identities, narrative repair*. Ithaca, NY: Cornell University Press.

Nesti, M. (2004). *Existential psychology and sport. Theory and application*. Abingdon: Routledge.

—— (2010). *Psychology in football. Working with elite and professional players*. Abingdon: Routledge.

Nike/Youth Sport Trust (2006). *Girls in sport monitoring and evaluation final report*. Loughborough: Institute of Youth Sport.

Nisbet, R. (1969). *Social change and history: Aspects of Western theory of development*. New York: Oxford University Press.

Papathomas, A. and Lavallee, D. (in press). Self-starvation and the performance narrative in competitive sport. *Psychology of Sport and Exercise*, http://dx.doi.org/10.1016/j.psychsport.2013.10.014.

Pensgaard, A-M. and Duda, L. (2002). 'If we work hard, we can do it': A tale from an Olympic (gold) medallist. *Journal of Applied Sport Psychology 14*, 219–236.

Phoenix, C. and Smith, B. (2011). Telling a (good?) counterstory of aging: Natural bodybuilding meets the narrative of decline. *The Journals of Gerontology Series B: Psychological Sciences and Social Sciences 66*, 628–639. http://bit.ly/YMhwe3.

Plummer, K. (2001). *Documents of life 2*. Thousand Oaks, CA: Sage.

Ratto, R. (2001). Language of sports forever changed. SF Gate, 16 September. www.sfgate.com (accessed 19 November 2013).

Ravizza, K. (2002). A philosophical construct: A framework for performance enhancement. *International Journal of Sport Psychology 33*, 4–18.

Richards, E. (2004). *Around alone*. London: Macmillan.

Richardson, L. (1994). Writing: A method of inquiry. In N. Denzin and Y. Lincoln (eds) *Handbook of qualitative research* (pp. 516–529). Thousand Oaks, CA: Sage.

Riessman, C.K. (2008). *Narrative methods for the human sciences*. Thousand Oaks, CA: Sage.

Ryba, T.V. and Wright, H.K. (2005). From mental game to cultural praxis: A cultural studies model's implications for the future of sport psychology. *Quest 57*, 192–212.

Sage, G.H. (1990). *Power and ideology in American sport: A critical perspective*. Champaign, IL: Human Kinetics

Schinke, R.J. and McGannon, K.R. (2014). The acculturation experiences of (and with) immigrant athletes. *International Journal of Sport and Exercise Psychology 12*, 64–75.

Schinke, R.J., Blodgett, A.T., Yungblut, H.E., Eys, M.A., Battochio, R.C., Wabano, M.J., Peltier, D.R., Stephen, R., Pickard, P. and Recollet-Saikonnen, D. (2010). The adaptation challenges and strategies of adolescent Aboriginal athletes competing off reserve. *Journal of Sport and Social Issues 34(4)*, 438–456.

Schinke, R.J., Michel, G., Gauthier, A.P., Pickard, P., Danielson, R., Peltier, D., Pheasant, C., Enosse, L. and Peltier, M. (2006). The adaptation to the mainstream in elite sport: A Canadian Aboriginal perspective. *The Sport Psychologist 20(4)*, 435–448.

Shogun, D. (1999). *The making of high-performance athletes: Discipline, diversity, and ethics*. Toronto, ON: University of Toronto Press.

Simon. J. (2013). 'A different kind of test match': Cricket, English society and the First World War. *Sport in History 33(1)*, 19–48, DOI:10.1080/17460263.2013.764922.

Smith, B. (1999). The abyss. *Qualitative Inquiry 5(2)*, 264–279.

—— (2007). The state of the art in narrative inquiry: Some reflections. *Narrative Inquiry 17(2)*, 391–398.

—— (2010). Narrative research: Ongoing conversations and questions for sport and exercise psychology research. *International Review of Sport and Exercise Psychology 3(1)*, 87–107.

Smith, B. and Sparkes, A.C. (2009a). Narrative inquiry in sport and exercise psychology: What can it mean, and why might we do it? *Psychology of Sport and Exercise 10(1)*, 1–11.

—— (2009b). Narrative analysis and sport and exercise psychology: Understanding lives in diverse ways. *Psychology of Sport and Exercise 10(2)*, 279–288.

Smith, G. (1973). The sport hero: An endangered species. *Quest 19*, 59–70.

Smith, J. (2009). Judging research quality: From certainty to contingency. *Qualitative Research in Sport and Exercise 1(2)*, 91–100.

Smith, S. and Watson, J. (2001). *Reading autobiography*. Minneapolis, MN: University of Minnesota Press.

Sparkes, A.C. (1992). The paradigms debate: An extended review and celebration of difference. In A. Sparkes (ed.) *Research in physical education and sport: Exploring alternative visions* (pp. 9–60). London: Falmer Press.

—— (1996). The fatal flaw. *Qualitative Inquiry 2(4)*, 463–494.

—— (1997). Reflections on the socially constructed physical self. In K.R. Fox (ed.) *The physical self* (pp. 83–110). Champaign, IL: Human Kinetics.

—— (1998). Athletic identity: An Achilles' heel to the survival of self. *Qualitative Health Research 8 (5)*, 644–664.

—— (2002). *Telling tales in sport and physical activity.* Champaign, IL: Human Kinetics.

—— (2004). Bodies, narratives, selves and autobiography: The example of Lance Armstrong. *Journal of Sport and Social Issues 28(4)*, 397–428.

—— (2009). Ethnography and the senses: Challenges and possibilities. *Qualitative Research in Sport and Exercise 1(1)*, 21–35.

Sparkes, A.C. and Douglas, K. (2007). Making the case for poetic representations: An example in action. *The Sport Psychologist 21(2)*, 170–189.

Sparkes, A.C. and Partington, S. (2003). Narrative practice and its potential contribution to sport psychology: The example of flow. *The Sport Psychologist 17*, 292–317.

Sparkes, A.C. and Smith, B. (2003). Men, sport, spinal cord injury and narrative time. *Qualitative Research 3(3)*, 295–320.

—— (2008). Narrative constructionist inquiry. In J. Holstein and J. Gubrium (eds) *Handbook of constructionist Research* (pp. 295–314). London: The Guilford Press.

—— (2014). *Qualitative research methods in sport, exercise and health: From process to product*. London: Routledge.

Spence, D. (1982). Narrative persuasion. *Psychoanalysis and Contemporary Thought 6*, 457–481.

Stewart, C., Smith, B. and Sparkes, A.C. (2011). Sporting autobiographies of illness and the role of metaphor. *Sport in Society: Cultures, Commerce, Media, Politics 14(5)*, 581–597.

Therberge, N. (1977). *An occupational analysis of women's professional golf.* Unpublished doctoral thesis. University of Massachusetts, Department of Sociology.

—— (1980). The systems of rewards in women's professional golf. *International Review of Sport Sociology 15(2)*, 387–393.

—— (2008). 'Just a normal bad part of what I do': Elite athletes' accounts of the relationship between sport participation and health. *Sociology of Sport Journal 25(2)*: 206–222.

Tiihonen, A. (1994). Asthma. *International Review for the Sociology of Sport 29(1)*, 51–62.

Trujillo, N. (1995). Machines, missiles, and men: Images of the male body on ABC's Monday night football. *Sociology of Sport 12(4)*: 403–423.

Tsang, T. (2000). Let me tell you a story. *Sociology of Sport Journal 17(10)*, 44–59.

University of Oxford (7 April 2012). Oxford prepares for the boat race. Produced by Angel Sharp Media, www.youtube.com/watch?v=mFStVsXqiDcandlist=TL75T9VgQ dRuFpupkqb3x5iTtjvFqtcjM4 (accessed 15 November 2013).

Vincent, J. and Crossman, J. (2012). Patriots at play: An analysis of the newspaper coverage of the gold medal contenders in men's and women's ice hockey at the 2010 Winter Olympic Games. *International Journal of Sport Communication 5*, 87–108.

Warriner, K. and Lavallee, D. (2008). The retirement experiences of elite female gymnasts: Self-identity and the physical self. *Journal of Applied Sport Psychology 20*, 301–317.

Washington, R. and Karen, D. (2010). *Sport, power, and society: Institutions and practices: A reader*. Boulder, CO: Westview Press.

Werthner, P. and Orlick, T. (1986). Retirement experiences of successful Olympic athletes. *International Journal of Sport Psychology 17*, 337–363.

White, M. and Epston, D. (1990). *Narrative means to therapeutic ends*. New York: Norton.

White, P., Young, K. and McTeer, W. (1995). Sport, masculinity and the injured body. In D. Sabo and F. Gordon (eds) *Men's health and illness* (pp. 158–182). London: Sage.

Wilkinson, A. (1998). Empowerment: Theory and practice. *Personnel Review 27(1)*, 40–56.

Williams, J.M. and Krane, V. (2001). Psychological characteristics of peak performance. In J.M. Williams (ed.) *Applied sport psychology: Personal growth to peak performance (*4th edn) (pp. 137–147). Mountain View, CA: Mayfield.

Williams, O. (2012). Olympics track cycling: Will technology win the war for GB? BBC Sport, www.bbc.co.uk/sport/0/olympics/19089259 (accessed 20 November 2013).

Williams, S. (1996). The vicissitudes of embodiment across the chronic illness trajectory. *Body and Society 2(2)*, 23–47.

Wolcott, H.F. (2002). *Sneaky kid and its aftermath: Ethics and intimacy in fieldwork*. Walnut Creek, CA: Alta Mira Press.

Index

Page numbers in *italics* denote tables.

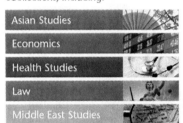